Lesbian and Gay Parents and Their Children

Contemporary Perspectives on Lesbian, Gay, and Bisexual Psychology

Gregory M. Herek, Series Editor

Series Titles

HIV+ Sex: The Psychological and Interpersonal Dynamics of HIV-Seropositive Gay and Bisexual Men's Relationships
Edited by Perry N. Halkitis, Cynthia A. Gómez, and Richard J. Wolitski

Sexual Orientation and Mental Health: Examining Identity and Development in Lesbian, Gay, and Bisexual People
Edited by Allen M. Omoto and Howard S. Kurtzman

Lesbian and Gay Parents and Their Children: Research on the Family Life Cycle
Abbie E. Goldberg

Lesbian and Gay Parents and Their Children

Research on the Family Life Cycle

Abbie E. Goldberg

American Psychological Association

Washington, DC

Second Printing, February 2010
Published by
American Psychological Association
750 First Street, NE
Washington, DC 20002
www.apa.org

To order
APA Order Department
P.O. Box 92984
Washington, DC 20090-2984
Tel: (800) 374-2721; Direct: (202) 336-5510
Fax: (202) 336-5502; TDD/TTY: (202) 336-6123
Online: www.apa.org/books/
E-mail: order@apa.org

In the U.K., Europe, Africa, and the Middle East, copies may be ordered from
American Psychological Association
3 Henrietta Street
Covent Garden, London
WC2E 8LU England

Typeset in Goudy by Stephen McDougal, Mechanicsville, MD

Printer: Edwards Brothers, Ann Arbor, MI
Cover Designer: Minker Design, Bethesda, MD
Technical/Production Editor: Kathryn Funk

The opinions and statements published are the responsibility of the authors, and such opinions and statements do not necessarily represent the policies of the American Psychological Association.

Library of Congress Cataloging-in-Publication Data

Goldberg, Abbie E.
  Lesbian and gay parents and their children : research on the family life cycle /
Abbie E. Goldberg. — 1st ed.
     p. cm.
  Includes bibliographical references and index.
  ISBN-13: 978-1-4338-0536-3
  ISBN-10: 1-4338-0536-7
  1. Gay parents. 2. Lesbian mothers. I. Title.

  HQ75.27.G65 2009
  306.874086'64—dc22   2009011724

British Library Cataloguing-in-Publication Data
A CIP record is available from the British Library.

Printed in the United States of America
First Edition

CONTENTS

Chapter 1.   Introduction: Lesbian and Gay Parents and Their
             Children—Research and Contemporary Issues   3

Chapter 2.   Partners but Not Parents: Intimate Relationships
             of Lesbians and Gay Men   15

Chapter 3.   From Partners to Parents: The Transition to
             Parenthood for Lesbians and Gay Men   49

Chapter 4.   Lesbians and Gay Men as Parents   89

Chapter 5.   Children of Lesbian and Gay Parents: Adjustment
             and Experiences   125

Chapter 6.   Young Adults and Adults With Lesbian and Gay
             Parents Speak Out   157

Chapter 7.   Conclusions and Future Directions   177

References   189

Index   223

About the Author   233

Lesbian and Gay Parents and Their Children

1

INTRODUCTION: LESBIAN AND GAY PARENTS AND THEIR CHILDREN— RESEARCH AND CONTEMPORARY ISSUES

Gay men and lesbians utilizing infertility clinics to have babies.
—*San Francisco Chronicle*, May 5, 2007

Gay wannabe dads still waiting for a baby.
—*Inside Out Australia*, May 6, 2007

Same-sex parents just as good.
—*Edmonton Journal*, Canada, May 7, 2007

The issue of gay parenting is one that is both highly current, in terms of media interest and political controversy, and historic, in that individuals with nonheterosexual attractions, identities, and behaviors have always been parents. Increased media attention to gay parenting is in part a response to the increased visibility of gay parents in society, which is in turn a function of (a) actual increases in the number of lesbian and gay parents, particularly those who become parents in the context of same-sex committed relationships (Gates & Ost, 2004), and (b) greater national and international acceptance of lesbians and gay men (G. R. Hicks & Lee, 2006)[1] and of a broader range of family forms (e.g., Thornton & Young-DeMarco, 2001).

---

[1]For example, a 2008 Gallup poll found that 48% of Americans considered homosexual relations to be morally acceptable, compared with 40% in 2001 (Saad, 2008). Additionally, national survey data indicate that in 2006, 36% of Americans believed that homosexuality is something that people are born with, compared with only 20% in 1985. Similarly, in 2006, 42% of Americans favored allowing

The current volume is a response to this increased interest in lesbian and gay parents and their children and to the corresponding growth in research on this topic. Although a number of journal articles and book chapters have summarized much of the research in this area (e.g., Gottman, 1990; Mooney-Somers & Golombok, 2000; C. J. Patterson, 2000; Stacey & Biblarz, 2001; Tasker, 1999), there has been no book-length synthesis or analysis to date. A full-length volume can provide a review of the research in a way that engages multiple perspectives (e.g., perspectives of both the children and parents who live in lesbian- and gay-parent households), includes topics that have rarely been discussed in the literature (e.g., divorce or relationship dissolution in lesbian- and gay-parent households; the perspectives of nonheterosexual children of lesbian and gay parents), and integrates the findings of both qualitative and quantitative research. In the current volume, I seek to provide a detailed and nuanced description of the research on lesbian and gay couples and parents and their children (which will include discussion of complex, under-studied, and sometimes controversial issues) and to offer insights and possible implications based on this research that will be useful to a broad audience. Specifically, I expect that researchers and graduate students in the social sciences (e.g., psychology, human development, family studies, sociology, women's studies) as well as scholars and students of legal studies and queer/gender studies will find the current volume of interest. Lawyers and policymakers, as well as family life educators, clinicians, health care professionals, child welfare professionals, and other practitioners who work with families in general and lesbian- and gay-parent families specifically may also call on this book as a source of information. Finally, this book will likely also be of interest to some lesbian and gay parents and prospective parents who wish to gain direct knowledge of the research studies that have been conducted on their families.

A NOTE ON TERMINOLOGY

In the current volume, I use the terms *female same-sex couples* and *male same-sex couples* interchangeably with the terms *lesbian couples* and *gay male couples*, respectively. These terms are notably imperfect, for several reasons. First, some sexual minorities do not identify with labels such as *lesbian* and *gay* (Fassinger & Arsenau, 2007). For example, some sexual minorities use the self-label *queer* because they prefer a "pan-descriptive term that embodies defiance of existing norms about gender and sexuality rather than a term

---

lesbians and gay men to adopt (up from 38% in 1999) and 54% favored civil unions for same-sex couples (up from 45% in 2003; The Pew Research Center, 2006). These data suggest a current trend toward increasing acceptance of sexual minorities in American society; however, many Americans do continue to hold ambivalent or hostile attitudes about homosexuality and the rights of sexual minorities (Stein, 2005).

claiming membership in a particular category" (Fassinger & Arseneau, 2007, p. 23). A second problem with these terms is that they are not explicitly inclusive of bisexual men and women. Although it might seem appropriate to use a more all-encompassing term such as *LGB*, use of such a term would be misleading in that studies of same-sex couples very rarely acknowledge, much less explore, the unique perspectives of bisexual men and women in their samples, as distinct from those of self-identified lesbian women and gay men. Rather, bisexual women and men in these studies are functionally treated as lesbian or gay by virtue of their membership in same-sex relationships. Similarly, bisexual men and women are rarely studied in the context of heterosexual relationships (but see Edser & Shea, 2002; Matteson, 1985; Reinhardt, 2002) because most studies of individuals in heterosexual relationships presume heterosexual identification. Thus, I refer to *LGB parents* only when this term is scientifically valid (i.e., when a study really did include self-identified lesbian, gay, and bisexual parents). Again, I realize that all of these terms are imperfect and overly simplistic and obscure tremendous variability and diversity in subjective experiences, but I use them here nevertheless to avoid overly long or unwieldy descriptors that might detract from the volume's readability.

This volume also reviews the very limited research on the experiences of transgender parents and their children. Transgender parents are not, by definition, sexual minorities; indeed, transgender parents may identify as heterosexual, lesbian, gay, bisexual, or queer, or they may prefer another descriptor (Devor, 1997, 2002; S. Hines, 2006a). However, transgender people and parents are often regarded (and regard themselves) as members of the broader gay/queer community in part because they share many of the same social and political concerns as LGB people (Devor, 2002). Indeed, sexual minorities and transgender people are both constructed as outside the mainstream of North American society, and they are routinely devalued and stigmatized on the basis of their marginalized identities (Dreschler, 2003). Thus, at times I refer to *LGBT parents* or the *LGBT community* typically in reference to the general community of LGBT parents or people being studied.

ORGANIZATION OF THE BOOK

The organization of the book mirrors the life cycle of the lesbian- and gay-parent family: that is, the research is discussed according to the life stage and developmental phase of the lesbian- and gay-parent family. Within each chapter, suggestions for future research and implications for practitioners are proposed. Concluding each chapter is a short list of practical resources (popular press books, Web sites, and videos) that may be of interest to the reader.

Chapter 2, titled "Partners but Not Parents: Intimate Relationships of Lesbians and Gay Men," discusses the research on the intimate relationships of same-sex couples[2] who are not parents, at least not yet. This chapter addresses questions such as, How do lesbian and gay couples meet? What are the characteristics of healthy or successful relationships among lesbians and gay men? How do lesbian and gay couples negotiate the division of paid and unpaid labor? How might marriage rights and other forms of legal recognition influence or change same-sex relationships?

Chapter 3, "From Partners to Parents: The Transition to Parenthood for Lesbians and Gay Men," discusses the literature on the transition to parenthood among sexual minorities. Among the questions that this chapter addresses are: How do lesbians and gay men decide to become parents? How do couples make decisions about what parenthood route to pursue (adoption, alternative issemination, surrogacy)? How do couples' relationships, roles, and identities change during this key life transition?

Chapter 4, "Lesbians and Gay Men as Parents," discusses the experiences, perspectives, and adjustment of lesbian and gay parents. Some of the questions this chapter addresses are: How do lesbians and gay men negotiate their roles as parents and partners? What are their experiences navigating the gendered meanings associated with motherhood and fatherhood? How do lesbian and gay parents manage the dissolution of their relationships in the absence of legal safeguards that protect both parents' rights? What are the parenting values and goals of lesbian and gay parents?

The questions considered in chapter 5, "Children of Lesbian and Gay Parents: Adjustment and Experiences," focus on the development and experiences of children raised in these families. For example, How do children feel about having lesbian and gay parents? Does their household composition affect their identity, mental health, and gender role orientation? In what ways? How do they negotiate issues unique to having lesbian and gay parents, such as coming out about their families?

Chapter 6, "Young Adults and Adults With Lesbian and Gay Parents Speak Out," describes the emerging research that privileges the voices of adults raised by lesbian and gay parents. Questions of interest include: How do adults with lesbian and gay parents perceive their growing-up experiences? How do they navigate issues of disclosure (i.e., coming out) about their families? What are the experiences of adults with lesbian and gay parents who identify as nonheterosexual themselves?

Chapter 7, "Conclusions and Future Directions," briefly summarizes the research findings to date and highlights several content areas within the field of lesbian and gay family studies that are particularly deserving of further research.

---

[2]In the current volume, the experiences of same-sex couples, as opposed to single lesbian and gay persons, are emphasized. This emphasis reflects the extant research, which has tended to focus on couples rather than singles.

CONCEPTUAL AND THEORETICAL FRAMEWORK

Scholars have emphasized the importance of bringing theory into the study of lesbian- and gay-parent families (e.g., Golombok & Tasker, 1994; Mooney-Somers & Golombok, 2000; Paechter, 2000). An integrative theoretical and conceptual framework guides the current volume. Specifically, several intersecting and complementary perspectives guide my writing, analysis, and presentation of this book.

An Ecological Perspective

An ecological perspective serves as one of the overarching frameworks to this volume (Bronfenbrenner, 1977, 1986). An ecological perspective emphasizes the importance of attending to the multiple contexts of individuals' lives in studying development. Bronfenbrenner (1977), Belsky (1984), and others have argued that understanding adaptation in one domain (e.g., the marital or couple relationship, child development, work functioning) requires an ecological or contextual analysis of multiple aspects of family life. A comprehensive understanding of human development, then, requires attention to multiple levels of analysis.

The term *microsystem* refers to the complex of relations between the developing individual and environment in an immediate setting that contains that person (e.g., family, school, workplace; Bronfenbrenner, 1977). The family is the principal context in which human development takes place, but it is one of several settings in which developmental processes can and do occur. The *mesosystem* encompasses the interrelations among major settings containing the developing person at a particular point in his or her life (e.g., for a 10-year-old daughter of two lesbian mothers, her family, her school, and the social organizations that she is involved in). The *exosystem*, an extension of the mesosystem, includes other specific social structures that do not contain the developing person but influence or encompass the settings that the person occupies. These include the neighborhood; the mass media; and local, state, and national governments (e.g., the laws pertaining to adoption and marriage rights have implications for sexual minorities' well-being and development). Similarly, the psychological development of children is affected by their environments as well as by what occurs in the varied settings that their parents occupy (e.g., their parents' work, their parents' social networks; Bronfenbrenner, 1977). Finally, the *macrosystem* comprises the overarching institutional patterns of the culture/subculture (e.g., economic, social, educational, legal, and political systems) of which micro-, meso-, and exosystems are the concrete manifestations (Bronfenbrenner, 1977). National sociopolitical ideologies and movements surrounding marriage rights for same-sex couples, for example, inevitably influence the varied settings in which individuals live and develop and, in turn, impact individual mental health and development.

The current volume attends to research that captures the varied contexts that shape, and are shaped by, lesbian and gay parents and their children. I have made an effort to situate individual outcomes and processes (e.g., dating relationships of lesbians and gay men, parenting experiences and values) within the broader social context and to examine the interrelationships among contexts (e.g., the couple and their extended families of origin, parents and their children's schools). Similarly, I emphasize research that theorizes the role of various contexts (e.g., family of origin support and involvement, laws and policies, cultural ideologies) in shaping the trajectories and outcomes of lesbian- and gay-parent families.

A Life Course Perspective

An additional context of interest is the context of time. A *life course perspective* (Elder, 1998a) acknowledges the importance of attending to, studying, and interpreting people's lives in the context of historical time. From this perspective, understanding development requires awareness not only of the broader contexts in which it occurs but also of the particular life stage an individual is in, how that stage is interpreted by the individual, and how the individual changes over time (Bengtson & Allen, 1993; Elder, 1998a). One major theme that is particularly distinctive of life course theory is the interplay of human lives and changing historical times and places (Elder, 1996). Indeed, varying years of birth expose individuals to different historical worlds, with distinctive priorities, constraints, and options (Elder, 1996, 1998a). Historical influences take the form of a cohort effect when social change differentiates the life patterns of successive cohorts (e.g., the gay baby boom in the 1980s). Lesbians and gay men who wish to become parents at the turn of the 21st century, for example, face a wider array of options than lesbians and gay men in the 1950s largely because of shifts in sociocultural attitudes toward sexual minorities (Savin-Williams, 2008). This volume, then, seeks to situate lesbian- and gay-parent families' experiences in terms of the unique social and historical trends that are occurring at the present time (e.g., increased options for becoming parents, the fight for same-sex marriage rights).

A life course perspective also emphasizes the *transitions* and *trajectories* that occur in a person's life. A single individual's life course can be viewed as a sequence of socially defined, age-graded events and roles (e.g., spouse, parent, employee) that the individual enacts over time (Elder, 1996, 1998a). Transitions into and out of social roles across the life span involve changes in personal and social status, sense of self, and identity. Becoming a parent, for example, involves gaining an entirely new role as well as making adjustments to already-held roles (e.g., partner, wife, husband; employee, supervisor, colleague). The *family life cycle* (Carter & McGoldrick, 2005) involves a finite number of normative family transitions, which may represent passage or change from one place or state to the next, or extended periods of change and disequilibrium between periods of stability and balance (P. A. Cowan & Cowan, 2003). Additionally, nonnormative or unexpected transitions may occur in the course of one's life (e.g., losing one's job, divorce). Normative and nonnormative transitions stimulate changes in roles and in the quality of close relationships, and they may also lead to the restructuring of one's psychological sense of self; for example, during the transition to parenthood, individuals restructure their identity to varying degrees to include that of "parent" (P. A. Cowan & Cowan, 2003).

Thus, the current volume aims to attend to the experiences of the multiple members of the family system (i.e., lesbian and gay parents and their offspring) during multiple transitional moments (e.g., for parents, the transition to couplehood and the transition to parenthood) and stages (e.g., for offspring, childhood, adolescence, and adulthood). Further, the experiences of individuals are understood to be linked, such that one person's experience of a particular transition or role necessarily impacts the experiences of the individuals with whom their lives are deeply entwined.

A Social Constructionist Perspective

A social constructionist approach also informs the writing and analysis of this book. A social constructionist perspective acknowledges families, sexuality, and gender as socially and materially constructed (Dunne, 2000; Oswald, Blume, & Marks, 2005). From this perspective, lesbian- and gay-parent families challenge and expose traditional conceptualizations of family (i.e., the ideological code that conveys what it means to be a family in legal, moral, and biological kinship terms) and highlight the ways in which "family" is subjectively constructed and interpreted (i.e., notions of family are neither objective nor ahistorical; Dunne, 2000; Stacey, 2006). Thus, from a social constructionist standpoint, lesbian- and gay-parent families, single-parent families, and other nonnuclear family arrangements do not represent the disintegration of family but, rather, constitute new and valid family forms (Cheal, 1993). Indeed, lesbian mothers and gay fathers can be viewed as actively disentangling heterosexuality from parenthood and, in many cases, biology from parenthood (e.g., in the case of nonbiological lesbian mothers and adoptive lesbian and gay parents), thereby challenging and perhaps even changing fundamental notions about parenthood, at least on a theoretical level. For example, many of the ways that lesbians and gay men achieve parenthood, such as alternative insemination or adoption, defy standard definitions of parenting as being the natural or inevitable consequence of biological relationships (Donovan, 2000). As Stacey (2006) noted in discussing postmodern transformations of parenthood: "Paths to parenthood no longer appear natural, obligatory, or uniform, but are necessarily reflexive, uncertain, self-fashioning, plural, and politically embattled. So too are parenting structures unmoored from marriage, coupling, or even biological reproduction" (p. 29). Lesbian and gay parents represent one striking example of the "self-fashioning" of parenthood, as well as the "unmooring" of parenthood from marriage or biological reproduction, and therefore serve as one embodiment of the diversity of postmodern families.

In addition to families, gender and sexuality are also understood by many feminist and queer theorists to be socially constructed (Ferree, 1990; Oswald et al., 2005). As West and Zimmerman (1987) argued, gender is not merely a defining feature of individuals (i.e., a personality characteristic or role) but is also created, constructed, defined, and sustained through daily interactions. Further, gender is embedded in the varied social processes of daily life and social organizations, and it is therefore socially constructed at the microlevel (family) and macrolevel (laws, ideology, culture; Ferree, 1990; Ridgeway & Correll, 2004; Risman, 2004; Thorne, 1992). Inequity in the division of household labor, for example, may therefore arise as a function of individuals' gendered selves, the immediate familial/couple context, cultural expectations, and the broader social structure (e.g., how men's jobs are organized). Lesbians and gay men are necessarily exposed to the same societal and cultural ideologies as heterosexual women and men (e.g., notions of women as nurturers and caretakers and men as workers and providers). However, their unique relational and social context may lead them to act in ways that fundamentally challenge traditional family relations and gendered notions of "the family" (e.g., the complex institutions of "motherhood" and "fatherhood") and disrupt and transform gender and gender relations, including intimate relationships and parent–child relationships. Thus, through acts and activities that resist or defy gender norms, "normal" sexuality, and traditional family relationships, individuals in lesbian- and gay-parent families may arguably deconstruct and reconstruct gender, sex, and family in complex ways (Goldberg, 2007a; Oswald et al., 2005).

Nevertheless, although it is important to examine the ways in which lesbian- and gay-parent families may construct and enact meaning in ways that resist heteronormativity and gendered relations, it is important not to take a reductionist approach that assumes that all lesbian- and gay-parent families actively and purposefully transform traditional notions of family, gender, and sexuality (Gabb, 2004a; Lewin, 1993). Such an approach is overly simplistic and ignores the ways in which the choices, behaviors, and roles of lesbian and gay parents and their families may be accommodating or assimilating rather than resistant and revisionist in nature. Thus, attention to the ways in which lesbian- and gay-parent families challenge traditional notions of family and gender is warranted, but not at the cost of reductionism. For example, Gabb (2004a) observed that lesbian- and gay-parent families are most often depicted as "egalitarian models that differ significantly from traditional heterosexual forms" and are cited as the "families of the future" (p. 168), but she pointed out that some data, including her own, paint a different picture, one that indicates that in some lesbian-parent families, the division of labor is fairly segregated and mirrors that of the traditional heterosexual male/female arrangement. Thus, just as heterosexual-parent families are overwhelmingly diverse, lesbian- and gay-parent families also represent an extremely heterogeneous group. Further, just as it is very difficult to generalize a particular descriptor or statement to all heterosexual parents or all heterosexual-parent families, it makes little sense to describe all lesbian- and gay-parent families as either assimilationist or radical. Lesbian and gay people and parents, like heterosexual people and parents, live their lives in varied, complex, and sometimes contradictory ways.

Further, it is possible that lesbian and gay parents and their families may simultaneously embody and enact both assimilationist and radical potentialities. Lesbian and gay parents (and their children, for that matter) necessarily negotiate parenthood within a societal system that is fundamentally gendered (e.g., biological motherhood is theoretically and culturally valued above any other type of motherhood or parenthood; Polikoff, 1990). In this way, it can be said that lesbians and gay men "do gender" by virtue of their participation in parenthood. And yet at the same time, they necessarily exist outside of the traditional gender and family system as "family outlaws" (Calhoun, 1997), thereby liberating them, at least theoretically, from some of the strictures of gendered parenthood; further, they enact and interpret their own parenting in the context of same-sex relationships. Thus, even while they actively "do gender" and "do parenthood," lesbian and gay parents and their families also challenge and expose the meaning and limits of gender—and, inextricably, standard or traditional conceptualizations of family—by virtue of their participation in parenthood.

METHODOLOGICAL LIMITATIONS OF EXISTING RESEARCH

Before reviewing the research and contemporary issues concerning same-sex couples and lesbian and gay parenting, it is appropriate to briefly discuss some of the major methodological problems and challenges in the research on lesbian and gay parents and their children. In discussing these issues, my purpose is not to invalidate or minimize the contributions of the research in this area thus far but, rather, to provide a context for interpreting the existing research.

Sampling in general is fraught with problems and challenges, particularly with populations that are hard to define, difficult to reach, or resistant to identification because of potential discrimination (Meezan & Martin, 2003; Meezan & Rauch, 2005). Such issues necessarily apply to research on sexual minorities and their families, and studies of lesbian and gay parents and their children have indeed been criticized for their use of small, volunteer samples (Belcastro, Gramlich, Nicholson, Price, & Wilson, 1993; Schumm, 2004). Some researchers have in turn questioned the validity of these studies' findings (Belcastro et al., 1993), and some critics of gay parenting have gone so far as to dismiss the entire body of literature as flawed (P. Cameron, 1999; P. Cameron & Cameron, 2002), although, notably, these authors typically fail to acknowledge that problems of small sample sizes and self-selection characterize much of the research in psychology (Herek, 2006; Tye, 2003), particularly studies of small, hard-to-reach populations (Meezan & Rauch, 2005). Indeed, some scientists tend to highlight the nonrepresentativeness of samples of lesbian- and gay-parent families in the context of questioning researchers' conclusions about the seemingly normal psychological adjustment of children of lesbian and gay parents (Belcastro et al., 1993) but tend to dismiss or overlook the nonrepresentative nature of these samples when arguing about the "social contagion" of homosexuality (P. Cameron & Cameron, 1996). For example, P. Cameron and Cameron (1996) noted that of the seven young adults reared by lesbian mothers depicted in Dorothy Chvatal's (1993) *Other Families* video, three (43%) became lesbian. This conclusion should raise eyebrows in light of P. Cameron and Cameron's frequent critiques of the sampling methods used by researchers who study lesbian- and gay-parent families. Further, invocation of percentages in the context of such a small sample is rarely warranted. (Readers should heed this latter point in evaluating the content of this book, which contains discussions of many qualitative studies that have used relatively small samples. When numbers are provided—for example, when 5 of 20 individuals gave a particular response—they are included for descriptive purposes and should not be generalized to the broader population.)

Critics have also often failed to acknowledge that recent studies of children of lesbian and gay parents that are based on random national samples have yielded findings that are remarkably consistent with earlier research (e.g., Wainright & Patterson, 2008; Wainright, Russell, & Patterson, 2004). For example, studies using nationally representative data sets have found that, consistent with earlier research, the peer functioning and psychological adjustment of children of lesbian and gay parents appear to be well within normal limits. Similarly, critics often highlight researchers' overreliance on self- and parent-reports but fail to acknowledge those studies that do utilize a wide variety of data collection methods (e.g., teacher reports of child behavior and functioning, observational data; see, e.g., Chan, Brooks, Raboy, & Patterson, 1998; Chan, Raboy, & Patterson, 1998; Roisman, Clausell, Holland, Fortuna, & Elieff, 2008).

Thus, the field has made a number of inroads in its sampling of lesbian and gay persons and their families. However, challenges certainly remain, not only in terms of the sophistication of data collection and analytic techniques but also in terms of reaching the broad spectrum of lesbian and gay persons and their families. Studies of lesbian and gay couples and their families have tended to include White, middle-class persons who are relatively "out" in the gay community and who are living in urban areas. Working-class sexual minorities, racial or ethnic sexual minorities, sexual minorities who live in rural or isolated geographical areas, closeted sexual minorities, and bisexual and transgender individuals have all been under-studied. This is particularly problematic when we consider how little we know about the experiences and coping strategies of individuals, couples, and families with few resources or who experience multiple forms of discrimination.

Sampling limitations are not the only problem facing research with sexual minorities. Few longitudinal studies are available, limiting insight into the ways that sexual minority individuals, parents, and families change over time and, in particular, during key life transitions to couplehood and to parenthood (Gartrell, Banks, et al., 1999, 2000; Gartrell et al., 1996; Goldberg & Sayer, 2006). Also, many studies collect data from only one partner in a relationship, thereby limiting researchers' ability to examine the ways in which partners mutually influence each other and their relationships, as well as the similar and divergent experiences of dyad members. Additionally, most research uses interviews and questionnaires; more innovative and creative research methods, such as ethnographic research (Carrington, 2002) and observational research (Roisman et al., 2008), are sorely needed to paint a more in-depth and nuanced portrait of both the processes and material conditions of lesbian and gay family life.

Finally, a larger problem that faces research on sexual minorities is the lack of professional recognition of the importance of this work, which is in turn reflected in the limited funding opportunities and publication outlets available to researchers. Despite shifts in attitudes about sexual orientation and the expansion of research on sexual minorities, empirical research on sexual minorities and their families has been hampered by limited funding as well as "heterosexist norms and policies that promote the exclusion of LGBT people from 'mainstream' . . . publications" (Harper, Jernewall, & Zea, 2004, p. 192). As Harper et al. (2004) noted, of the 14,482 empirical articles published in American Psychological Association (APA) journals between 1992 and 2002, only 124 were lesbian or gay-specific (and of these, only 6 focused on people of color). Further, empirical research on transgender people is virtually nonexistent in APA journals (Harper et al., 2004). The absence of adequate funding for research on sexual minorities, as well as the lack of inclusion of such research in mainstream journals, further perpetuates the invisibility of sexual minorities and their families and also serves to discourage scholarship in this area.

SUMMARY: APPROACH TO THIS BOOK

As outlined previously, I have attempted to present the material in this book with special attention to the role of multiple contexts (including state and national governments, the family environment, and the work environment) in shaping the lives and development of lesbian and gay parents and their children. I also expand the definition of context to include consideration of time and timing in the lives of lesbian and gay parents and their children, as well as the role of gender in shaping family and relationship dynamics and processes. Given, too, that "social experience and lived realities are multi-dimensional and. . . our understandings are impoverished and may be inadequate if we view these phenomena only along a single dimension" (Mason, 2006, p. 10), I recognize the importance of addressing and exploring the qualitative research on these families, which is often left out of traditional meta-analyses and literature reviews. Presentation of both quantitative and qualitative reports enables researchers to probe the incongruities and query the inconsistencies in the research and may therefore move our theorizing, empirical study, and discussion of lesbian- and gay-parent families forward.

2

PARTNERS BUT NOT PARENTS: INTIMATE RELATIONSHIPS OF LESBIANS AND GAY MEN

A significant literature has begun to emerge, particularly in the past several decades, on the intimate partner relationships of lesbians and gay men. The themes and foci of this research have varied as a function of historical context. Early research on homosexuality and same-sex relationships must be contextualized in terms of the significant clinical, social, and political debate that preceded and followed the removal in 1973 of the term *homosexuality* from the *Diagnostic and Statistical Manual of Mental Disorders* (3rd ed.; *DSM–III*; American Psychiatric Association, 1980). This removal meant that homosexuality was no longer considered a mental illness by clinical diagnostic standards. However, debate continued to rage—as it still does today—about whether homosexuality in fact represents an inferior or pathological condition. Researchers were charged with the task of answering some very basic questions about the nature and quality of homosexual identity and homosexual relationships, while remaining cognizant of their own biases and orientations (Safer & Riess, 1975).

Thus, early research on same-sex couples and relationships (i.e., research done in the 1970s and 1980s) focused on issues such as stages of coming out (E. Coleman, 1981), establishing a gay identity (L. Lewis, 1984; Troiden, 1979), sexual exclusivity versus openness in gay male relationships (Blasband & Peplau, 1985), and "sex role" identity and behavior (Cardell, Finn, & Marecek, 1981; R. W. Jones & de Cecco, 1982). Although these themes still appear in the current literature, recent research is far more varied, and more attention is being paid to the diversity among lesbians and gay men (as well as, increasingly, among individuals who identify as bisexual and transgender or gender queer) and the intersections among various aspects of identity (sexual orientation, gender, race, and social class). Even so, more work is needed that explores such diversity. This chapter provides a review of the research on same-sex relationships, focusing on research areas that have received the most attention. Within each area, an effort is made to elucidate the ways in which findings appear to or might actually differ according to the nexus of social and relational identities (e.g., social class, race, age). In addition, both qualitative and quantitative sources of data are reviewed, with attention to points of convergence and divergence. This chapter, as well as the chapters that follow, is guided by a framework characterized by attention to social context, time, and gender.

COURTING AND COUPLING:
A SOCIAL–HISTORICAL PERSPECTIVE

Understanding of the development and maintenance of same-sex relationships is enhanced by attending to the broader sociopolitical climate—specifically, the dominant cultural norms and practices that govern behavior in a particular time and place (James & Murphy, 1998). In addition, many lesbians and gay men belong to other subcultures or subgroups whose values and orientation may be similar to or very different from those of the dominant culture. For example, lesbians' and gay men's membership in certain racial/ethnic or religious groups may serve to exacerbate or buffer the homophobic attitudes they confront in the broader society. Lesbians' and gay men's age, social class, and (dis)ability represent additional personal characteristics that serve to contextualize and shape their experiences. Other relevant contexts of the same-sex couple include the family of origin, which may be a source of support or nonsupport, and the gay community; indeed, some sexual minorities, particularly in rural settings, may not have access to a gay community. Furthermore, partners may differ from each other in terms of personal and demographic characteristics, experiences in family of origin, and identification with the gay community; such differences also may pose challenges to the couple.

Notably, the changing social context has had a powerful influence on how same-sex relationships develop. Until relatively recently, opportunities for lesbians and gay men to congregate were quite limited, and the gay bar represented one of the few public places for men and women to interact and socialize (James & Murphy, 1998). Although the gay bar served an important purpose, it may not have represented the ideal context for meaningful social interaction and relationship development, at least for lesbians. For example, an early study by Peplau, Cochran, Rook, and Padesky (1978) suggested that lesbians seeking long-term relationships were more likely to meet their partners in contexts other than bars (e.g., at feminist or lesbian activities or events). Similarly, Bryant and Demian (1994) studied 1,749 lesbians and gay men and found that lesbian partners typically met through work or through friends, whereas gay men were most likely to have met in a bar or some other sexually charged arena.

Currently, lesbians and gay men have many more opportunities for meeting potential partners. Bars still have their place in the lesbian and gay dating scene, but the growing visibility of sexual minorities (and, in turn, of gay communities) has facilitated the development of gay political organizations and activities, gay cruises, gay church groups, and many other activities, avenues, and institutions for interaction. Gay–straight alliances and gay youth groups are now commonplace in many areas of the country in both high schools and colleges (James & Murphy, 1998). The explosion of the Internet as a dating tool has also had an effect on the gay community: Sexual minorities (and gay men in particular) are increasingly turning to online dating as a means of meeting potential romantic and sexual partners (Davis, Hart, Bolding, Sherr, & Elford, 2006).

Increased opportunities for dating have occurred alongside increasingly tolerant attitudes with regard to lesbian and gay rights, especially pertaining to marriage and adoption (Herek, 2006; Savin-Williams, 2008). For example, a 2008 Gallup poll found that 89% of Americans believed that sexual minorities should have equal rights in terms of job opportunities (Saad, 2008). However, public attitudes about the morality of same-sex sexuality and sexual behaviors are much more negative. For example, the same survey found that 48% of Americans considered homosexual relations to be morally wrong, and 40% of Americans believed that homosexual relations between consenting adults should be illegal. Thus, while the climate has improved, negative attitudes continue to exist and therefore shape the experiences of sexual minorities with regard to feelings of safety, decision making about whether to come out in various situations, decision making about whether to demonstrate physical affection with partners in public, and numerous other domains (Peplau, Fingerhut, & Beals, 2004).

Bearing in mind both historical and social-contextual influences on same-sex relationships, I turn now to a discussion of the coming-out process for lesbians and gay men—a process that may precede or unfold in tandem with the formation of a same-sex relationship.

COMING OUT AND BEING OUT

Individuals who possess concealable stigmas (Goffman, 1963) routinely confront situations in which they must decide whether to disclose the source of their stigma. For sexual minorities, this disclosure process is often referred to as *coming out*. Perhaps the best-known framework for understanding the coming out process is Cass's (1979) stage model. According to the model, individuals move from confusion to acceptance and tolerance to pride and synthesis of their sexual minority identity. Thus, the coming out process is conceived of as consisting of a series of relatively linear and continuous stages. Contemporary scholars, however, have suggested that coming out is an ongoing process for sexual minorities (Oswald, 2002) that is not necessarily linear and is often marked by contradiction and change and both pride and shame (Dindia, 1998). Further, outness may vary considerably according to social context (Oswald, 2002): For example, men and women are more likely to be out to friends than to family members (e.g., Morris, Waldo, & Rothblum, 2001).

Additionally, scholars have highlighted the importance of considering the varied situational and contextual forces that affect an individual's decision to come out. In deciding whether to disclose their sexual orientation, lesbians and gay men must consider numerous factors, including their immediate social context (and potential threats associated with disclosure, e.g., harassment), how well they know the individual at hand, and the ease of concealment (Herek, 1996). Broader contextual factors, such as characteristics of one's family and community, will also influence coming out processes. Individuals from highly religious or politically conservative families, for example, may be particularly cautious about coming out for fear of lack of support (Boon & Miller, 1999). They may also face the challenge of reconciling their own religious upbringing with their emergent sexual identity (Schope, 2002). Coming to terms with sexual feelings that are discouraged by one's religion can create intrapersonal tension, particularly for highly religious individuals, who may be plagued with questions about their own self-worth, the validity of their religious beliefs, and what it means to be a "righteous" person (Schuck & Liddle, 2001). Factors such as social class and occupation may also impact the degree to which individuals are out in various aspects of their lives. For example, working-class sexual minorities, who are often employed in male-dominated, blue-collar workplaces where heterosexuality is heavily regulated, may experience less freedom to be out at work than their middle-class counterparts (McDermott, 2006; Taylor, 2005).

Race and ethnicity also may influence coming out. Research has established that sexual minorities who are also racial or ethnic minorities often experience double discrimination: They confront racism in the gay community, and they also face homophobia[1] and marginalization within their own

---

[1]I use the related terms homophobia and heterosexism in the current volume. Homophobia is generally understood as the irrational hatred and fear of lesbians and gay men (Pharr, 1988), which

families and communities (A. I. Green, 2007; Greene, 2000a; Loiacano, 1989; Mays, Chatters, Cochran, & Mackness, 1998; Pearlman, 1996). As an example, people who are members of both racial/ethnic and sexual minorities encounter multiple forms of racism in gay bars that serve predominantly White clienteles: They may be stared at or whispered about or refused entry (indirect and direct racism, respectively; A. I. Green, 2007; Greene & Boyd-Franklin, 1996; Han, 2007). Furthermore, lesbians and gay men from racial/ ethnic minorities are vulnerable to being either ignored or eroticized in the mainstream gay community (Han, 2007). They are generally aware of the homophobia in their extended families and churches, but are nonetheless grateful for the material and emotional sources of support that these communities provide and consequently may feel intrapersonal conflict with regard to coming out (A. I. Green, 2007). Indeed, for lesbians and gay men of color, their heterosexual identification may seem to represent one of the few sources of societal power they possess, and coming out may mean the loss of valuable social, community, and economic resources. They may also hesitate to come out to family out of respect for their cultural upbringing. For example, Merighi and Grimes (2000) found that African American, Mexican American, and Vietnamese American gay men struggled with wanting to establish their own gay identity while also respecting certain cultural norms and ideals. They were aware that their families would respond to their coming out as the end to the family line and that coming out might bring shame and embarrassment not only to their immediate families but also to the extended family and members of their cultural communities. Men therefore hesitated to place such a heavy burden on their families.

Nevertheless, coming out may be considered worth the risk, for multiple reasons. First, failure to do so may restrict individuals' opportunities to find potential partners and their ability to maintain healthy relationships. Second, closeting greatly limits the amount of social support available to sexual minorities as they develop as individuals and partners (Caron & Ulin, 1997). Also, perhaps in part as a function of diminished social support, as well as intrapersonal conflict and internalized homophobia, closeting may be associated with reduced well-being (Garnets & Kimmel, 2003; Lane & Wegner, 1995). However, it is important to acknowledge that concealment of one's sexual orientation is a functional and protective strategy in certain contexts (R. J. Green, 2000), and, in turn, men and women who are not out in all areas of their lives are not necessary less psychologically healthy than

---

can exist both in a society and within an individual (i.e., internalized homophobia). Heterosexism is rooted in a set of beliefs that define heterosexuality as the only normal, acceptable, and moral form of human sexuality (Pharr, 1988; Rich, 1981). This compulsory view of heterosexuality (Rich, 1981) results in the stigmatization of all persons with nonheterosexual identities, behaviors, or attractions, as well as the devaluing of all families that exist outside of the heterosexually married nuclear family. Together, homophobia and heterosexism form a complex system of prejudice against sexual minorities that pervades social, legal, religious, medical, educational, and societal institutions (Blumenfeld, 1992; Herek, 2007).

those who are. Indeed, sexual minorities who closet their sexual orientation in certain situations and settings do not necessarily experience ambivalence or intrapsychic conflict. In a study of 40 lesbian women, Anderson and Holliday (2004) found that all of the participants had purposefully "passed" as heterosexual at some point in their lives. Most women felt that such passing was understandable and appropriate given the social pressures at hand (e.g., concerns about safety, concerns about being fired from a job); only 19% of women had mixed or ambivalent feelings about passing. That is, they were angry and sad that they had to do it but recognized that it was often essential to survival.

As stated earlier, the coming out process may precede or unfold alongside the formation of same-sex relationships. While sharing many commonalities with heterosexual relationships, same-sex unions are characterized by certain unique factors, including the stigmatized nature of the relationship and, thus, potential barriers to relationship development and maintenance. Next, the creation and maintenance of same-sex relationships are discussed, with attention to factors within and outside of the couple that shape the quality and dynamics of relationships.

GETTING TO KNOW YOU: LESBIAN AND GAY DATING

Coming out may occur before or during initial dating experiences with same-sex partners. As individuals begin to explore their sexuality, they may feel the need to inform their friends and family members; however, they may also delay coming out until they enter into a serious dating relationship. Little research has examined the dating experiences of lesbians and gay men, in contrast to a sizeable literature on courtship among heterosexual women and men (Christopher & Sprecher, 2000; Surra, Gray, Boettcher, Cottle, & West, 2006). Much of the research in this area has been conducted by Suzanna Rose and her colleagues (e.g., Klinkenberg & Rose, 1994; Rose & Zand, 2000), who have published several studies that address lesbians' (and to a lesser extent, gay men's) use of dating and romance scripts. A *script* refers to "a set of stereotypical actions defined by cultural norms that serve as a guide for what feelings and behaviors should occur in a specific situation" (Rose & Zand, p. 79). Questions of particular interest to Rose and her colleagues have been, How do lesbians and gay men construct their dating experiences? Do they draw from gendered dating scripts (e.g., man makes the first move)? If so, how does this play out or unfold in the context of same-sex relationships? In one study by Klinkenberg and Rose (1994), 51 gay men and 44 lesbians completed a questionnaire on dating experiences. Half of the participants were asked to describe what a man and woman would typically do on a first date, whereas the other half described their own most recent first date. The authors found that gay men's scripts tended to be more sexually oriented than those of lesbians (i.e., gay men tended to emphasize the sexual aspects of the date such as having sex and staying over), whereas lesbians were more likely to emphasize the emotional aspects of the date. Such findings, then, mirror and may reflect the influence of stereotypes about heterosexual dating and sexuality: for example, notions of men as sexually dominant and sexually driven in relationships and women as more attuned to the emotional nuances of relationships. These findings are also consistent with other research that finds that lesbians tend to prioritize romance over sexual activity in their intimate relationships (Gordon, 2006).

In a later, more in-depth study, Rose and Zand (2000) interviewed 38 lesbians, aged 22 to 63, about their dating histories, in an effort to examine lesbian dating and courtship among young adult women, adult women, and women in midlife. The authors were particularly interested in exploring women's use of three possible courtship scripts: a romance script, a friendship script, and a sexually explicit script. According to Rose and Zand, the lesbian romance script depicts emotional intimacy and physical or sexual attraction as being intertwined in women's attraction to each other. Dating proceeds quickly toward commitment (hence, the stereotype of lesbians moving in with one another after the third date). The friendship script emphasizes emotional intimacy over sexuality. According to this script, two women become friends, fall in love, and enter into a relationship with one another. In the sexually explicit script, two women who are attracted to each other initiate sexual contact with no apparent goal of a future relationship.

Rose and Zand (2000) found that about 74% of lesbians reported having been friends with a woman before entering into a romantic involvement with her, whereas 55% had at some point used the romance script, and 63% had engaged in a sexually explicit script. Younger lesbians, in particular, were likely to use the friendship script. In the absence of clear and widely available scripts for same-sex romance, young women may initially label same-sex attraction as close friendship (Diamond, 2000). Indeed, research has demonstrated that the boundaries between friendship and sexual relationships are complex and sometimes frustratingly unclear, particularly for women, who have been socialized to value intimacy and connectedness in relationships to a greater extent than sexuality (Diamond & Dube, 2002); in turn, some lesbians report not knowing when they are on a date and when they are going out as friends (Gordon, 2006). Confusion about one's sexual orientation and anxiety about potential victimization may also contribute to the more frequent reliance on the friendship script (Savin-Williams, 1995). Additionally, Rose and Zand found that the majority of women tended to prefer to wait until someone else initiated courtship (i.e., asked them on a date), which the authors interpreted as reflective of gender socialization: Men are expected to initiate the relationship, whereas women are expected to wait passively for men's overtures of interest. Further, women in the study tended to use nonverbal cues to indicate interest (e.g., eye contact, light touch) rather than to engage in a direct, verbal approach (asking for a date). Of note, however, lesbians in midlife were the most likely to ask other women for dates and therefore appeared to engage in more "purposeful" dating, perhaps due to having established a strong sense of self and a stronger identity as a lesbian (Rose & Zand, 2000).

These data hint at important interconnections among life stage, age, length of time being out as a lesbian, personal gender socialization and beliefs, and attitudes and approach to dating and relationships. They also highlight a theme that permeates the literature on same-sex relationships: that is, the simultaneously liberating and challenging aspects of being a member of a group (sexual minority) that lacks established guidelines or rules about behavior and identity (i.e., gendered role scripts for same-sex couples). Sexual minorities are, Adam (2006) suggested, "'condemned to freedom' in the sense of innovating relationships without many of the signposts familiar to heterosexual kinship, but are at the same time now able to avail themselves of new opportunities for constructing relationships without much of the 'baggage' of patriarchy and traditional gender expectations" (p. 6). Even so, these data suggest that lesbians' gender socialization and gender beliefs do have powerful effects on their dating behaviors, in the absence of firmly established personal or sexual identities, at least among younger lesbians. Indeed, these dating patterns—younger women's reliance on the friendship script and preference for passive dating behavior, and older women's preference for more direct dating behavior—appear to be shaped less by social–historical factors (e.g., an increasingly tolerant social climate) than by age and length of time being out. Younger lesbians, by virtue of their limited life experience and short length of time away from their families of origin, may continue to be affected by and to conform to gender-related expectations and scripts (i.e., women should not be too aggressive or sexual), whereas older lesbians may experience more freedom to pave their own way (Rose & Zand, 2000).

The Internet has introduced many new opportunities for dating, meeting sexual partners, and "hooking up." Both lesbians and gay men use the Internet for meeting potential partners, although gay men appear to do so more often than lesbians (Henrickson, 2007): One study found that about 40% of gay men reported having used the Internet to find sexual partners (Liau, Millett, & Marks, 2006). Some scholars have been concerned that Internet dating may lead to increased rates of HIV/AIDS (Davis et al., 2006). There is evidence that the anonymity of the Internet may facilitate greater numbers of high-risk sexual encounters (Davis et al., 2006), and use of the Internet to meet sexual partners may lead to sexual mixing between persons who have engaged in high-risk behaviors and those who have not (Wohlfeiler & Potterat, 2005).

LESBIANS AND GAY MEN IN COMMITTED RELATIONSHIPS

Despite the prevalence of stereotypes of sexual minorities (particularly gay men) as fickle and unstable in their intimate relationships (Baker, 2005), many lesbians and gay men are in fact in committed same-sex relationships. Data from the U.S. Census (2000) indicate that at least 1.2 million people reported being in same-sex intimate partner relationships and sharing a household (Simmons & O'Neill, 2001). However, that figure is regarded as a fairly conservative estimate because some same-sex couples likely chose to conceal their relationships on the Census. Indeed, some survey data suggest that U.S. Census numbers for same-sex couples probably undercount them by at least 16% and as much as 28% (Badgett & Rogers, 2003).

A rich literature has begun to emerge on lesbians and gay men in committed relationships. This research has begun to answer some interesting questions about how the relationships of same-sex couples are similar to and differ from those of heterosexual couples, as well as what factors appear to be related to satisfaction and longevity in same-sex relationships. Before turning to a discussion of the nature and quality of committed same-sex relationships, it is important to highlight that not all same-sex couples are monogamous. In fact, there is evidence that sexual exclusivity is not the norm in gay male couples in particular (although the AIDS epidemic has led some gay men to limit their number of sexual partners and to pursue committed relationships; Herdt, 1992). For example, Hickson et al. (1992) found that of 252 men with a regular partner, 56% had a nonmonogamous relationship. Similarly, Julien, Chartrand, and Begin (1996) found that 62% of the 41 gay male couples they interviewed reported having had sex with people outside the relationship. Finally, Solomon, Rothblum, and Balsam (2005) found that slightly more than half of gay men with regular partners had had sex outside of their primary relationship, compared with about 15% of married heterosexual men. However, a 2007 study of lesbian and gay youth found that, among boys, 61% hoped to be monogamously partnered in the next 5 years and 82% expected to be monogamously partnered after age 30 (percentages for girls were 82% and 92%, respectively; D'Augelli, Rendina, Grossman, & Sinclair, 2007). These data point to the possibility of generational effects in attitudes toward sexual exclusivity among gay men and suggest that the emerging cohort of gay men may value monogamy to a greater degree than did prior generations.

Even if the parameters of gay male relationships may deviate somewhat, on average, from the heterosexual norm of marriage and monogamy, sexual exclusivity in such relationships does not appear to be related to relationship satisfaction. Many gay male couples in open relationships experience these relationships as rewarding and satisfying (Kurdek, 1988; Ridge & Feeney, 1998), and some research has found no differences in relationship satisfaction among gay men in open as opposed to closed relationships (Peplau

& Cochran, 1981). Such findings are not particularly surprising, given that gay male partners often discuss and negotiate rules regarding sexual exclusivity and openness with one another (Peplau et al., 2004). For example, Hickson et al. (1992) studied 252 gay men with a "regular partner" and found that 56% of these men also had a nonmonogamous relationship. Most of these men had "contracts" with their regular partners that dictated the boundaries of their nonmonogamy (e.g., they had rules regarding honesty, emotional attachment to other partners, and safe sex). Likewise, Adam (2006) interviewed 70 gay men and found that gay men in open relationships described these relationships as characterized by "a set of tacit and/or explicit understandings that differentiate the primary partner from others, and typically communicate priority for the partner in house" (p. 18). Thus, sexual nonexclusivity in gay male partners is not typically equivalent to "cheating" or "infidelity" and, by itself, does not represent a threat to relationship stability or satisfaction.

Compared with gay couples, lesbian couples are more likely to be monogamous. Bryant and Demian (1994) found that 91% of lesbians reported that their current relationship was sexually exclusive. Moreover, lesbians in exclusive relationships tend to be more satisfied than lesbians with multiple partners (Ridge & Feeney, 1998). However, the findings of at least one study indicate that patterns of sexual exclusivity among lesbians may be more variable than prior research has suggested, and beliefs and practices regarding monogamy may vary in part according to race or ethnicity. Peplau, Cochran, and Mays (1997) studied 398 Black lesbians in relationships and found that 46% acknowledged that they had had extradyadic sex, typically with only one person. These findings caution us to seriously consider the limited generalizability of our findings in this area, given that much of the research on lesbian and gay couples has used samples of White, middle-class individuals.

The differences between lesbians and gay men regarding sexual exclusivity are at least in part a reflection of male–female differences. Men in general demonstrate higher levels of sexual desire compared with women on both self-report measures and physiological indicators, and men also tend to have more permissive attitudes toward premarital and extramarital sex (Baumeister, Catanese, & Vohs, 2001). Women tend to prefer sex in the context of a committed relationship, as opposed to sex with multiple partners or sex with a stranger (Peplau, 2003). Both biological sex differences (men are hormonally predisposed to experience higher levels of sexual desire and arousal) and gender socialization effects (sexuality, desire, and arousal are socially constructed, and women have been socialized to experience shame about their sexuality) have been offered as explanations for these differences (Tolman & Diamond, 2001). Regardless of causality, however, the existing data imply that two men in a relationship are more likely to mutually pursue an arrangement that involves sex with multiple partners, whereas two women in a relationship are more likely to mutually desire monogamous sex. Beyond gender, societal ideologies and discourses, as well as more localized attitudes and norms, also serve to influence sexual and relationship behavior. Heterosexual married men are less likely than gay male partners to have extradyadic sex not only because there is a woman in the relationship, but also because their relationships are governed by a discourse of romance and commitment that positions monogamy as expected, central, and necessary to functional relationships. Gay men, on the other hand, are aware of romance scripts that prescribe sexual exclusivity and commitment, but they are also influenced by the norms and attitudes that characterize contemporary gay male culture (e.g., sexual consumerism; Adam, 2006). Indeed, the "fast-lane sexuality" (Connell, 1992) that characterizes many gay communities may be perceived as a threat to the maintenance of monogamous relationships, and gay men who value sexually exclusive relationships may distance themselves from these communities once they enter into a committed relationship (J. Meyer, 1989). Lesbian couples do not appear to confront these same pressures. In fact, not only are lesbians more likely to be monogamous, but, perhaps because, as two women, they are socialized to value the symbolism of marriage, they are also more likely to choose to legalize their relationship, when options such as civil union or marriage are available (Oswald, Goldberg, Kuvalanka, & Clausell, 2008; Rothblum, Balsam, & Solomon, 2008).

Regardless of whether relationships are open or closed, many lesbians and gay men are in committed, satisfying relationships (Bryant & Demian, 1994; Mackey, Diemer, & O'Brien, 2004). The fact that so many lesbians and gay men are able to sustain lasting relationships in spite of opposition from family members, societal stigma, and the absence of the legal and structural supports that benefit married couples is particularly remarkable. It is important to understand (a) how, and in what ways, same-sex couples differ from heterosexual couples and (b) what factors are associated with relationship quality and satisfaction in these couples. With these aims in mind, this chapter now turns to a discussion of intimate relationship quality and satisfaction among same-sex couples. It must be noted that because few researchers actually ask about relationships outside the primary relationships, studies of committed same-sex couples' relationship outcomes do not necessarily take into account the presence and nature of other relevant relationships. Thus, the data that are reported typically reflect lesbians' and gay men's primary relationships.

Relationship Quality

Although relationship quality and satisfaction have been studied extensively in heterosexual couples (Cordova, Gee, & Warren, 2005; Whisman, Uebelacker, & Weinstock, 2004), studies have only recently begun to examine these domains among same-sex couples, and in turn, to compare the relational health of same-sex and heterosexual couples. The majority of these studies have found few differences between the two types of couples. In one study of long-term relationships (average duration 30 years), about 85% of respondents reported satisfaction with their relationship; no differences were found between heterosexual men, heterosexual women, lesbians, and gay men (Mackey et al., 2004). Other studies have reported that lesbian couples report higher relationship quality than heterosexual couples (Balsam, Beauchaine, Rothblum, & Solomon, 2008; Kurdek, 2001, 2003), a finding that may in part reflect the absence of structural barriers that govern heterosexual relationships (i.e., fundamental relationship constraints such as legal support, family support, and children, without which relationships that are unrewarding or conflictual are more easily terminated). Alternatively, this finding may also reflect something uniquely protective about the presence of two women in a relationship: Women are known to strongly value communication and emotional intimacy in relationships, and thus the presence of two women may lead to enhanced communication and relationship stability (Kurdek, 1998).

Studies have also examined how same-sex couples' relationships change over time. Kurdek (1998) studied heterosexual married couples and lesbian and gay cohabiting couples and found that over a 5-year period all couples tended to show a decrease in relationship satisfaction; there were no differences among groups in their rates of change. Other studies (e.g., Kurdek, 2003) have found the reported relationship quality of lesbian partners to be higher initially than that of gay male couples and to decline more slowly, again suggesting that the presence of two women exerts a buffering effect on relationships.

As noted, lesbian and gay couples lack institutionalized barriers to leaving their relationships. It is possible that the absence of such barriers (e.g., marriage), which confer legal, social, and/or religious support and which therefore function to stabilize relationships, may lead lesbian and gay partners to end their unions during times of crisis, stress, or dissatisfaction. In an effort to examine the viability of this hypothesis, several studies have compared rates of relationship dissolution among gay, lesbian, and heterosexual couples. A study by Kurdek (2006) found that gay and lesbian couples were indeed more likely to separate than were heterosexual married couples with children—who are, almost by definition, couples with multiple institutionalized barriers to leaving. Further, Balsam et al. (2008) conducted a longitudinal study of same-sex couples in Vermont and found that couples who had obtained civil unions were less likely to have ended their relationship than couples who had not, which may point to the potential stabilizing effect of civil unions. (Importantly, however, this study did not establish a causal relationship between civil unions and relationship commitment: It is possible that couples who obtained civil unions—many of whom resided in other states, rendering their unions purely symbolic in nature—were more committed to their relationships in the first place.) Research is needed to explore whether same-sex couples with children are less likely to dissolve their relationships than same-sex couples without children; perhaps children exert a partial stabilizing function. A related question is how relationship dissolution rates among same-sex couples who have children and who have legalized their relationships (e.g., by civil union or marriage) compare with rates among heterosexual couples with children. Of course, even if rates of dissolution among same-sex couples are higher, this may suggest more about the broader social context, which continues to undermine same-sex unions, than about anything inherent to same-sex relationships themselves. This is an intriguing area for future study.

Psychological Intimacy and Autonomy

An important aspect of relationship quality is *intimacy*, or the merging of the self and the other. Intimacy has been studied fairly extensively in heterosexual couples (Lemieux & Hale, 2000; Prager & Buhrmester, 1998) and more recently in lesbian and gay couples (Eldridge & Gilbert, 1990; Mackey, Diemer, & O'Brien, 2000). Researchers (e.g., Kurdek, 1998) have hypothesized that because lesbian couples are made up of two women who have been socialized to orient themselves to relationships, to value intimacy and connection, and to define themselves in terms of their relationships (see Burch, 1985), lesbian relationships may benefit from "a double dose of relationship-enhancing influences" (Kurdek, 1998, p. 554). From this perspective, the relational orientation of women (i.e., an orientation that is characterized by a valuing of mutuality rather than of autonomy within relationships) may nurture the development of psychological intimacy in women's relationships. In line with such predictions, Kurdek (1998) found that lesbians had higher levels of psychological intimacy than partners in heterosexual relationships and gay male relationships. Schreurs (1994) also found that lesbians' relationships were characterized by higher levels of emotional intimacy compared with heterosexual men and women. Finally, qualitative research by Connolly (2005) on long-term lesbian couples further suggests that stable lesbian relationships are characterized by high mutuality and psychological intimacy. An important component of relationship quality, psychological intimacy has in turn been linked to relationship stability and satisfaction. For example, Mackey et al. (2004) found that psychologically intimate communication and minimal conflict were the most powerful contributors to relationship satisfaction for heterosexual, gay, and lesbian couples.

Researchers have observed that too much psychological intimacy may be damaging to lesbian relationships. Some theorists have argued that high levels of psychological intimacy, combined with little support from or contact with the outside world, can result in *fusion,* a state of psychological unity between people in which individual ego boundaries merge (Burch, 1985).

Presumably, lesbian couples are more vulnerable to fusion than other types of couples because of their common gender socialization and, by extension, their strong orientation to relationships and relating. Fusion has been blamed for contributing to low sexual desire and infrequent sexual activity in lesbian relationships; indeed, some research has found that of all couple types, lesbian couples tend to have the lowest frequencies of sexual contact (e.g., Blumstein & Schwarz, 1983; but see A. K. Matthews, Tartaro, & Hughes, 2003). However, empirical research on fusion suggests that despite its frequent mention in theoretical writings on lesbian relationships, it does not characterize lesbian relationships in general (Hill, 1999).

Another dimension of relationships that has been studied extensively is autonomy, or the degree to which one maintains a sense of self separate from the relationship (i.e., independence; Goodman, 1999; Tower & Krasner, 2006). Many theorists have posited that men, gay and heterosexual, are socialized to value independence and separateness in their relationships (e.g., Gilligan, 1982). Assuming this is true, perhaps gay male couples should report greater autonomy because they experience a "double dose of individual-enhancing influences" (Kurdek, 1998, p. 554). Consistent with this hypothesis, some studies have found that gay male partners have higher levels of autonomy than heterosexual partners (Kurdek, 1998, 2001). This finding would seem to suggest differences based on gender rather than sexual orientation. However, some studies have also found that lesbian partners have higher levels of autonomy than heterosexual partners (Kurdek, 1998). Kurdek suggested that lesbians' socialization as lesbians may be relevant in understanding this finding. As part of their journey to self-identifying as lesbians, women confront the reality that they cannot and will never be reliant on men to support them (Fassinger, 1995; Morgan & Brown, 1991), a realization that may promote the development of emotional and financial independence, which are characteristics of autonomy.

Autonomy, at high levels, may be a barrier to relationship durability and commitment. Kurdek's (2000) study of gay and lesbian couples found that possessing a high level of autonomy was linked to perceiving few attractions to the relationship. High levels of autonomy have also been linked to lower relationship satisfaction in lesbian couples (Eldridge & Gilbert, 1990). Further, an increase in personal autonomy over time appears to be associated with a greater risk of relationship dissolution in lesbian and gay couples (Kurdek, 1996). As stated earlier, high levels of autonomy are particularly characteristic of gay male couples (Kurdek, 1998) and appear to be linked to negative relational patterns such as emotional distancing (Levine, 1979), which may become mutually reinforcing and lead to impaired communication (Mackey et al., 2000). Indeed, Mackey, O'Brien, and Mackey (1997) interviewed lesbian and gay couples about their communication over the course of their relationship and found that gay couples tended to report a decline in the quality of their communication over time, such that 54% of gay men compared with 85% of lesbians were satisfied with their communication at the time of the study. The double dose of autonomous influences that characterizes gay male relationships may also have direct implications for commitment processes, insomuch as commitment implies mutual dependence. For example, Kurdek (2001) found that gay male couples demonstrated lower levels of commitment in comparison with heterosexual couples. Of course, many other factors also influence gay men's commitment levels and processes, including family support for the relationship and the attitudes and norms of the gay community and the broader community. For example, gay men who live in urban areas that valorize open relationships and nonmonogamy may be less likely to form committed relationships; alternatively, those who do may be rejected from the single-oriented gay male community (J. Meyer, 1989). As marriage rights and civil unions become more prominent, it is possible that both lesbian and gay couples will demonstrate higher levels of commitment.

Conflict in Relationships

Few couples can avoid any conflict in their relationships. Indeed, lesbian, gay male, and heterosexual couples tend to report similar frequencies of arguments in their relationships (Peplau & Fingerhut, 2007). Observational studies of lesbian, gay, and heterosexual couples (i.e., studies that observe couples during laboratory interactions) also suggest few differences in the nature and quality of conflict interactions (Julien, Chartrand, Simard, Bouthillier, & Begin, 2003), although one study found that lesbian couples worked together more harmoniously when asked to discuss an area of disagreement in their relationship than did gay male and heterosexual couples (Roisman, Clausell, Holland, Fortuna, & Elieff, 2008), and another study found that lesbian and gay partners were more likely to maintain a positive tone while discussing problems in their relationships than were heterosexual partners (Gottman et al., 2003). Studies also indicate that same-sex and heterosexual couples also appear to disagree about similar topics: Finances, sex, and household tasks top the charts for both types of couples (Kurdek, 1994, 2006).

Given the unique relational context of same-sex relationships (e.g., partners' shared gender socialization and minority sexual orientation), it seems likely that lesbian and gay couples might encounter certain unique interpersonal challenges or demonstrate some unique patterns with regard to conflict resolution style. Mackey et al. (1997) found that gay men in long-term relationships tended to avoid discussing their thoughts and feelings about conflicts until difficulties threatened their relationships. This may be interpreted as a function of the double dose of male socialization that characterizes gay men's relationships (Kurdek, 1998). Lesbian couples in Mackey et al.'s (1997) study encountered challenges in other areas: Specifically, in the early stages of their relationships, women avoid confronting interpersonal differences, preferring to maintain relational harmony. As their relationship progressed, women became less avoidant of confrontation about such differences. The authors suggested that declining fears of being abandoned by their partners may have facilitated this change.

Although lesbian and gay partners within relationships share several important factors (e.g., their gender socialization, their status as a stigmatized minority in society), their differences from one another can create conflict. Partners may come from different social class backgrounds, which may create chronic misunderstanding and tension (Hall & Greene, 2002). For example, one partner's high career investment may be cast as evidence of advanced (and taken-for-granted) class standing (Rutter & Schwartz, 1996). Similarly, racial or ethnic differences between partners can create stress. As noted, racial/ethnic minorities who are also sexual minorities may contend with lack of support and discrimination in multiple communities: the broader racial/ethnic group to which they belong, and the gay community (Loiacano, 1989; Mays, Cochran, & Rhue, 1993; Pearlman, 1996). Racial/ethnic minorities who are also sexual minorities with White partners may experience alienation and isolation within their relationships if they feel that their partners cannot empathize with or understand the intersecting forces of sexism, heterosexism, and racism that they face on a daily basis (Pearlman, 1996). Likewise, White partners may feel guilty about racism and attempt to compensate for their privilege, a strategy that will ultimately be unsuccessful and may leave both partners feeling angry and frustrated. Furthermore, interracial same-sex couples may be more identifiable than two women or men of the same ethnic group, thereby eliciting strong homophobic and racist reactions from outsiders (Greene & Boyd-Franklin, 1996). Such reactions may lead interracial couples to "manage" their visibility by seeking out racially mixed lesbian or gay spaces or choosing to pass as heterosexual friends, particularly when in racially segregated or hostile social terrain (Steinbugler, 2005). However, despite the challenges that interracial same-sex couples face, at least one study found that interracial couples did not differ from same-race couples in terms of relationship satisfaction, suggesting that many interracial same-sex couples successfully navigate their differences (Peplau, Cochran, & Mays, 1997). More research is needed that examines the experiences of interracial same-sex couples. Indeed, although researchers of same-sex couples have begun to acknowledge that gender, sexuality, race, and class are linked systems, very little work has begun to specify how these distinct social locations intersect and interact (Gamson & Moon, 2004).

A final source of difference and potential conflict in intimate same-sex relationships concerns partners' individual preferences about how "out" to be about the relationship (Bepko & Johnson, 2000; Rutter & Schwartz, 1996). In one study of lesbians and gay men, J. Cameron and Hargreaves (2005) found that an imbalance between partners in managing secrecy and openness was a key source of conflict in many participants' relationships. Some participants spoke about the challenge of having to protect their partner's need for secrecy when they themselves would prefer to be open; for example, being introduced as a friend when the open partner wished to be identified as someone closer was sometimes experienced as hurtful. As Bepko and Johnson (2000) noted, the anxiety and stress of continually navigating such issues can cause distance and defensiveness in couples. Thus, couples who mutually resolve their differing preferences and concerns about openness are likely to enjoy more stable and harmonious relationships.

Equality and Power

The same-sex nature of lesbian and gay relationships may have implications for how couples navigate issues of equality and power in their relationships. A number of scholars have theorized that, as women, lesbians have experienced unfairness and oppression in multiple contexts throughout their lives and may therefore possess a heightened awareness of issues of inequity and inequality compared with heterosexual couples (e.g., Blumstein & Schwartz, 1983; Dunne, 2000). In turn, lesbians may be especially likely to value and facilitate equality in their intimate relationships (Blumstein & Schwartz, 1983; Riggle, Whitman, Olson, Rostosky, & Strong, 2008). In line with this suggestion, empirical research has found that, compared with gay male partners, lesbians tend to place more value on equality in their appraisals of "ideal" relationships (Kurdek, 1995). Caldwell and Peplau (1984) conducted a study of 77 lesbians in committed relationships and found that 97% of lesbians thought that both partners should have "exactly equal" say in their relationship, although not all women believed that their current relationship matched this ideal. Notably, when perceptions of imbalance in power occurred, the partner who was regarded as having more power in the relationship was typically the partner who was relatively less involved in and less committed to the relationship. Relational power was also related to structural variables, such that women who possessed fewer personal resources (less education, less personal income) than their partners tended to have less power in the relationship. Compared with other types of couples, though, lesbians do tend to demonstrate greater equality in their relationships. Specifically, when perceptions of equality in the relationship (i.e., equal power and equal contributions to the relationship) are assessed, lesbian couples tend to report more equality in their relationships than heterosexual couples (Kurdek, 1998) and gay male couples (Kurdek, 2003).

Division of Labor

One important and frequently studied aspect of power is the division of labor. In heterosexual couples, labor is often divided up according to sex (difference). Women are expected to maintain more of the responsibility for unpaid work, such as housework, and men to assume more of the responsibility for paid work (Coltrane, 2000). Even in dual-earner heterosexual couples, in which women and men work roughly the same amount of hours, women often assume a greater proportion of the unpaid or household labor (Kitterod & Pettersen, 2006). Because unpaid labor is often regarded as a devalued and unappreciated form of labor (Ferree, 1990), women's disproportionate responsibility for housework can be regarded as reflecting an imbalance in status and power. Given that lesbian and gay couples cannot rely on sex difference as a guide for how to allocate paid and unpaid work responsibilities, it follows that they may do so more equally.[2] Consistent with this notion, research has found that same-sex couples, and particularly lesbians, are more likely to share housework equally compared with heterosexual couples (Balsam et al., 2008; Kurdek, 1993; A. K. Matthews et al., 2003; Solomon, Rothblum, & Balsam, 2004; Solomon et al., 2005). Some research suggests that lesbian partners tend to share tasks, whereas gay male partners are more likely to specialize in certain tasks (Kurdek, 1993). Where task specialization occurs, lesbians and gay men often tend to emphasize work schedules, interests, and skills as factors that influence the division of tasks (Bialeschki & Pearce, 1997; Kurdek, 2005).

Qualitative work by Carrington (2002) paints a somewhat different picture, however. In his in-depth ethnographic study of 52 lesbian and gay couples (all but 3 of whom did not have children living in the home), Carrington found that many couples failed to make a clear distinction between what they considered equal and what they considered fair. That is, many couples did not seem to have achieved equality, but because they considered the division of labor fair (i.e., equitable), they often spoke of their arrangements as equal. Furthermore, Carrington observed that one person tended to "specialize" in unpaid labor in about three 3 of 4 of the couples studied (namely, 38 of 52 couples). He found that the longer the couple had been together, the more pronounced the specialization had become. Carrington observed that in most cases, the person with less earning power or with less occupational prestige performed the majority of the domestic work, a finding he suggested could be explained by the "relative resource" model (partners with fewer financial resources make up for it with greater investment in unpaid labor) or a "time availability" explanation (the person with less time investment in paid work does more unpaid labor; pp. 187–188). Further, Carrington suggested that equal sharing is strongly facilitated by financial, educational,

[2]In addition, because, as noted, lesbians cannot expect to be financially dependent on men, they must assume that they will always be their own primary source of financial support. This reality is reflected in employment rates of approximately 70%–90% in most lesbian samples (Morgan & Brown, 1991). Indeed, U.S. Census data suggest that 69% of lesbians with partners worked full-time compared with only 47% of married women and 74% of married men (Human Rights Campaign, 2003, as cited in Peplau & Fingerhut, 2004). In turn, most lesbians ultimately occupy dual-earner relationships, such that both partners feel obligated to provide financially (Morgan & Brown, 1991).

and social resources: He found that equal sharing of domestic duties was most common among affluent couples who relied on paid help (e.g., housecleaners, laundry workers) and among couples in which both partners had flexible schedules.

Thus, it seems that middle- to upper middle-class same-sex couples are advantaged in multiple ways, including their capacity to buy their way out of routine, dull, and undesirable work. The allocation of work to other sources may serve to minimize the degree of struggle and conflict that couples experience over the division of labor and may ultimately contribute to greater equality. Working-class same-sex couples cannot afford to allocate labor to other sources and must therefore negotiate the full spectrum of household tasks. As a result, they may experience more conflict about certain tasks or types of work.

Differences in earning potential within the couple may also have implications for the division of labor. Solomon and colleagues (2005) compared lesbians, gay men, and heterosexual men and women in committed relationships and found that doing "women's housework" (i.e., the routine, repetitive tasks such as cleaning and cooking) was negatively associated with income (a form of power) and income difference (i.e., when partner earns more money than participant). Doing "men's housework" (i.e., infrequent tasks such as taking out the garbage and household repairs) was positively correlated with personal income, being in a lesbian relationship, and working full-time. Thus, the authors suggested that while lesbian and gay couples may divide chores more equally than heterosexual couples do, power differences within the relationship may, on some level, influence who does what.

A 2007 study of lesbian and gay couples suggests the potential mechanisms by which the division of labor and perceptions of power and equality might be related to each other and to perceptions of relationship quality (Kurdek, 2007). Kurdek found that satisfaction with the division of housework was associated with relationship satisfaction, such that individuals who were more dissatisfied with the division of chores were more dissatisfied with their relationships. However, this association was mediated by perceptions of equality in the relationship; that is, dissatisfaction with the division of housework exerted an effect on relationship dissatisfaction through appraisals of inequality in the relationship. Thus, lesbians' and gay men's subjective assessments of the division of labor (i.e., satisfaction with the division, as well as the degree to which imbalances in the division of labor are viewed through the lens of equality or inequality) may be as or more important than the actual division of labor, in terms of its impact on relationship outcomes.

Role Playing and Gender Performance

Because female same-sex couples (and to some extent, male same-sex couples) are often presumed to value and embody egalitarianism in their intimate relationships, lesbian couples whose gender performance is perceived as mirroring or emulating heterosexual relationships have long been the subject of scrutiny and, often, criticism (see Faderman, 1991), particularly from White, middle-class feminists (Moore, 2006). Specifically, lesbians who enact butch–femme identities or who are viewed as engaging in role playing are often criticized for replicating and reifying heterosexual relationship structures and heteronormativity. Specifically, *butch women*—that is, women who reject feminine ways of dressing and acting—are viewed as imitating men, and *femme women*—that is, women whose self-presentation aligns more closely with stereotypically female ways of dressing and acting—are seen as enacting scripted heterosexual female behavior with a woman (Faderman, 1991; Levitt & Horne, 2002). According to some feminist scholars, such behaviors serve to maintain and celebrate heterosexuality as the only natural and normative expression of human sexuality and to mark all other expressions as deviant (Rich, 1981). Other feminist theorists (e.g., Rubin, 1992) have argued that lesbian roles challenge the constructed nature of heterosexual roles and function to subvert and destabilize dominant conceptions of gender categories. Still other theorists (e.g., Butler, 1991) believe that lesbian identities and butch–femme roles are simultaneously derivative of and subversive of heterosexuality.

A historical perspective is necessary to contextualize the evolution and meaning of butch–femme roles and identities. Nestle (1992) and Faderman (1991) provided accounts of the historical influences and social context that shaped and were shaped by the emergence of butch–femme identities and role playing in the 20th century. In the 1960s, these identities emerged in the context of the "political lesbianism" movement and were not so much about desire as they were about challenging and transforming gender oppression (Faderman, 1991). However, by the 1970s, White lesbian feminists were often disparaging toward feminine and masculine gender displays among lesbians, and they pushed women to move toward more androgynous gender presentations, thereby silencing butch–femme roles in many communities (although Black lesbians, who were somewhat distanced from the feminist movement, were less influenced by these pressures; Moore, 2006). In the 1980s, the butch–femme culture began to reemerge in many lesbian communities. However, the assumption of these identities was less a political enterprise and was more motivated by desire (Levitt & Hiestand, 2005; Nestle, 1992), and researchers therefore saw more choice in the types of gender presentation that lesbians were creating (Stein, 1992).

It is not entirely clear to what extent lesbians today endorse butch–femme identities, and how and to what extent gender presentation continues to structure relationships in contemporary lesbian communities. The empirical work that has explored these questions is limited. Some studies have not found much evidence of butch–femme roles (e.g., Caldwell & Peplau, 1984; Smith & Stillman, 2002), whereas others have found that such roles characterize some lesbians' relationships but not all. For example, Levitt and

Horne (2002) conducted a study of 149 (primarily White) lesbian, bisexual, and queer-identified women and found that, in terms of gender expression, 16% identified as butch, 31% identified as femme, 31% identified as androgynous, and 15% identified as other. Notably, butch-identified women, who visibly defied heterosexual gender norms, reported higher rates of discrimination based on their gender expression. Thus, these data indicate that if requested, many lesbians can indeed align themselves with a category of gender presentation; however, it is unclear from these data how meaningful such descriptors are in the lives of these women or how such identifiers structure their relationships and identities. Indeed, Levitt and Hiestand (2005) conducted qualitative research with 12 butch-identified women and 12 femme-identified women and found that, contrary to stereotype, women do not necessarily pair with their "opposite"—that is, some femme women were attracted to and had been in relationships with other femme women; likewise, some butch women had been or were currently involved with other butch-identified women. Importantly, all of the women in this study viewed their gender performance as challenging traditional gender and sexual orientation boundaries, and they did not conceive of their relationships as imitative of heterosexual relationships.

Moore (2006) studied over 100 Black lesbians and used participants' self-descriptions and her own observations to categorize women into three categories: femmes or feminine women (48%); "gender-blenders," somewhat similar to what the literature has termed *androgynous*; (34%); and "transgressives," or masculine–butch (18%).[3] She found that these women often rejected labels such as butch–femme, even when their gender presentation (hairstyle, clothes, physical mannerisms) seemed to embody such descriptors. According to Moore, these women's gender displays often appeared to structure social interactions and dating practices. For example, gender-blenders and transgressives often dated women who were more feminine than themselves, and women who desired a particular type of woman (e.g., a feminine type of woman) sometimes made special efforts to attract them. For example, by dressing in a nonfeminine way, they could win the attention of feminine women, who tended to find that gender display highly desirable.

Notably, physical gender display categories were not accompanied by, and did not map onto, gendered personality traits. That is, "traits such as

---

[3]Femmes in this study, according to Moore (2006),

> wear dresses or skirts, form-fitting jeans, tops that are low cut or that show cleavage, makeup, jewelry, and accessories such as a purse or high-heeled shoes that display a sense of femininity. This gender presentation is limited to how they look physically and is not necessarily connected to any specific personality traits or ideologies about gender display. Gender-blender is a style related to but distinct from an androgynous presentation of self . . . rather than a de-emphasis on femininity or masculinity, gender-blenders combine specific aspects of both to create a unique look. . . . Transgressive women . . . wear men's clothes and shoes and coordinate these outfits with heavy jewelry, belts with large, masculine buckles, and ties or suspenders. . . . Clothes are never form-fitting. (pp. 124–125)

straightforwardness, assertiveness, being highly emotional, or being a particularly rational thinker did not reveal themselves in any consistent way with the three gender display categories" (Moore, 2006, p. 127). Nor was there any consistent trend for the gender-blenders or transgressives to assume the role of sexual aggressor in their relationships. Thus, these categories were defined only by a mix of style, symbols, and mannerisms, and in part, patterns of physical attraction—not personality. Bailey, Kim, Hills, and Linsenmeier (1997) also suggested the importance of teasing apart physical appearance and personality/behavioral traits in understanding patterns of attraction and pairing. Bailey et al. found that, on average, their sample of mostly White lesbians preferred women who were feminine-*looking* but were not opposed to pairing with a woman who was masculine-*acting*.

Thus, it can be concluded that (a) butch–femme identities and roles characterize the dynamics of some but certainly not all lesbian relationships; (b) there are inconsistencies and divergences in the degree to which women identify with these identifiers and the degree to which these identifiers explain patterns of attraction and pairing; (c) these inconsistencies and divergences are likely the result of, and reflect, variability in the ways in which both researchers and participants have conceptualized these identifiers (e.g., as indicative of gender identity, gender display, patterns of attraction, and personality); and (d) studying diverse groups of lesbians, with regard to race, social class, urbanity, and culture will help to expand our understanding of roles and gender display in lesbian relationships. Indeed, Crawley (2001) suggested that social class may represent one variable that shapes the degree to which butch–femme labels are embodied and embraced. Specifically, Crawley's research indicates that contemporary middle-class lesbians are more likely to reject the butch–femme classification than are working-class lesbians, which Crawley suggested may be related to the fact that working-class lesbians "have very little privilege to protect . . . they have less to lose than middle-class women" and therefore are less invested in "assimilationist gender representations" than middle-class women (p. 188). Likewise, Weber (1996) studied 235 lesbian women and found that education was the most significant predictor of whether women identified themselves as butch, femme, or neither, such that women with higher levels of education were less likely to identify as butch or femme.

Less attention has been paid to gay men's gender presentation and role playing, although some work has explored gay men's identification with different types of masculinities. Research suggests that gay men often identify with particular categories of gender performance and acknowledge attraction to particular categories of gender performance—for example, some gay men espouse a preference for "straight-acting" or "straight gay" homosexual men and condemn any gender performances that they label "in your face" gayness (i.e., "queens"; Clarkson, 2006; Connell, 1992). In turn, some gay men have been found to actively revise their own style and appearance to appear "less gay and more 'normal'" in an effort to attract the attention of more masculine and straight-acting men (Clarke & Turner, 2007, p. 272). Many gay men appear to eroticize masculine gender displays and criticize effeminate gender presentations, a practice that both reflects and reifies dominant notions of hegemonic masculinity (Clarkson, 2006).[4]

Some research has explicitly focused on gendered role playing in gay male relationships. For example, an early study by Jay and Young (1979) asked gay men, "How often do you 'role-play' (butch–femme, masculine–feminine, husband–wife, dominant–submissive) in your relationships?" The most common responses were "never" (47%) and "very infrequently" (23%). Other research has explicitly explored whether specific sexual acts and preferences tend to map onto general patterns of masculinity and dominance in gay male relationships. Blumstein and Schwartz (1983), for example, examined whether gay men who tended to take the "inserter" role (i.e., "tops") in anal sex were more masculine than gay men who tended to take the "receiver" role (i.e., "bottoms"). They did not find strong evidence that sexual practices tend to be associated with general patterns of masculinity/dominance and femininity/submissiveness in gay male relationships. Wegesin and Meyer-Bahlburg (2000) also found few differences in feminine–masculine gender identity among bottoms, tops, and versatiles (who have an equal preference for both roles), although their qualitative data suggest that many gay men nevertheless possess a stereotype of "bottoms" as feminine. One problem with efforts to dichotomize gay men into masculine and feminine roles is that not all gay men label themselves as inserters or receivers—that is, many gay men consider themselves to be versatiles (Hart, Wolitski, Purcell, Gomez, & Halkitis, 2003; Moskowitz, Rieger, & Roloff, 2008). For example, Hart et al. (2003) studied 205 gay men and found that the majority (47%) identified as versatiles; 23% identified as bottoms, 18% identified as tops, and 12% reported that these labels did not apply to them.

UNIQUE CHALLENGES: SYMBOLIC AND STRUCTURAL SUPPORTS AND RECOGNITION

Thus far, this chapter has addressed the dynamics of same-sex couples and relationships. However, these couples and their relationships exist in a broader societal context, which necessarily has an impact on sexual minorities and the dynamics and stability of their relationships. Discrimination and lack of recognition occur at the broadest level (e.g., in the form of state and

---

[4]Interestingly, some research suggests that gay men who possess traditional masculinity ideologies (e.g., they avoid femininity, value self-reliance and achievement/status) tend to engage in more high-risk sexual activity (Halkitis, 2001) and to report lower quality romantic relationships (Wade & Donis, 2007). Thus, strong adherence to hegemonic masculinity norms may have detrimental effects on gay men's well-being and relationships.

federal laws and practices) and at the most immediate level (e.g., in one's family of origin) and pose challenges for same-sex couples and the families that they create.

The Social–Legal Context

Lesbian and gay couples reside virtually everywhere in the United States: the 2000 Census established that same-sex couples live in 99.3% of all U.S. counties (Pawelski et al., 2006). Nevertheless, same-sex couples continue to be denied many of the legal protections and supports that are afforded to heterosexual couples (Herek, 2006; Pawelski et al., 2006). Denial of such protections is often defended on the grounds that to protect same-sex couples would be to approve of or encourage such relationships; furthermore, protecting such relationships is viewed as a threat to the institution of marriage and the stability of family life (Clarkson-Freeman, 2004). Currently, policymakers at all levels of government have moved to enact legislation to prohibit any type of legal recognition of same-sex partnerships and parenting (Pawelski et al., 2006). For example, constitutional amendments that prohibit same-sex civil marriage, civil union, and domestic partnership have been pursued, and passed, in multiple states. The enactment of such marriage amendments formally halts the possibility of obtaining a variety of legal and financial rights and protections, including eligibility for public housing and housing subsidies, automatic financial decision-making authority on behalf of one's spouse, the ability to make medical decisions for an incapacitated partner, access to spousal benefits of worker's compensation, the ability to file joint income tax returns and benefit from family-related deductions, and many other benefits (Pawelski et al., 2006). As Pawelski et al. pointed out, the current national political debates about same-sex marriage occur in the context of, and thereby serve to intensify, an already unfavorable social climate for lesbians and gay men. Societal intolerance and the absence of legal and symbolic supports serve to undermine the commitment that lesbian and gay partners have made to each other and threaten their emotional and relational well-being. Legal and social recognition (e.g., in the form of marriage) would arguably improve both the physical and emotional well-being of lesbians and gay men by conferring health benefits, reducing discrimination, and increasing the stability of same-sex relationships (King & Bartlett, 2005). Furthermore, provisions of formal recognition and support for same-sex unions take on new and important meaning in the context of raising children, which is discussed in subsequent chapters of this volume.

However, the prohibitive measures that are increasingly being pursued in many states have been introduced alongside legislation favorable toward civil marriage and civil unions. For example, on November 18, 2003, the Massachusetts Supreme Judicial Court ruled that prohibiting same-sex couples from civil marriage violated the state's constitution, and on May 20, 2004,

Massachusetts began issuing marriage licenses to same-sex couples. Likewise, on May 15, 2008, the California Supreme Court overturned the same-sex marriage ban (although this decision was undermined by the passage of Proposition 8 in the November 2008 election, which aimed to ban same-sex marriage in California). And, on October 10, 2008, Connecticut became the third state to legalize same-sex marriage in a 4 to 3 decision by the state Supreme Court. (Of course, these states' marriage laws are not recognized by the federal government as this book goes to press, and therefore they do not entitle lesbian and gay married couples to any of the federal rights, benefits, or protections that are afforded to heterosexual married couples.) Furthermore, a number of states (e.g., New Jersey, Vermont) have legalized civil unions, which provide many of the benefits of civil marriage but are regarded as separate and distinct from the institution of marriage. Of course, a number of countries other than the United States, namely, the Netherlands, Belgium, Canada, Spain, and South Africa, permit same-sex couples to marry legally.

Only a few studies have explored the experiences of same-sex couples who have pursued civil unions and marriage and the effects of civil unions and marriage on the relationships of lesbians and gay men. Solomon, Rothblum, and Balsam (2004) compared lesbian and gay couples with civil unions to lesbian and gay couples without civil unions in an effort to identify factors that distinguished these two groups. They found that gay men in civil unions were more likely to be fathers, compared with gay men not in civil unions. This indicates that, at least among gay male partners, having a child may create additional impetus to seek legal and social recognition for their union (Oswald et al., 2008). Additionally, Solomon et al. (2004) found that gay men in civil unions were closer to their families of origin than gay men not in civil unions, and lesbians in civil unions were more open about their sexual orientation than lesbians not in civil unions. These data suggest that relationship visibility and efforts at legal recognition are related. Indeed, it is possible that couples that are more out are thereby more oriented toward seeking legal recognition for their relationships; conversely, obtaining legal recognition may lead to greater visibility in their families and communities.

In their 2005 article, Solomon et al. reported that 54% of same-sex couples perceived positive changes in their love and commitment for each other as a result of having a civil union (although, interestingly, no differences in relationship quality were found several years later between couples who had obtained civil unions and couples who had not obtained civil unions; Balsam et al., 2008). The findings of Solomon et al. (2005) are consistent with the argument made by Herek (2006) and others that the execution of legal documents may have a protective and stabilizing function with regard to couple relationships. Also, qualitative research by Alderson (2004) provides evidence of some of the perceived effects of civil marriage among lesbians and gay men. Alderson interviewed married lesbians and gay men in

Canada and found that, for many participants, getting married created an added sense of security that was deeply felt and greatly appreciated. Consistent with the findings of Solomon et al. (2005), Alderson also found that many participants felt that marriage brought greater depth and completion to their relationships, cementing them in both financial and emotional ways. They also understood their marriage as symbolizing monogamy and as providing recognition for them as a family.

However, the legalization of same-sex marriage is not considered desirable by all sexual minorities. In fact, the subject of same-sex marriage is considered highly controversial by both heterosexual and sexual minority individuals (Yep, Lovaas, & Elia, 2003). Some lesbian and gay activists and scholars have questioned whether movements to secure same-sex marriage rights are assimilationist in nature and have wondered whether the gay community might be better off advocating for rights that are not so mired in the legacy of patriarchy that dominates heterosexual marriage: Marriage has historically been a vehicle for securing male status and privilege and the role of women as property (Peel & Harding, 2004b). Elizabeth Peel (Peel & Harding, 2004a) problematized the issue of civil marriage, suggesting that

> imposing a fundamentally straight framework . . . is very problematic from lesbian feminist and/or "queer" perspectives. Civil partnership could quash the "diversity" in lesbian and gay male relationships, because (in part) it embodies assumptions and exclusivity. Would civil partnership not inevitably merely attempt to mimic heterosexual marriage? (p. 42)

Thus, Peel questioned whether the institution of marriage, with its traditional meaning of monogamy, may have a homogenizing and destructive effect on gay communities. Walters (2000) held a similar position, stating that

> gay marriage might grant visibility and "acceptance" to gay marrieds, but it will not necessarily challenge homophobia or the nuclear family. Indeed, it might demonise not-married gays as the "bad gays." . . . Participation in the institution not only assimilates us into the dominant heterosexist way of relating, but gives further credence to an institution that has been built on the backs of sexism and heterosexism. (p. 55)

This position—that the pursuit of same-sex marriage rights is assimilationist and misguided—is not uncommon among lesbians and gay men (Yep et al., 2003; Yip, 2004). Yip (2004) studied lesbian, gay, and bisexual Christian men and women and found that some participants rejected marriage because of its heterosexual connotations: that is, it was perceived as oppressive and unequal. Other respondents favored the abolition of marriage altogether, for themselves and heterosexuals. They felt that it was a problematic, dysfunctional, and outdated social institution that should be replaced with civil marriage or registered partnerships because these arrangements did not have the "cultural baggage" of marriage (p. 175).

Indeed, many critics of same-sex marriage are critics of marriage in general (Peel & Harding, 2004a; Walters, 2000). Card (2007), for example, argued for the abolishment of the legal regulation of marriage, noting that the auxiliary benefits that are currently attached to marriage (e.g., health care coverage) can mean the difference between life and death. According to Card, legally regulated marriage supports a profoundly unjust distribution of benefits that disadvantages all unmarried persons, heterosexual or nonheterosexual, but particularly the poor.[5] The possibility that same-sex marriage would create a greater polarization of wealth and poverty within the gay community has been cited as a major reason for why gay equality advocates should abandon their efforts on behalf of same-sex marriage and focus on securing rights that would benefit all sexual minorities, regardless of partnership status. In arguing for domestic partnership benefits, broadly defined, Christopher Carrington (see Haddock, 2003), pointed out that

> the assumption is . . . that the commitments that are made in the marital dyad trump all other obligations. . . . It confuses and offends me that people in relationships should be entitled to lower automobile insurance rates than my best friend who is not in a relationship. One of the real strengths of gay and lesbian culture, as it exists now, is that we have been able to transgress these nuclear-family boundaries and understand our obligations more broadly. . . . I believe that broadly defined domestic partnership policies and benefits [are therefore] the correct way to go. (pp. 73–74)

Thus, the perspectives of Peel, Walter, Card, and Carrington highlight a perhaps obvious but often misunderstood point: Lesbian and gay activists and scholars, even those who are the most critical of same-sex marriage, typically agree that sexual minorities should have access to all of the practical benefits that are conferred on married or cohabiting heterosexual couples (Peel & Harding, 2004b). The fact that these benefits are often tied to marriage in heterosexual couples—a system that disadvantages the poor and people who are not in monogamous committed relationships—has therefore led some activists to limit their support for same-sex marriage and to advocate for other, alternative solutions (e.g., universal domestic partnership benefits).

Social Support

Another potential vulnerability that same-sex couples face is lack of social support from their families and communities, which is important given

---

[5]Poor and working-class lesbians and gay men face double disadvantage in the absence of marriage rights. The legal safeguards that same-sex couples often pursue in an effort to alleviate the vulnerability that they face in the absence of marriage are quite costly. Estate planning tools (e.g., wills, living trusts), powers of attorney for health care and finances, the naming of a health care surrogate, and advanced medical directives are some of the documents that same-sex couples can initiate at a price (Riggle & Rostosky, 2005). Lesbian and gay persons and couples who cannot afford the services of a lawyer, then, are rendered particularly vulnerable.

that social support is strongly related to well-being for both heterosexual and sexual minority individuals (Wayment & Peplau, 1995). A number of studies have found that lesbian and gay partners perceive less social support from family members than do heterosexual couples (e.g., Bryant & Demian, 1994; Kurdek & Schmitt, 1987; Kurdek, 2001). For example, Bryant and Demian (1994) surveyed lesbian and gay partners and found that both women and men reported relatively low levels of support from their relatives—less than they received from coworkers. In fact, they ranked their relatives as the third greatest challenge in their relationship, and fewer than 10% of partners had sought relationship help or advice from relatives. Notably, sexual minorities who receive little support from family may compensate by forming strong networks of friends (Kurdek, 2006). Indeed, some studies have found that lesbian and gay male partners perceive higher levels of support from friends than do heterosexual nonparent partners (Kurdek, 2001).

Several studies have also examined the association between perceived social support and lesbian and gay couples' relationship quality. Research results on the relationship between social support from family and intimate relationship quality have been mixed: The association between these two variables has emerged as nonsignificant in some studies (Kurdek & Schmitt, 1987) and significant in others (Caron & Ulin, 1997; Smith & Brown, 1997). For example, Caron and Ulin (1997) studied 124 middle-class lesbians and found that specific family behaviors (e.g., inviting a family member's lesbian partner to family events) had an influence on the quality of the lesbian couple's relationship, such that women who perceived more behavioral affirmations of their relationship reported higher relationship quality. Qualitative research mirrors these discrepant findings. Some research suggests that many same-sex couples perceive the presence or absence of family support as impacting the quality of their couple relationship (Rostosky et al., 2004), whereas other research suggests that same-sex couples do not tend to feel that their relationships are significantly impacted by family disapproval or nonsupport (LaSala, 2002). However, compared with support from family, social support from friends is more consistently linked to relationship quality for lesbians and gay men (Elizur & Mintzer, 2003; R. J. Green, 2000).

Qualitative data suggest that one reason for the mixed findings regarding the association between family support and relationship quality is that sexual minorities cope with and respond to lack of family support in a variety of ways. Connolly (2005) interviewed long-term lesbian couples (i.e., couples who had been in their current relationships for 10–24 years) and found that although external stressors, such as experiences with societal pressures and family prejudice, were seen as having placed strain on their relationships, these women also unified themselves against these stressors, thereby promoting resilience, closeness, and intimacy. In this way, lack of support from family may have the potential to create both stress and enhanced intimacy. A qualitative study of 14 lesbian couples conducted by Rostosky et al. (2004)

provides further insight into the divergent ways in which lesbian couples co-construct, respond to, and cope with familial nonsupport. The researchers found that some couples tended to resign themselves to their family's lack of support, simultaneously reaffirming the relationship by discrediting family members' negative opinions or expressing their belief in the worth of the relationship. Other couples tended to respond to nonsupport by hiding their relationship; others attempted to change their families' beliefs and opinions; some rejected their families; others tended to internalize their families' negative attitudes toward homosexuality; and still others responded by blaming their partners for their families' nonsupport. Thus, same-sex couples may respond to nonsupport from their families of origin in a number of ways, many of which may be inherently adaptive and protective. Further, as noted, in the absence of supportive and involved families of origin, many sexual minorities seek to create their own chosen families, made up largely of friends (Oswald, 2002), which may buffer the effects of familial nonsupport.

As mentioned earlier, lesbians and gay men from racial/ethnic minorities often receive even less support from their families and communities (Greene, 2000a), although some groups, such as Native American sexual minorities, have been found to report relatively high levels of support and respect from their families and spiritual communities (B. Adams & Phillips, 2006). Also, as noted, lesbians and gay men in interracial relationships may be particularly vulnerable to lack of support and antagonism from their families of origin and from each individual's racial/ethnic community, as well as from the gay community (Greene, 2000a, 2000b). Bisexual women and men are also at particular risk of nonsupport and rejection from both their families and the gay community at large (Firestein, 2007). Indeed, research suggests that bisexuality, particularly female bisexuality, is controversial and stigmatized within the gay community (Firestein, 2007). One study of 346 lesbians found that most participants endorsed the beliefs that bisexual women were "in transition," not as committed to other women as lesbians, and more likely to want to pass as heterosexual than lesbians (Rust, 1993). Moreover, Rust (1995) found that more than half of the 332 lesbians in her sample preferred other lesbians as friends and tended to avoid bisexual women as friends. Thus, bisexual women are at risk of nonsupport within the gay community, within their families, and from mainstream society, which has tended to stereotype bisexuals as promiscuous or confused (Firestein, 2007).

HIV/AIDS

A final challenge that may face gay male couples in particular is HIV/AIDS, which has had devastating effects on gay men in the United States. Gay men with AIDS may confront numerous stresses, including loss of financial resources, disfigurement, and the physiological consequences of the disease (Kadushin, 1996), although recent advancements in treatments for

HIV have slowed the progression of the illness and have contributed to improved quality of life for many gay men (Liu et al., 2006). Furthermore, the stigma of AIDS, which is associated in the public mind with evil, deviance, promiscuity, and above all else, homosexuality, means that these stresses are often accompanied by, and exacerbated by, social isolation. Indeed, gay men in general tend to experience lower levels of support from family and community members than heterosexual men; this lack of support is magnified and intensified in the context of HIV/AIDS. As a result, gay men who are HIV-positive are more likely to seek and receive social support from friends and partners instead of family members and tend to regard their friends and partners as their primary social support systems and caregivers (Bor, du Plessis, & Russell, 2004; Haas, 2002; Hays, Catania, McKusick, & Coates, 1990). For example, Haas (2002) found that gay HIV-positive men perceived their partners as their greatest source of support, followed by close friends, and then members of their families of origin. Importantly, though, most of the gay men in Haas's study felt that their family members were at least somewhat supportive in contrast with the findings of previous studies, which Haas suggested may indicate a slow shift toward increased HIV education and acceptance of family members with HIV or AIDS.

Advancements in treatment options for HIV have had significant implications for the psychological functioning and relationship maintenance of individuals living with HIV: Indeed, the medications that are currently used for treating HIV are better than those used even a decade ago; thus, gay men who are living with HIV today enjoy improved quality of life and increased life expectancy (Moyle et al., 2008). No longer regarded as a death sentence, HIV is now viewed as a chronic illness that can be managed with medication (Holt & Stephenson, 2006). In turn, individuals with HIV can expect to have an almost normal life expectancy (Biswas, 2007), which, of course, means that millions of persons with HIV will continue to engage in sexual relationships for decades after their diagnosis (Kippax, Aggleton, Moatti, & Delfraissy, 2007). In turn, gay HIV-positive men must negotiate complex issues of sexual safety in both their casual and committed partner relationships.

It appears that sexual safety is sustained in relationships in different ways, depending on the HIV status of the two partners. Many HIV-positive people seek partners with concordant status, thus rendering unprotected sex in such relationships "acceptable" (Cusick & Rhodes, 2000; Davis et al., 2006). Indeed, as Cusick and Rhodes (2000) pointed out, given the emotional and psychological rewards of primary intimate relationships, the popularity of unprotected sex in primary intimate relationships, and the importance of avoiding transmission to HIV-negative partners, it is unsurprising that many HIV-positive individuals deliberately seek out longer term relationships with other HIV-positive persons. Fear of rejection by HIV-negative individuals may also prompt some HIV-positive persons to seek out other HIV-positive partners (Rutledge, 2007). Of course, some HIV-positive individuals do partner with HIV-negative individuals. These HIV-discordant couples face the challenge of negotiating safe sex practices in order to avoid potential transmission (Cusick & Rhodes, 2000). HIV-negative men in relationships with other HIV-negative men also negotiate issues of sexual safety (Prestage et al., 2008). They may have informal or formal agreements or contracts that define the parameter of sex both within and outside of the relationship, in an effort to protect both partners in the relationship.

Couples in long-term relationships in which one or both members are HIV-positive face the reality that one partner may need to take on significant caretaking responsibilities at various points during the relationship, or at least later in life. Such caregiving responsibilities are often experienced as stressful by "well" partners; the boundaries between partner and caregiver roles may become blurred, and well partners may feel more like nurses than companions at times (Palmer & Bor, 2001). Ideally, couples will anticipate and prepare for the grief that the surviving partner will experience in the wake of death, as research suggests that men who lose a partner to AIDS tend to suffer significantly in terms of mental health and health outcomes (Mayne, Acree, Chesney, & Folkman, 1998).

CONCLUSIONS AND RECOMMENDATIONS

The research on same-sex couples has widespread implications in a variety of domains. First, the data suggest that many female and male same-sex couples enjoy long-term, fulfilling relationships. Furthermore, researchers have found few differences in the relationship outcomes of same-sex and heterosexual couples. Nevertheless, the fact that same-sex couples are able to maintain satisfying relationships in the absence of societal legitimacy and structural-legal support for their relationships does not render acceptable the practice of denying these couples basic human rights. As Patricia Hill Collins (1992) wrote in regard to Black mothers, "Black mothers' ability to cope with race, class, and gender oppression should not be confused with transcending those conditions" (pp. 234–235). The same message applies to same-sex couples: Their ability to cope with heterosexism does not negate the fact that they continue to suffer because of heterosexism. Access to relationship recognition in a form that carries all the benefits of heterosexual marriage would arguably benefit individuals' subjective and objective sense of security and well-being. By extension, it would communicate a powerful social message about human equality, and systemic forms of discrimination and oppression might gradually be mitigated. This, in turn, would have important physical and mental health consequences for sexual minorities: Indeed, exposure to heterosexism (e.g., in the form of exclusion and violence) has consistently been linked to poorer mental health among sexual minorities (e.g., Szymanksi, 2005).

Future research on same-sex couples would benefit from attention to the inherent diversity within the population. For example, research is needed that explores more fully how partners of different social class, racial, cultural, religious, and geographical backgrounds experience their relationships. Additionally, little is known about the experiences of couples in which one partner identifies as bisexual and the other as lesbian or gay or about the experiences of same-sex couples in which one partner undergoes a gender transition. Examination of such intracouple variability would provide unique insights into the relational dynamics of gender and sexuality. Furthermore, research is needed that explores the experiences, challenges, and strengths of different cohorts of same-sex couples. How are the experiences of same-sex couples who are beginning their relationships today, for example, uniquely different from those couples who paired up 20 years ago? Finally, much more research is needed that examines relationship trajectories for lesbian and gay persons in multiple (i.e., nonmonogamous) relationships.

Turning to practice implications, therapists and practitioners who work with same-sex couples should be attentive to the unique dimensions of their relationships as compared with heterosexual relationships, while remaining cognizant of the ways in which same-sex couples' relational difficulties may reflect universal relationship conflicts. Furthermore, therapists should be sensitive to the many variables that affect the formation, nature, and stability of same-sex relationships, such as partners' personalities, partners' commitment to the relationship, and similarities and differences between partners in terms of internalized homophobia, outness, race, ethnicity, social class, HIV status, and so forth. Practitioners are encouraged to investigate partners' and couples' attitudes about open versus closed relationships and to avoid assumptive leaps (e.g., presuming that gay men who engage in open relationships are less healthy or less satisfied with their relationships). Finally, practitioners who work with same-sex couples may find it useful to investigate what social supports both partners have access to, in order to gain a comprehensive picture of the kinds of social-contextual forces that are operating on the couple. For example, the therapist might inquire about the extent to which family members and friends are relied on as sources of support, as well as the extent to which partners feel supported by their broader communities (e.g., do partners perceive places of worship, social and civic organizations, and so forth as welcoming and accessible?).

In the following chapter, I discuss the transition to parenthood for same-sex couples and address a series of vital questions. How do same-sex couples decide to become parents, and what factors they consider in choosing a particular route to parenthood (e.g., alternative insemination, adoption, surrogacy)? How do couples' relationships change during this key life transition, what factors are related to relationship outcomes, and how do these processes mirror or deviate from the patterns observed among heterosexual couples? Does parenthood transform the division of labor—that is, do same-sex couples' relationships continue to be characterized, on average, by a relatively egalitarian division of labor? In what ways? Finally, do lesbians' and gay men's experiences of becoming parents differ from one another? In what ways?

PRACTICAL RESOURCES

Coming Out

Book: Wunder, K., & Stevens, T. (2002). *How to be a happy lesbian: A coming out guide.* Asheville, NC: Amazing Dreams Publishing.

Summary: A humorous book with advice on how to "make it" in a predominantly homophobic world. It includes advice on coming out to family, friends, and coworkers, and it contains a list of additional resources (e.g., books, organizations, support groups).

Marriage

Web site: http://www.marriageequality.org (Marriage Equality, Inc.)

Summary: Marriage Equality, Inc., began as an idea in 1996 with a handful of activists believing that same-sex couples should have the freedom and the right to civil marriage and angry that the federal government wanted to pass a law barring lesbian, gay, bisexual, and transgender (LGBT) people from this right.

Film (DVD): de Seve, J. (Director). (2003). *Tying the Knot.* New York: New Video Group.

Summary: The documentary presents a detailed account of the struggle to legalize gay marriage in the United States, beginning with the Hawaiian union of Nina Baehr and Genora Dancel, which prompted the creation of the Defense of Marriage Act (which was signed into law in 1996 by President Bill Clinton).

Legal

Book: Clifford, D., Hertz, F., & Doskow, E. (2007). *A legal guide for lesbian and gay couples* (14th ed). Berkeley, CA: Nolo.

Summary: This practical guide shows lesbian and gay couples how to (a) make practical decisions about living together; (b) obtain domestic partner benefits; (c) make medical decisions for each other when needed; (d) leave property to each other; and (e) have and raise children through adoption, donor insemination, surrogacy, and foster parenting.

Web site: http://www.gaylawnet.com (Gay Law Net)

Summary: This site provides general information, news, and resources concerning the law as it affects the global gay, lesbian, bisexual, transsexual, and intersex community and facilitates access to a gay or lesbian (or gay- or lesbian-friendly) lawyers.

Web site: http://www.thetaskforce.org (The National Gay and Lesbian Task Force)

Summary: The mission of the National Gay and Lesbian Task Force (NGLTF) is to build the grassroots power of the LGBT community. NGLTF does this by training activists and equipping state and local organizations with the skills needed to organize broad-based campaigns to defeat anti-LGBT referenda and advance pro-LGBT legislation.

3

FROM PARTNERS TO PARENTS: THE TRANSITION TO PARENTHOOD FOR LESBIANS AND GAY MEN

Homosexuality and the family have often been viewed as incompatible and exclusive categories (Allen & Demo, 1995), and social and political rhetoric has perpetuated a myth of lesbians and gay men as "antifamily." In consequence, up until the past few decades, many lesbians and gay men who wished to become parents entered into marriage as a means to an end, as this was the only well-known route to parenthood. Recent advancements in reproductive technology, as well as social and political progress, have created a climate in which lesbians and gay men are increasingly aware of a wider range of parenting options, which has led to the rising number of intentional, or planned, lesbian- and gay-parent families. The growing number of lesbians and gay men who are becoming parents in the context of committed same-sex relationships (as opposed to having children in the context of heterosexual relationships and then coming out after the dissolution of these relationships) has in turn contributed to the growing visibility of gay parenting in the media and society at large. In becoming parents, lesbians and gay men destabilize the associative interdependence of "the family," heterosexuality, and reproduction and therefore serve as vivid examples of the socially constructed nature of families. Furthermore, they directly challenge the necessity of conventional (hetero)sexual relations for reproduction (Agigian, 2004; Michelle, 2006).

How many lesbian- and gay-parent families are there in the United States, and how have these numbers changed over the past several decades? Estimates based on U.S. Census data suggested that approximately 1 in 20 male same-sex couples and 1 in 5 female same-sex couples were raising children in 1990; in 2000 these figures had risen to 1 in 5 for male couples and 1 in 3 for female couples (Gates & Ost, 2004). Furthermore, more than half of gay men (52%) wanted to become parents at some point in their lives, compared with two thirds of heterosexual and bisexual men. Similarly, 41% of lesbians said that they would like to have a child, compared with 53% of heterosexual women and 59% of bisexual women (Gates, Badgett, Macomber, & Chambers, 2007).[1] Importantly, of the quarter million children who were living in U.S. households headed by same-sex couples, 4.2% were either adopted or foster children, almost double the figure for heterosexual couples (Gates & Ost, 2004). Importantly, these estimates were conservative and may have failed to capture a large number of lesbian- and gay-parent families by virtue of undercounting the number of same-sex couple households (Badgett & Rogers, 2003).[2] What is relatively certain, however, is that the number of lesbian- and gay-parent households is steadily increasing—a shift that corresponds to the increasing visibility of lesbian and gay parents in society. Moreover, while these families are most tightly clustered in progressive, urban areas of the United States like Austin, San Francisco, and Seattle, lesbian and gay parents are virtually everywhere: They are represented in every state and almost every county in the country (Gates & Ost, 2004; Gates, 2007).

This chapter examines the transition to parenthood experience for lesbians and gay men. Obviously, many lesbians and gay men do not ever be-

---

[1] These numbers can be further broken down into those men and women who already are parents versus those without children. Among gay men with children, 25% want to become parents again, and among gay men without children, 57% want to become parents. Among heterosexual men, these figures are 44% and 87% respectively, and among bisexual men, they are 55% and 70%, respectively. Among lesbians with children, 49% wish to become parents again, and among lesbians without children, 37% want to become parents. Among heterosexual women, these figures are 37% and 84%, respectively, and among bisexual women, they are 40% and 75%, respectively (Gates et al., 2007).
[2] Beginning in 1990, the U.S. Census form permitted respondents to describe another household member as an "unmarried partner," thereby allowing the Census to determine the number of same-sex couples by comparing the sexes of the household members who called themselves unmarried partners. However, many same-sex couples were likely left out of the 1990 Census estimates because they did not check the unmarried partner box; for example, some men and women might have checked some other relationship category such as "married," while others likely chose not to identify themselves as unmarried partners because of concerns about confidentiality (Badgett & Rogers, 2003). In the 2000 Census, same-sex couples were also permitted the option of identifying another same-sex household member as "husband" or "wife"; as a result, the counts since 2000 have included some couples who were excluded from the 1990 enumeration. Thus, because of the changes in the Census Bureau's coding procedures, the 1990 data are not directly comparable with the 2000 data.

come parents; thus, this chapter focuses on the subset of lesbians and gay men who ultimately do become parents. Although there is no set period of time that defines *transition to parenthood*, in general this term is used to refer to the transitional stage between non-parenthood and parenthood. In the current chapter, I begin by addressing some of the factors that may influence sexual minorities' decision-making about whether to pursue parenthood, as well as what parenthood route to pursue. Second, I discuss some of the unique challenges and characteristics associated with each major route to parenthood, most commonly, alternative insemination, adoption, and surrogacy. Third, I discuss the transition to parenthood experience for same-sex couples, with special attention to how couples' division of labor, perceived social support, and intimate relationship quality may change during this key life transition. I focus on couples' experiences from the point at which they begin to consider parenthood until their children's early toddlerhood. Chapter 4 of this volume focuses on the experiences of lesbians and gay men with children of toddler age and older.

DECISION-MAKING: TO PARENT OR NOT TO PARENT?

Recent social, cultural, and technological shifts have, as noted earlier, raised awareness of parenthood options among lesbians and gay men. Even so, many lesbians and gay men ultimately decide not to become parents. Their choice to parent or not to parent raises important questions. How do lesbians and gay men choose to become parents in the first place? What factors are relevant in determining who will ultimately pursue parenthood?

Internalized Homophobia

A significant challenge that lesbians and gay men face as they consider parenthood is internalized homophobia (Gianino, 2008). Growing up in a heterosexist society, many sexual minorities have internalized a complex set of interrelated societal notions: that (a) homosexuality is wrong; (b) lesbians and gay men are less fit to parent than heterosexual women and men; (c) every child needs a mother and a father; and (d) growing up with lesbians and gay men is harmful to children. Thus, many sexual minorities may question whether they have a right to bear or adopt children, may worry that the barriers to becoming a gay parent are insurmountable, and may be concerned about the discrimination that a child might face in the context of growing up with nonheterosexual parents. Indeed, they may have realistic worries about the stigma that a child with lesbian or gay parents will encounter, and they may therefore wonder whether their becoming parents is fair to the child. They may also worry about their capacity to construct their children's gender identity according to the norms of mainstream society (Berkowitz & Marsiglio,

2007). Gay men in particular must also struggle with the strong societal bias against men in general (and gay men specifically) as nurturers and caretakers of children (Mallon, 2004). Thus, internalized homophobia represents a major barrier to pursuing parenthood among some lesbians and gay men.

Presence of an Equally Motivated Partner

Another barrier to (shared) parenthood among lesbian and gay couples is the presence of a less motivated partner. Upon realizing or acknowledging their own desire to parent, some lesbians and gay men may discover, or have their suspicions confirmed, that their partners are not equally committed to becoming parents, and in some cases they may be vehemently opposed to the idea (Pies, 1990). This may initiate a process of discussion and negotiation that may result in the dissolution of the relationship, if the conflict over whether or not to parent together cannot be resolved (Morningstar, 1999; Stacey, 2006). The more motivated partner may then pursue parenthood alone or may wait to pursue parenthood with a future, child-oriented partner (Lev, 2004).[3] In other cases, however, the process of discussion and negotiation may result in the less motivated partner developing a greater interest in the prospect of parenthood: Indeed, the resistant partner may ultimately match the other's enthusiasm, so that both partners are equally committed to parenthood (Herrmann-Green & Gehring, 2007). Some partners, however, will fall short of this commitment. They may agree to be supportive in their partner's quest to parent, and perhaps to help out, but may ultimately reject the possibility of parenthood as a joint endeavor (Pies, 1990). Still, there is evidence that even among lesbians and gay men who start out significantly less invested in parenthood than their partners, some may come to enjoy and even embrace parenting. Reimann (1997) studied 25 lesbian couples who had their children by alternative insemination and found that in 8 couples the nonbiological mother was initially strongly opposed to having children because she did not feel equipped to be a good parent or she was concerned that her life would change too significantly. After considerable deliberation, however, these eight women decided to support their partner's decision to have a child, and, ultimately, they came to enjoy parenting.

Geographical Location and Lack of Resources

Another barrier to lesbian and gay parenthood is lack of access to information and resources about how to become a parent. Lesbians and gay men who live in remote, rural, or politically conservative regions of the country,

---

[3]Of course, this process of negotiation is not unique to same-sex couples. Heterosexual couples in which one partner is less motivated to parent also encounter similar dynamics whereby the couple must decide whether to split up, stay together and remain child-free, or stay together and become parents together.

for example, may not have access to a visible and organized gay community (Oswald & Culton, 2003) and to gay parenting–specific resources (e.g., "Maybe Baby" groups for gay prospective parents; gay-friendly adoption agencies and fertility centers). Of course, the Internet can provide important information to rural or remote lesbians and gay men who are seeking advice and information as to the basic how-to of becoming parents (e.g., Lev et al., 2005). However, once armed with this information, lesbians and gay men may be in the unavoidable predicament of having to interface with their local communities to pursue their parenthood goals; their communities, in turn, may be unsupportive, ignorant, or unhelpful, thereby thwarting their parenthood aspirations.

Furthermore, lesbians and gay men may experience their geographical location as a barrier to shared parenthood inasmuch as many states' adoption laws (discussed in greater depth later in this chapter) prohibit both partners from legally adopting their children. Some couples may therefore be hesitant to pursue parenthood because of legal insecurities. And of course, up until September 10, 2008, when Florida's ban on adoption by lesbians and gay men was ruled unconstitutional, openly gay persons in Florida could not become adoptive parents.

Internalized homophobia, the presence of a resistant partner, and inhospitable geographical location are not the only factors that may serve to limit which lesbians and gay men ultimately become parents. Other factors, such as age (in the case of lesbians and gay men who only begin to consider parenthood later in life), may also affect lesbians' and gay men's parenting decisions.

Turning Points

Experiences that challenge internalized homophobia or that raise awareness of lesbian and gay parenthood can function as turning points in the lives of sexual minorities (Elder, 1998b). That is, lesbians and gay men who experience internalized homophobia, who lack the motivation to parent, or who lack access to a visible gay community may encounter people, experiences, and events that redefine or shift their life course, leading them to seriously consider and investigate parenthood. Such turning point experiences include meeting and forming friendships with other lesbian and gay parents (Berkowitz & Marsiglio, 2007; Chabot & Ames, 2004), being exposed to other people's children (Berkowitz & Marsiglio, 2007), experiencing a growing awareness of one's own desire to parent (Berkowitz, 2007; Chabot & Ames, 2004), and meeting the "right" partner (i.e., someone who is equally interested in and committed to parenthood; Baetens, Camus, & Devroey, 2002; Berkowitz & Marsiglio, 2007; Chabot & Ames, 2004; Gagnon, Riley, Toole, & Goldberg, 2007). Such intrapersonal and interpersonal experiences challenge sexual minorities to (re)consider the possibility of parenthood, and they stimulate a process of integrating one's ideas about motherhood or fatherhood with one's lesbian or gay identity (Lewin, 1993). Notably, however, this process of considering parenthood is not necessarily without tension. Berkowitz (2007), in speaking about contemporary gay men's emergent "procreative consciousness" (i.e., their drive to become parents), observed:

> On the one hand, they are being exposed to a wide array of right-wing political discourse that refuses to acknowledge the rights of gay parents. On the other hand, they are hearing and learning about varying opportunities permitting them parenthood. What results is that gay men end up mentally juggling contradictory ideological discourses as they construct fantasies about their future families. (p. 175)

Of course, such juggling is likely to continue once lesbians and gay men become parents. Sexual minorities who become parents in the current sociopolitical climate may encounter more support than in decades past, but they are nevertheless vulnerable to stigmatization and marginalization by dominant societal institutions and ideologies, which continue to condemn and denigrate lesbian- and gay-parent families.

DECISION-MAKING: ROUTES TO PARENTHOOD

Once lesbians and gay men have made the decision to pursue parenthood, the decision about how to become parents becomes paramount. The most frequent and most frequently discussed routes to parenthood (other than heterosexual marriage) include alternative insemination, adoption, and foster care. However, there are several other paths to parenthood that lesbians and gay men may consider. First, some lesbians engage in heterosexual sex in order to become parents (e.g., because it is seen as more natural or because women feel that it may increase the chances of conception; Lev, 2004). Second, some lesbians and gay men pursue surrogacy, whereby a third-party carries a baby who will be raised by the couple. Third, some lesbians and gay men pursue more complex parenting arrangements (e.g., a lesbian couple coparenting with a gay couple; a single lesbian coparenting with lesbian or gay friend[s]). A number of factors influence individuals' and couples' decision-making about which route to take.

One of the major factors that influence sexual minorities' decision-making about parenthood is finances. Alternative insemination, using banked sperm, costs approximately $500 to $1,000 for the first insemination cycle and from $300 to $700 for each cycle thereafter (Agigian, 2004). These estimates include health tests, registration at a sperm bank or clinic, the cost of frozen semen, and ovulation predictor kits. They do not include fertility treatments or medications, which may be necessary and are somewhat costly. For example, clomiphene (Clomid), which produces the hormones that trigger ovulation, averages about $50 per cycle; this does not include doctor's visits or ultrasounds of the ovaries (BabyCenter, 2007). The cost of in vitro fertilization (IVF) is much more significant: A single cycle of IVF averages from $8,000 to $10,000 (Advanced Fertility Center of Chicago, 2007). Only men and women of some financial means, then, are able to access and take advantage of advanced reproductive technologies (Agigian, 2004; Boggis, 2001), thereby highlighting the social class–infused nature of parental decision-making. Sexual minorities who desire a biological child but who lack the money to pursue surrogacy or physician-assisted alternative insemination using approved sperm may consider alternative pathways, including heterosexual contact—which is, understandably, unattractive to many sexual minorities—or, for lesbians, self-insemination at home with unchecked, unapproved sperm, often from a known donor. Importantly, both unprotected sex and self-insemination with unchecked sperm carry risks of HIV and other sexually transmitted diseases (STDs). Low-income women, while aware of these risks, are also aware of their limited options. Thus, they are sometimes so grateful to the sperm donor that they do not always insist on HIV and STD testing (Agigian, 2004). Inseminating outside of the medical system and engaging in heterosexual contact also carry legal risks, as well as threats to personal and relational integrity. When a coupled lesbian engages in heterosexual sex to become pregnant, for example, this threatens both the legal and symbolic parental role of her partner, in that the biological father is often awarded greater symbolic and legal recognition than the nonbiological lesbian partner (Boggis, 2001).

Private adoption is also an expensive route to parenthood. The cost of licensed private agency adoptions ranges from $5,000 to $40,000, and the cost of independent, private adoptions (i.e., through a lawyer) typically ranges from $8,000 to $40,000. International adoption is also expensive, ranging approximately from $7,000 to $30,000 (Child Welfare Information Gateway, 2004). However, men and women can stay within the lower end of the financial continuum (e.g., $7,000–$10,000) by cutting costs; for example, couples who pursue private domestic open adoption can choose to manage their own advertising to birth mothers, as opposed to enlisting agency services. Thus, the variability in cost estimates is in part a function of the actual agency services used. Other sources of variability in cost are the race of the child (i.e., children of color are considered harder to place and are therefore sometimes available for placement at a reduced cost compared with White children) and the financial needs of the birth mother. The cheapest option, of course, is adoption through the child welfare system. Costs of adoptions through the public sector typically range from nothing to $2,500. Yet while many lesbians and gay men view child welfare adoptions as financially attractive, they often perceive numerous disadvantages that prevent them from pursuing this route (Downing, Richardson, & Goldberg, 2008). They may consider the low availability of infants available for placement through the child welfare system; the potential for severe emotional and behavioral challenges in the child, possibly related to prior abuse or neglect; and legal uncertainties. For example, regarding legal uncertainties, foster parents who wish to adopt must wait until the legal rights of the child's biological parents are terminated, a process that can take many months or even years. Lesbians and gay men with such concerns who also have financial resources, then, are more likely to pursue private adoption; of course, for those with few financial resources, such concerns may be less influential.

Finally, surrogacy tends to be more expensive than either alternative insemination or adoption. The cost of surrogacy services through Growing Generations (the world's first gay-owned surrogacy agency that serves an international gay clientele),[4] for example, ranges from $115,000 to $150,000 (see http://www.growinggenerations.com). These high costs are prohibitive for most individuals and couples, and thus surrogacy is favored by only a small number of relatively affluent lesbians and gay men.

Another factor that will influence lesbians' and gay men's decision making about what route to pursue is the relative importance of having a *biogenetic relationship* to one's child—that is, passing on one's genes or physically resembling one's child. Lesbians and gay men who strongly desire a biogenetically related child tend to favor alternative insemination or surrogacy over adoption (Berkowitz & Marsiglio, 2007; Chabot & Ames, 2004; Goldberg, Downing, & Richardson, in press). Indeed, to the extent that this is a valued component of parenthood, lesbians and gay men may be willing to make personal and financial sacrifices to increase the chances of having a biological child, although among same-sex couples, a child can typically be related to only one of the partners.[5]

For lesbians, the relative importance of experiencing pregnancy and childbirth may also be influential in their decision making regarding what route to choose (Goldberg et al., in press). Studies of lesbian mothers who had their children by alternative insemination have revealed that they often cite the desire to experience pregnancy and childbirth as a principal reason for having pursued alternative insemination (Chabot & Ames, 2004; Daniels, 1994; Goldberg et al., in press; Harvey, Carr, & Bernheine, 1989; Kranz & Daniluk, 2006; Reimann, 1997). Lesbians may also opt for alternative insemination over adoption because they wish to control their child's genetic background and prenatal care (Wendland, Byrn, & Hill, 1996), or they strongly desire the experience of raising a child from infancy (Herrmann-

---

[4]Growing Generations was founded in 1996 and has since worked with approximately 500 families and birthed 230 babies (Lev, 2006).

[5]Some lesbian couples ensure that they are both genetically related to the child by having a brother or other male relative of the nonbiological mother donate the sperm. In this way, the child also shares some genetic material with the comother. Likewise, gay couples can feasibly have one man's sister or other female relative donate the eggs and have the other man donate the sperm.

Green & Gehring, 2007). Additionally, some lesbians and gay men may pursue biological parenthood as opposed to adoption because they believe that their family members are more likely to accept a child who is biogenetically related to them than an unrelated adopted child. That is, they perceive their families as more likely to overlook or tolerate their sexual orientation in order to have a relationship with a "real" grandchild or niece or nephew but not necessarily with an unrelated stranger. Finally, some lesbians anticipate greater barriers and discrimination in the adoption process than the insemination process, leading them to view the latter path as easier (Goldberg et al., in press; Kranz & Daniluk, 2006).

Lesbians and gay men who do not feel strongly about having a biogenetically related child or, in the case of lesbians, experiencing pregnancy and childbirth are often more oriented toward adoption (Gagnon et al., 2007; Goldberg et al., in press). Indeed, in some lesbian couples, neither woman has a strong desire to be pregnant (Pies, 1990). Furthermore, some couples may opt for adoption over alternative insemination because they want each parent to have an equal connection to the child (Goldberg et al., in press). Altruistic motivations, too, may underlie some sexual minorities' interest in adoption: Rather than bringing another child into the world, they may wish to parent a child who does not have a permanent home (Gagnon et al., 2007). Some lesbians may also turn to adoption because of their age (i.e., they believe they are "too old" to conceive) or because prior attempts to conceive were unsuccessful (Goldberg et al., in press; Goldberg & Smith, 2008a; Shelley-Sireci & Ciano-Boyce, 2002).

Finally, in choosing a route to parenthood, lesbians and gay men may also be influenced by the choices and trajectories of the lesbians and gay men in their immediate social network, in their communities, or in the media (Herrmann-Green & Gehring, 2007). As Chabot and Ames (2004) found in their qualitative study of 10 lesbian mothers, talking to, hearing about, and reading about lesbians who had children by insemination led women to view alternative insemination specifically as a viable and attractive route to achieving parenthood. Similarly, lesbians and gay men who pursue adoption often cited their friends and acquaintances as valuable sources of information and resources about adoption, leading them to view adoption (as opposed to insemination or surrogacy) as the easiest and most straightforward route to parenthood (Pedrick & Goldberg, 2008).

Each of the major routes to parenthood (alternative insemination, adoption, and surrogacy) is characterized by unique choices and challenges. Each of these major routes, as well as their associated characteristics, is discussed next.

Alternative Insemination: Choices and Challenges

Having made the decision to have a child, and to pursue insemination specifically, lesbian couples face a range of subsequent decisions; many of them involve continued negotiation over time, but others need to be made fairly quickly. Such decisions include who should carry the child; donor type (whether it should be known or unknown); if donor type is known, who it should be and what the donor's role should be; and the desired characteristics of the donor.

Who Should Carry the Child

Among lesbians who pursue parenthood with a committed partner, the decision of who should carry the child is a significant one. The nonbiological mother faces social and legal invisibility during the pregnancy and beyond: Her status as an expectant and actual parent often goes unrecognized by friends, family members, and the broader social and legal infrastructure. The birth mother, in contrast, receives recognition of her parental status during pregnancy because of her growing belly and, as a parent, as a function of the biological and legal bond that she shares with her child, which is often signified by their physical resemblance to one another. In addition to being a marker of parenthood, pregnancy is also a public symbol of femininity (Gross & Pattison, 2007) and also, however illusory, heterosexuality. Thus, the decision of who will carry the child carries notable implications for how each partner will be viewed by the outside world.

Some research has explored lesbian couples' decision making about who will conceive, carry, and bear their children. In Goldberg's (2006) study of 29 lesbian couples' transition to parenthood, couples' explanations of how they decided who would carry the child fell into several general categories. In 41% of couples, the birth mother's greater desire to bear a child (to experience pregnancy and childbirth, and in some cases to have a genetic connection to the child) was the most important factor in their decision.[6] For 14% of couples, fertility was the major determinant: The nonbiological mother had tried to become pregnant without success; thus, her partner became the birth mother by default. The remaining 45% cited a range of reasons, including health, age (the older of the two women was chosen to try first, with the plan of having the younger partner bear a second child, or the younger of the two women was chosen on the basis of the couple's perception that the older partner was unlikely to be successful because of her age); and career (e.g., one partner's job was more flexible, paid less, or was less personally rewarding,

---

[6]Of interest is what other factors might be related to "desire to bear a child." One question that has as of yet been relatively unexplored is whether, how, and to what extent women's gender identity (i.e., their sense of themselves as feminine or masculine subjects) interplays with their desire (or lack of desire) to experience pregnancy and childbirth. Indeed, Epstein (2002) discussed the experience of a sample of butch mothers, some of whom were repelled by the idea of pregnancy but others of whom actively sought out and enjoyed pregnancy. Other research (Singh, Vidaurri, Zambarano, & Dabbs, 1999) has suggested that butch lesbians may have less of a desire to give birth than femme lesbians but do not differ from femme lesbians in their desire for children per se. More research is needed that explores how women's gender identity maps on to their desire to give birth and/or be pregnant—experiences that are hallmarks of culturally dominant notions of femininity and motherhood.

thus making her a better candidate to take parental leave or reduce her work hours to care for the child).

Most couples in this study experienced the decision of who would carry the child as relatively easy. However, couples who chose the birth mother because of the nonbiological mother's fertility problems sometimes experienced the decision-making process as painful and challenging. The nonbiological mother was initially chosen to bear the child because of her greater interest in experiencing pregnancy and childbirth; thus, her inability to conceive was sometimes emotionally difficult and hard to accept. Some birth mothers noted that their partners had been so focused on getting pregnant that they had often lost sight of their common goal: to have children. This sometimes caused strain between partners, which was largely alleviated when the nonbiological mother finally allowed the birth mother to try.

Chabot and Ames (2004) identified similar patterns in their study of 10 lesbians. Four women noted that they and their partners decided who would carry based on one partner's greater desire, while the other couples cited age, health considerations, work considerations (including who had the better health insurance plan), and also family-of-origin issues (if one partner was not out to her family of origin, the other partner was chosen to carry the child). When women felt similarly in terms of their desire to be pregnant and bear a child, and were of similar age and had similar employment situations and benefits, the decision-making process was experienced as more difficult, and couples tended to engage in a lengthier period of discussion and negotiation before deciding who would try first. Such a situation is probably more of an exception than the norm: In a study of 95 Belgian lesbian couples seeking donor insemination services, in only 14% of couples did both partners wish to become pregnant; in the remaining 86% of couples, only one partner wished to become pregnant (Baetens et al., 2002). In all cases in which both partners wished to become pregnant, the older partner was chosen to try first. Likewise, Goldberg et al. (in press) studied 30 lesbian couples and 30 heterosexual couples who were in the process of adopting for the first time. All couples had arrived at adoption because of difficulties in conceiving. Notably, however, in only 3 of the 30 lesbian couples did both partners try to conceive before turning to adoption. In the other 27 couples, the trying partner had typically had a greater desire to be pregnant than her partner; most non-trying partners had no interest in being pregnant or giving birth and had been open to adoption all along.

Donor Type

Another major decision that lesbians face is whether to inseminate using the sperm of a known donor (e.g., an acquaintance, friend) or an unknown/anonymous donor. Studies of lesbian mothers have examined women's preferences and decisions with respect to donor type. In contrast to heterosexual married couples, who typically select unknown donors for their chil-

dren (Brewaeys, Ponjaert-Kristoffersen, Van Steirteghem, & Devroey, 1993; Scheib, Riordan, & Rubin, 2005), lesbians' donor selection choices are more varied. In her prospective study of lesbian mothers, Gartrell et al. (1996) found that 47% preferred an unknown donor, 45% preferred a known donor, and 8% had no preference. Similarly, Goldberg (2006) studied pregnant lesbians and their partners and found that 59% of women chose an unknown donor, 31% chose a known donor, and the remaining 10% chose an "ID release" or "Yes" donor (i.e., a donor who agreed to be contacted when the child reached some specified age, usually 18 years old).

Lesbians weigh many competing fears and desires in selecting a donor type. Women who choose an unknown donor often cite legal reasons (i.e., there is no father who can claim rights to the child) and their desire to raise their child without outside interference (Goldberg, 2006; Haimes & Weiner, 2000; Kenney & Tash, 1992; Kranz & Daniluk, 2006). Indeed, lesbian couples are often wary of selecting a known donor and facing a custody dispute. Nonbiological mothers may feel particularly strongly about choosing an unknown donor, in that their status as a full and equal coparent is at least symbolically threatened by the presence of a known donor (Ben-Ari & Livni, 2006; Goldberg, 2006; Reimann, 1997). Women may also feel that choosing a known donor is antithetical to their goal of creating an intentional two-mother family, and they may worry that such a choice would imply "some kind of shortcoming in the family" (Ben-Ari & Livni, 2006, p. 525). Finally, some women may choose an unknown donor because they lack friends or acquaintances whom they feel they could ask to be the donor (Goldberg, 2006).

Women who choose a known doctor typically do so because they want their child to know who their biological father is and to be able to have some contact with them. However, women who choose known donors do not necessarily want these men to be involved as fathers—that is, as equal counterparts (Gartrell et al., 1996; Goldberg, 2006; Haimes & Weiner, 2000; Hertz, 2002; Morningstar, 1999; Touroni & Coyle, 2002). Lesbian couples who use known donors often do so for the psychological health of their children (e.g., they may feel that their child deserves to know about his or her other biological half or that it is in the child's best interest to know about his or her biological heritage) but do not feel that it is necessary for their child to have an active father per se (Almack, 2006; Goldberg & Allen, 2007; Ryan-Flood, 2005). Some women also choose to inseminate with the sperm of a known donor because they desire more control over the insemination process or wish to avoid interacting with potentially heterosexist institutions such as fertility clinics, which may, for example, fail to acknowledge the non-inseminating partner as a valid coparent (Almack, 2006; Chabot & Ames, 2004; Touroni & Coyle, 2002). Women also cite health reasons for pursuing a known donor: that is, they desire the security of knowing that, should they need to access additional health information about the donor, they will be able to find him (Goldberg, 2006). Limited access to information regarding

genetic risk factors and history is regarded as a serious disadvantage associated with donor anonymity (Kenney & Tash, 1992).

Women who desire a known donor but are concerned about legal risk sometimes choose a gay donor because, should the question of custody arise in the future, a gay man is less likely than a heterosexual man to be awarded custody over a lesbian (Haimes & Weiner, 2000; Ryan-Flood, 2005). Some lesbians also desire gay men as donors because they view them as better role models of masculinity than heterosexual men—that is, they serve to challenge traditional notions of masculinity, thus serving a role-breaking function (Donovan, 2000; Goldberg & Allen, 2007; Ryan-Flood, 2005). Furthermore, some lesbians may seek out gay men as donors (and as potential coparents) out of recognition that these men might otherwise not have the opportunity to parent (Pies, 1988). Lesbians may also wish to share the parenting role with someone who shares the experience of homophobic oppression and who understands the challenges of parenting in a heterosexist society (Ryan-Flood, 2005).

Lesbians who pursue known donors face the additional task of negotiating the extent and nature of the donor's involvement. Such negotiations are ongoing, often persisting throughout the child's life, but are typically initiated early in the parenting process (e.g., before conception, during the pregnancy). Lesbians who wish to use a known donor may feel that the act of simply providing semen does not entitle the donor to assume either the role or title of father (Goldberg & Allen, 2007; Haimes & Weiner, 2000; Hertz, 2002). To avoid confusion and miscommunication, women may find it useful to discuss their expectations with their donors, who are often friends or acquaintances, early on. For example, women may seek to clarify the parameters of their donor's involvement, as well as their role and title; for example, they may carefully designate them as family friends rather than as daddies per se (Haimes & Weiner, 2000).

The extent to which lesbians desire relatively involved donors (e.g., donors who take on coparenting responsibilities) versus relatively uninvolved donors may in part depend on their broader social, cultural, and national contexts. Ryan-Flood (2005) conducted a qualitative study of donor preferences and ideologies among Irish and Swedish lesbians and found that Swedish lesbians were far more likely to choose involved, known donors than Irish lesbians, who tended to opt for unknown donors or known donors who were relatively uninvolved. Swedish lesbians explained their preference by emphasizing the importance of their children having access to their biological origins, which the authors interpreted as reflecting broader discourses about the significance of fatherhood and the centrality of biological relatedness in Swedish society. In contrast, Irish women emphasized the importance of remaining the primary parents and caretakers in their children's lives. They did not want male coparents, in part because of their lack of trust in the legal system (Ireland is significantly less progressive than Sweden in its recognition of same-sex relationships and its protection of lesbian- and gay-parent families; Ryan-Flood, 2005). These findings highlight the importance of considering how national and localized ideologies and discourses shape lesbians' (and gay men's) preferences and decisions with respect to family building. They also suggest that it may be inappropriate to generalize the findings from studies of lesbians' donor insemination practices in countries other than the United States, given that the legal, political, and cultural meanings of such practices necessarily vary as a function of geographical context.

Donor Characteristics

Lesbian couples must also decide what donor characteristics are important to them. Both heterosexual and lesbian couples who pursue donor insemination often attempt to match the physical characteristics of the donor to the physical characteristics of the recipients (i.e., the family purchasing the sperm; Chabot & Ames, 2004; C. Jones, 2005). Specifically, heterosexual couples often attempt to obtain sperm from a donor who looks like the father, and lesbian couples may engage in a similar practice of trying to match the characteristics of the donor to those of the nonbiological mother, thus facilitating a "reproduction of their image" (C. Jones, 2005, p. 255). Jones (2005) suggested that this practice is often pursued in part as a means of allowing donor-conceived children to "pass" as genetically related members of the family. That is, the practice of matching physical characteristics serves to construct genetic continuity among family members, by establishing quasi-biogenetic ties between the nonbiological mother and the donor-conceived child. Lesbian couples often seek donors who are similar to the nonbiological mother in hair color, eye color, and race; they may also attempt to match on other factors such as religious background (Chabot & Ames, 2004; C. Jones, 2005).[7] In this way, the links they seek to establish are not just physical in nature but also cultural; for example, a Jewish donor might be chosen because of the nonbiological mother's Jewish background. Finally, in addition to selecting for physical and background characteristics, lesbians also consider the medical history of the donor, as well as education, intelligence, and talents and interests (Herrmann-Green & Gehring, 2007; Mamo, 2002, as cited in Agigian, 2004).

Barriers in the Insemination Process and Beyond

Historically, lesbians have encountered difficulties in accessing clinic- and hospital-based donor insemination services because of the currency among health care professionals of legal, ethical, and moral arguments against les-

---

[7]Some lesbian couples may consider asking a male relative of the nonbiological mother, such as the brother, to be the donor; however, couples typically decide against this option because of the complicated nature of such an arrangement. For example, they worry about the possibility that the donor will want more involvement than the couple is comfortable with or that their families of origin will treat the donor as more of a parent than the nonbiological mother (Kranz & Daniluk, 2006).

bian insemination (Agigian, 2004). As Haimes and Weiner (2000) pointed out, the relatively higher degree of acceptance of heterosexual donor insemination suggested that lesbian donor insemination was often resisted simply because it transgressed too many boundaries: "the ideological, because of its apparent flouting of the importance of fathers; the structural, because of its advocacy of either one-parent or two-mother households; and the biogenetic, because of its avoidance of sexual intercourse" (p. 478). Social change, combined with the increasing visibility of lesbian mothers, has facilitated more sensitive treatment of lesbians who seek out donor insemination (McManus, Hunter, & Renn, 2006), although challenges do still exist, and reports of insensitive and inappropriate treatment by health care providers continue to appear in the literature (Wilton & Kaufman, 2000).[8]

For example, in Goldberg's (2006) sample, 2 of 29 couples encountered doctors who refused to inseminate expressly because of the couples' sexual orientation. In a third case, a birth mother's insurance company would not cover insemination costs for same-sex couples. Indeed, some insurance carriers justify the decision to only cover married women on the basis that they treat infertility and that when a woman in a married couple seeks alternative insemination it is because of a medical problem in the couple (e.g., genetic risk) or because of infertility in the couple (e.g., the husband is infertile; Agigian, 2004). The fact that lesbian couples are not considered "infertile couples" is an example of what Agigian referred to as *medical heterosexism* (p. 45). Lesbian couples are technically not medically infertile, but they do experience social infertility, a condition that arguably warrants medical assistance and intervention, if it is desired.

Ross and Steele (2006) and Ross, Steele, and Epstein (2006) conducted focus groups with lesbians in Canada who were parents or who were trying to conceive, and they found that lesbians' quest to obtain assisted reproduction and fertility services often brought them into contact with insensitive or ignorant providers. Fertility support services were often targeted to heterosexual women (see also Chabot & Ames, 2004); clinic forms were often inappropriately designed for lesbian and bisexual clients (e.g., they assumed a heterosexual, two-parent family); and health care providers sometimes failed to acknowledge the nonbirthing partner in office visits and prenatal classes (see also Goldberg, 2006; Wilton & Kaufmann, 2000). Similarly, Harvey et al. (1989) found that although over 83% of the lesbians in their sample felt that their health care providers provided competent care to them during pregnancy and childbirth, over half rated their providers as inadequate to poor on their practical knowledge of lesbian health issues, their awareness of homophobia, and their comfort level in providing care to lesbians.

---

[8]A 2008 decision made by the California Supreme Court ruled that physicians are not permitted to discriminate on the basis of sexual orientation. The Supreme Court decision can be found at http://www.courtinfo.ca.gov/opinions/documents/S142892.PDF

An additional challenge that lesbian inseminating couples face is legal barriers—that is, the fact that state laws undermine the nonbiological mother's relationship to her child. When a child is born to a lesbian couple, the biological mother is typically the sole legal parent. Ideally, the nonbiological mother can obtain a second-parent adoption, which allows her to adopt her partner's child without requiring the birth mother to give up her own parental rights. In this way, the child comes to have two legal parents. Historically, second-parent adoptions have been used most often by heterosexual stepparents (typically stepfathers) who wish to adopt their spouse's children (Connolly, 2002a), but they are now increasingly being used by lesbians as a means of ensuring legal recognition of the nonbiological mother.[9] Still, fewer than half of U.S. states have granted second-parent adoptions to lesbians and gay men (Pawelski et al., 2006), and practices vary significantly even within state borders, as in different jurisdictions or counties. Some courts choose to reject the analogy that is made between lesbian second-parents and heterosexual stepparents by ruling that their respective laws mandate marriage as a prerequisite before conferring stepparent status, whereas other courts choose to ignore the requirement that a petitioning stepparent has to be married to the biological or primary adoptive parent (Connolly, 2002a). When possible, second-parent adoption proceedings are typically initiated soon after the birth, once the donor, if known, has relinquished his parental rights and responsibilities. The process typically takes several months (but varies among jurisdictions) and involves a home study, in which a social worker visits the home of the couple, interviews and evaluates the nonbiological mother, and then writes a report on the basis of his or her impressions. The home study fee ranges from $1,500 to $3,500; thus, some couples may find it challenging to pay for this service, particularly if they have already spent their savings on efforts to conceive. Many couples also find this experience invasive and unfair: Although grateful that they live in a place where they are able to pursue such protections, they are angered by the fact that they must pay for the legal rights that (biological) heterosexual parents enjoy automatically (Connolly, 2002b).

In the absence of such protections (i.e., in states in which lesbians have not been successful at obtaining second-parent adoptions), couples often secure other legal safeguards, such as wills and powers of attorney for the

---

[9]Second-parent adoptions are also used to ensure legal recognition of the nonlegal adoptive lesbian or gay partner (in cases in which only one partner can legally adopt, such as international adoption and certain U.S. states). Second-parent adoptions protect the rights of both parents and allow both of them to claim their child as a dependent for tax purposes, to provide health insurance to their child from their employers, to take their child to the hospital for emergency care, and to share child custody and support in the event that their relationship dissolves. Couples that live in states that do not permit second-parent adoptions by lesbian or gay partners are therefore subject to additional vulnerability, in that they lack many of the rights and protections that are available to heterosexual-parent families.

nonbiological mother (Goldberg, 2006). Such protections provide some security, albeit limited, to families (see chap. 2, this volume).

Adoption: Choices and Challenges

Like lesbians who decide to pursue insemination, lesbians and gay men who decide to adopt face a number of subsequent decisions. These decisions include the type of adoption to pursue (e.g., domestic vs. international; if international, what country to use; if domestic, private vs. public; if private adoption, open vs. closed), willingness to adopt a child with special needs (e.g., prenatal drug exposure, emotional and behavioral problems, physical and medical problems), and desired or optimal child characteristics (e.g., the race and sex of the child). Notably, little research exists on lesbian and gay adoptive parents, and almost no research exists on their decision-making about adoption. Thus, much of the data reported here are from my own study of the transition to adoptive parenthood among lesbian and gay couples. This study follows lesbian and gay couples from the preadoptive stage to the postplacement phase, and it includes couples who are adopting internationally and domestically.

Type of Adoption

A variety of factors may be influential in lesbian and gay couples' decision making about what type of adoption to choose. Lesbians and gay men who choose private domestic, open adoption, in which the birth mother or birth parents choose the adoptive parents, often do so in part because they are attracted to the possibility of maintaining contact with their child's birth parent(s) or being able to provide their child with information, possibly ongoing, about the child's birth parent(s) (Downing et al., 2008). Some lesbian and gay couples feel that the philosophy of open adoption fits perfectly with their desire to be out and honest about their sexual orientation and relationship status during the adoption process (Goldberg, Downing, & Sauck, 2007; Downing et al., 2008). For them, international adoption is not attractive because it requires couples to closet themselves, that is, to choose one partner to pose as a single parent, in order to adopt (Goldberg et al., 2007; Mallon, 2007). Also, many lesbians and gay men are drawn to private domestic, open adoption because of their desire to adopt an infant (Downing et al., 2008; Nugent & Goldberg, 2008); indeed, children adopted internationally are typically somewhat older (e.g., between 6 and 24 months; Brooks, Simmel, Wind, & Barth, 2005), and few infants are available through foster care.

Men and women who do choose international adoption sometimes report doing so because of a special relationship with a country. For example, some couples choose a country that family members came from or in which they themselves have lived (Goldberg, 2009). Some lesbian and gay couples perceive international adoption as easier and more straightforward than private domestic adoption. For example, they suspect that birth mothers are less likely to choose a gay couple and that they will end up "waiting forever" for a child (Goldberg et al., 2007; Goldberg & Smith, 2008a). Some lesbians and gay men may choose international adoption because they perceive the only alternative to be open, domestic adoption—indeed, fully closed adoptions are increasingly rare—and they are anxious about the possibility that birth parents might come looking for the children that they have given up (a scenario that is not typical but which has been highly publicized in the media; e.g., Garcia, 2008). Finally, some individuals and couples may adopt internationally if they wish to adopt a child of a particular race; for example, a Vietnamese American lesbian couple might choose to pursue international adoption through Vietnam, in light of the fact that there are relatively few Vietnamese children available for adoption in the United States. Notably, lesbians and gay men are currently encountering new ethical and legal barriers in the international adoption process. For example, China and Guatemala now require affidavits of heterosexuality from single adopters, making it increasingly difficult for same-sex couples to adopt from those countries, and there are others with comparable restrictions.

Lesbians and gay men who adopt through the public welfare system may be motivated by finances (Downing et al., 2008; Nugent & Goldberg, 2008) or the altruistic desire to give a child a permanent home (Brooks & Goldberg, 2003). Another reason some individuals offer for pursuing public adoption is a desire to adopt an older child. Of course, in some cases, lesbians and gay men have had very few choices about what avenue they pursue. In Florida, for example, a ban on adoptions by lesbians and gay men was enacted in 1977 and was in place until September 2008, when it was ruled unconstitutional. During this 31-year period, lesbians' and gay men's only option was to become foster parents through the public welfare system, but they were not permitted to adopt those children.

Child Characteristics

Lesbians and gay men who seek to adopt must, like heterosexual prospective adoptive couples, think carefully about what kind of child they are interested in and willing to raise. Issues concerning the health of the child warrant serious consideration; for example, prospective adoptive parents are asked to consider the level of risk that they are willing to consider with respect to drug and alcohol exposure. For individuals and couples who are adopting older children either domestically or internationally, applicants also must consider whether they are open to adopting a child with known emotional or physical handicaps, and if so, what level and type of difficulties they feel they can manage. Historically, lesbians and gay men have been more willing to adopt children with special needs (Mallon, 2004) in part because of the fact that they are competing against heterosexual couples (who are regarded as more "ideal") for children. Indeed, some sexual minorities report feeling that they are expected to be more open to adopting children with special needs: that is, they wonder whether agencies that push high-risk children on them are attempting to match the least desirable applicants with the least desirable children (Goldberg et al., 2007; J. D. Matthews & Cramer, 2006). Some lesbians and gay men, though, are likely open to adopting a child with special needs out of a desire to make a difference in the world and because they empathize strongly with the "unwanteds" in society (Lassiter, Dew, Newton, Hays, & Yarbrough, 2006).

Lesbians and gay men also face decisions about the race of the child that they are willing to adopt. There is some evidence that same-sex couples are more likely than heterosexual couples to adopt transracially, at least with regard to international adoption (Gates et al., 2007; Shelley-Sireci & Ciano-Boyce, 2002). Furthermore, in a 2009 study of 54 lesbian and 93 heterosexual preadoptive couples, Goldberg explored (a) whether there were different rates of willingness to adopt transracially in the two groups and (b) couples' explanations for why they were willing or unwilling to adopt transracially. Findings revealed that lesbians were significantly more likely to be willing to adopt transracially than were heterosexual couples. Lesbian and heterosexual couples cited the following reasons for being open: (a) they lived in a racially diverse community, and therefore they felt they could provide an environment that supported and reflected their child's race/ethnicity; (b) their families or friendship networks were racially diverse; and (c) they perceived their family members as supportive (i.e., not racist) and were confident that their families would accept and love a family member who was racially different. Some lesbians also felt that it would not be fair to discriminate against a child on the basis of race in light of their own experiences of discrimination. Reasons for being unwilling to adopt transracially included: (a) a lack of racial/ethnic diversity in their communities; (b) lack of support from or racism within their families of origin; (c) personal internalized racism; and (d) the sense, from lesbians, that having gay parents, being adopted, and being racially different from one's parents was simply too much for a child to handle.

Lesbians and gay men also may spend time thinking about the sex of the child that they wish to adopt. Although agency personnel may caution applicants not to be unnecessarily selective in their preferred child characteristics (indeed, the family that is waiting for a blond-haired male infant may be waiting for quite some time), some lesbians and gay men, by virtue of the fact that only one sex is represented in the parental unit, may engage in thoughtful consideration about their ability and desire to raise a boy or girl. Some research suggests that lesbians tend to have a preference for adopting girls (Gartrell et al., 1996; Shelley-Sireci & Ciano-Boyce, 2002).[10] It is pos-

---

[10]Interestingly, women who conceive by insemination have an elevated (approximately 65%) chance of bearing a son. This is because sperm that carry a Y chromosome (the chromosome that determines a

sible that gay men tend to exhibit a similar pattern of preferring a same-sex child, perhaps because of internalized societal assumptions that they will not be able to provide proper gender socialization to a girl. Alternatively, dominant (and unfounded) stereotypes of gay men as perverts and child molesters might lead some men to exhibit or report a preference for girls, at least at the application stage of adoption (S. Hicks, 2005a). At the mercy of adoption personnel to approve or reject them as prospective adoptive parents, gay men and lesbians also may feel that they cannot afford to fulfill negative stereotypes.

Of course, some lesbians and gay men likely prefer girls and boys, respectively, for reasons other than fear of disapproval by society and adoption agencies. Some women and men may truly feel that they are better equipped to raise a child of the same sex because of their own insider knowledge regarding body parts, gender development, and gender socialization (Mallon, 2004). Additionally, some sexual minorities may worry about garnering "appropriate role models" for an opposite-sex child (Goldberg & Allen, 2007), and some lesbians may prefer girls because they perceive a lack of acceptance of boys and sons within the lesbian community (Chrisp, 2001). Alternatively, some lesbians and gay men may prefer to raise an opposite-sex child, perhaps in part because of their own self-perceived nonconformity with the gendered norms associated with their sex. They may wonder whether they might be better parents to, or have greater enjoyment in raising, an opposite-sex child.

Barriers in the Adoption Process and Beyond

Once a couple has decided to adopt, distant systems become highly relevant in shaping the experiences and trajectories of lesbians and gay men. At the broadest level, court decisions regarding adoption by lesbians and gay men at the local, county, and state levels play a significant role in either alleviating or exacerbating the stresses associated with adoption (Hunter & Mallon, 1998). Although every state allows individual, unmarried adults to petition to adopt a child, which presumably includes lesbian and gay individuals, a limited number of states have demonstrated by judicial rulings (a) an openness to adoption by openly lesbian and gay individuals and (b) an openness to adoption by openly lesbian and gay couples (Human Rights Campaign Foundation, 2002). The latter states specifically allow both partners to adopt a child together, at the same time; this is often referred to as *joint* or *coparent adoption*. In states that are unlikely to grant coparent adoptions, lesbian and gay couples typically choose one partner to officially adopt, as a single parent; later, the other partner may petition to adopt his or her partner's

---

male child) weigh less than sperm that carry the X chromosome (which determines a female child). The lighter-weight Y chromosome can swim faster (Erwin, 2007). Thus, lesbians who strongly prefer a female child may be better off adopting.

child with a second-parent adoption, if this is possible in the couple's state. Of course, there are many states where second-parent adoptions are rarely granted, leading to a situation in which there is one legal parent and one nonlegal, unrecognized parent. Indeed, the absence of legal structures and supports that acknowledge both partners' commitment to parenthood functions to undermine and challenge the stability of couple and family relationships (Herek, 2006; Pawelski et al., 2006).

At a more immediate level, adoption agencies and services can serve as potential supports, or additional barriers, in lesbians' and gay men's quest to adopt. There is tremendous variability in adoption agency practices with regard to adoption by lesbian and gay persons and couples. The Evan B. Donaldson Adoption Institute conducted a nationwide analysis to assess the attitudes and practices of private and public adoption agencies with respect to lesbian and gay adoptive parents (Brodzinsky, 2003). The researchers found that 65% of agencies accepted applications from lesbians and gay men, and about 39% of agencies had made at least one placement with lesbians or gay men in the past year. About 20% of agency representatives reported that their agencies had rejected applications from lesbian or gay individuals or couples on at least one occasion. Of course, practices likely vary within adoption agencies as well, such that some social workers will actively advocate for lesbian and gay prospective adoptive parents and others will resist making placement recommendations with sexual minorities. Research has suggested that adoption workers often make decisions on the basis of their own religious or moral beliefs; such workers, then, would presumably avoid placing children with gay parents (Berkman & Zinberg, 1997).

Adoption agencies that do accept applications from lesbian and gay prospective adopters are not necessarily affirming and sensitive in their practices. Matthews and Cramer (2006) examined barriers to adoption from the perspective of 16 gay male adoptive parents who retrospectively reported on their experiences during various phases of the adoption process. Some men reported that some of the agencies they encountered discouraged openness about sexual orientation during the preplacement stage (i.e., they operated on an informal "don't ask, don't tell" basis), and the men recalled the experience as confusing and upsetting. Indeed, lesbians and gay men often receive conflicting messages about whether or not they should disclose their sexual orientation during the adoption process (Mallon, 2004). Several men in Matthews and Cramer's study also reported feeling put off by insensitive application forms that seemed to focus on heterosexual applicants only. With regard to placement, several men felt that social workers pushed them to take children who were older or had special needs. Also, several men reported that support groups were more geared toward heterosexual couples, in that they presumed infertility.

Because of their vulnerability in the adoption process, it is not surprising that many lesbians and gay men expend significant time and effort researching potential adoption agencies (Gianino, 2008; Goldberg et al., 2007). In selecting an agency, a primary consideration for many sexual minorities is the perceived gay-friendliness of the agency. Among the factors they might consider are: Do the agency's materials (e.g., Web site, printed materials, office signage) contain images of same-sex couples? Does the agency explicitly state its openness to working with lesbians and gay men (i.e., in their materials, on their Web site, in their mission statement)? Are staff members friendly and respectful in initial in-person and telephone interactions? Does the agency have specialized support groups or services for gay adoptive parents and prospective parents? Does the agency actively engage with and recruit from the gay community? Agencies that receive high marks in these categories tend to be perceived as gay-friendly, and are thus more likely to be selected by lesbians and gay men (Goldberg et al., 2007).

Of course, some lesbians and gay men are limited by financial resources and geographic location, such that they have few choices in choosing an adoption agency. As a result, they may elect to remain closeted throughout the process, for fear of jeopardizing their chances of adopting (Mallon, 2004). For this reason, social workers and adoption agencies that are open to and accepting of lesbians and gay men as prospective adoptive and foster parents should make an effort to clearly communicate this openness—in their language, affect, and overall demeanor—starting in their very first encounters with couples and individuals (Mallon, 2007). Furthermore, because applicants may not be out in the first interview, it is important for social workers not to presume heterosexuality (e.g., to assume that a single man is necessarily heterosexual).

Surrogacy

Finally, in addition to seeking alternative insemination and adoption services, some sexual minorities, especially men, choose to pursue surrogacy.[11] In the gay male couple context, surrogacy involves a pregnancy created by the insemination of one or both of the gay men's sperm into the surrogate; thus, the child is the biological child of the surrogate and one of the partners (Lev, 2004). Gay men may pursue surrogacy over adoption because they desire a biological connection to their child; they wish to raise a child from birth; they perceive the surrogacy process as being less complex and allowing them more control, compared with the adoption process; and they worry about the emotional difficulties that a child might experience as a result of having been relinquished for adoption by birth parents (Lev, 2006).

---

[11]Options for both gay men and lesbians are traditional surrogacy, whereby the surrogate mother is genetically related to the baby, or gestational surrogacy, whereby the baby is carried by the surrogate but is genetically related to another woman, who has donated the egg.

However, the pursuit of surrogacy can be challenging for several reasons. First, it is extremely costly, possibly requiring significant financial sacrifices on the part of all but the most affluent lesbians and gay men. Second, surrogacy involves complex legal issues (Hollandsworth, 1995). Eleven states and the District of Columbia ban surrogacy completely, and several of these states criminalize it (Wald, 2007). Only six states have explicitly approved surrogacy contracts through their courts and/or legislatures; the remaining states have yet to take a position on the legality of surrogacy.

Lesbians and gay men who pursue surrogacy face both the typical legal challenges associated with surrogacy and the challenges related to their sexual orientation. As Wald (2007) observed, surrogacy agencies may be open to working with sexual minorities but may not have the legal know-how to match a gay man from State A with a surrogate from State B. Indeed, the initial determination of parentage for any baby (e.g., a baby born to a birth mother or surrogate) generally happens in the state in which the baby is born. Thus, if a couple from New York (where surrogacy is illegal) contracts with a surrogacy agency in California, which in turn matches them with a surrogate in Ohio, the initial determination of parentage should occur in Ohio. This is presumably what would happen with a heterosexual couple who are becoming parents through surrogacy. However, Wald warned that this scenario would play out somewhat differently for a same-sex couple because Ohio is a super-DOMA (i.e., Defense of Marriage Act) state (i.e., Ohio prohibits same-sex couples or unmarried heterosexual couples from enjoying the same benefits as married couples). Under Ohio law, a heterosexual couple using a gestational carrier could claim parentage from birth "based on a combination of genetics and marital presumptions" (Wald, 2007, para. 7). A same-sex couple would not be able to make this same claim because of the Ohio DOMA as well as the fact that Ohio does not allow adoptions by same-sex couples. Thus, a same-sex couple using an Ohio surrogate would need to establish legal parentage for at least one of the partners in a different state, where surrogacy is legal (Wald, 2007).

There is a notable dearth of empirical research on lesbians' and gay men's use of surrogacy, although several books address the subject: for example, Diane Ehrensaft's (2005) book *Mommies, Daddies, Donors, Surrogates: Answering Tough Questions and Building Stronger Families* addressed surrogacy in the context of both heterosexual- and sexual minority–parent families. In her discussion of the complexities of surrogacy, Ehrensaft intimated that surrogacy is a lot like insemination: It allows one partner to be biologically related to the child, and like insemination, it involves a biological "other" to provide the other half of the genetic material, and, in this case, to carry the child. It follows, then, that many of the same complexities that accompany alternative insemination are also relevant in the surrogacy context. Surrogacy introduces a *genetic asymmetry* among same-sex couples, such that only one partner has a biological bond to the child. This may lead couples to wonder whether the child is more one partner's than the other's and to consider whether the genetic connection will or should affect bonding or who has more say in parenting decisions (Ehrensaft, 2005). Like insemination, surrogacy also raises questions about the symbolic other—that is, how to tell the child about how he or she came to be, how to tell the child about his or her other genetic half, what to tell, and so on. Unlike insemination, though, the child grows in another's body, often a stranger's body; thus, the couple is waiting for the child to be birthed by an other and then delivered to them as their child. It follows that same-sex couples who use surrogates may experience anxiety about the surrogacy arrangement. For example, they may wonder whether the child will develop a bond to the surrogate, only to be taken away from her (Ehrensaft, 2005).

Notably, gay male couples' experiences with surrogates may be different from those of heterosexual couples and lesbian couples. First, having no female partner in the equation presumably might make some surrogates feel more comfortable. In her study of gay fathers, some of whom had become parents through surrogacy, Stacey (2006) found evidence that some surrogates may prefer to work with gay men because, as one surrogate stated, "The mother . . . can get a little jealous and a little threatened, because she's already feeling insecure about being infertile and having another woman having that process. . . . With a gay couple . . . there's no exclusion, and there's no threatened feelings" (p. 35). Thus, in theory, some gay men may enjoy more harmonious relationships with their surrogates, in that they did not arrive at surrogacy because of infertility and there is no symbolic or actual female for the surrogate to compete with or feel challenged by.

BECOMING PARENTS: THE TRANSITION TO PARENTHOOD FOR LESBIAN AND GAY COUPLES

In this section, I discuss the transition to parenthood experience for same-sex couples, paying attention to the ways in which same-sex couples' experiences are likely similar to and different from those heterosexual couples. In addition, I attend to the varied contexts that uniquely define lesbian and gay people's transition to parenthood, highlighting the significant variability within lesbian and gay people's experiences.

The transition from couplehood to parenthood has been extensively studied in heterosexual couples (C. P. Cowan & Cowan, 1988; Gjerdingen & Chaloner, 1994; Goldberg & Perry-Jenkins, 2004). This literature suggests that becoming a parent is a challenging and potentially stressful life transition that is often marked by increased strain between work and family responsibilities (Costigan, Cox, & Cauce, 2003; Schulz, Cowan, Cowan, & Brennan, 2004), decreased relationship quality (Belsky & Rovine, 1990; Krieg,

2007), and compromised well-being, particularly for women (Ballard, Davis, Cullen, Mohan, & Dean, 1994; Matthey, Barnett, Ungerer, & Waters, 2000). While studies of heterosexual couples have identified factors that facilitate an easier transition to parenthood (e.g., a strong preexisting marital relationship, social support from family members and friends; Feldman, Sussman, & Zigler, 2004; Morse, Buist, & Durkin, 2000), such findings cannot be assumed to unilaterally apply to same-sex couples or single lesbians and gay men. Same-sex couples carry with them unique strengths and potential vulnerabilities, which may shape their transition to parenthood. For example, it is possible that lesbians' (and to some degree, gay men's) shared gender socialization, valuing of egalitarianism, and fluidity in roles may function as protective factors with regard to adjustment.[12] Likewise, because men in general earn more income than women, regardless of sexual orientation (Badgett, 1998), gay male couples' greater earning potential may also be viewed as a potential strength. But, as discussed in chapter 2 of this volume, lesbians and gay men do not benefit from the societal support that heterosexual couples receive when they become parents, and, thus, relative nonsupport may represent a risk factor for sexual minorities during the transition to parenthood. Indeed, lesbians and gay men are vulnerable to discrimination in the process of becoming parents; they also may lack support from family members. Furthermore, on the broadest level, they must navigate state laws and policies that systematically thwart their efforts to become parents.

Very little research has examined the transition to parenthood experience of lesbian and gay couples, and the research that has been conducted is limited in many ways. First, there is no research at all (with the exception of my current ongoing study) that prospectively examines gay men's transition to parenthood, although some research has examined men's retrospective accounts of this transition (Berkowitz & Marsiglio, 2007; Gianino, 2008; Mallon, 2004; J. D. Matthews & Cramer, 2006). Second, no research has examined this transition among bisexual men and women or transgender persons, and this omission limits our understanding of how people of diverse sexualities and gender expressions experience this key life event. Third, the research on lesbian couples' transition to parenthood has largely addressed the experiences of White, relatively affluent, inseminating couples (Gartrell et al., 1996, 1999; Goldberg, 2006; Goldberg & Perry-Jenkins, 2007; Goldberg & Sayer, 2006), although data are emerging on lesbian couples' transition to adoptive parenthood (Goldberg & Smith, 2008a). Thus, although the data presented here are by no means comprehensive, they do provide insights into the experience of becoming parents for lesbians and, to some extent, for gay men.

---

[12]Of course, as discussed in chapter 2 of this volume, not all same-sex couples necessarily value or enact egalitarianism in their relationships. This is discussed further in chapter 4, in the context of lesbian and gay parenting.

The transition to parenthood for heterosexual couples has been examined most extensively with regard to changes in relationship quality, well-being, and the family roles and division of labor. In the following section, these domains are discussed, as well as others that are especially relevant in the lesbian and gay parent context, such as social support, that may have implications for adjustment.

Social Supports: Family, Friends, and Others

Heterosexual parents, and, in particular, heterosexual mothers, receive significant validation from their families and from the broader society regarding their parenthood roles and identities. Lesbian mothers and gay fathers challenge and contradict the norms that govern heterosexuality, reproduction, and the family, and, in turn, may face nonsupport and resistance from other (heterosexual) parents, as well as their own family members. Indeed, notions of lesbian motherhood and gay fatherhood may activate deep-seated moral resistance in some family members. Furthermore, some family members may worry that they themselves will be outed as the mother, father, sister, or brother of a lesbian woman or gay man. Sexual minorities, then, can face a withdrawal of or lack of support from their families just when they desire it the most—as they anticipate and then experience the life-changing event of becoming parents. Alternatively, it is also possible that lesbians' and gay men's sexual orientation becomes less of an issue to some family members as they embark upon parenthood. Perhaps what may emerge as most salient to many family members is the new, adorable addition to their family.

Some research sheds light on these issues. Gartrell et al. (1996) conducted one of the few longitudinal studies of the transition to parenthood among lesbian couples. They first interviewed their predominantly White, middle-class sample of lesbian mothers (84 families: 70 included a birth mother and comother, 14 were single mothers) during the insemination or pregnancy stage. Most (62%) of the sample were first-time parents. Prebirth, about 78% of women expected at least some relatives to accept their child. Gartrell et al. (1999) reinterviewed these women when their children were toddlers and found that the majority of women did feel supported by at least some family members; furthermore, 69% of the sample felt that having a child had enhanced their relationships with their own parents. Notably, birth mothers tended to rate their parents as closer to their child than did nonbiological mothers. These data are consistent with those of Goldberg (2006), who interviewed lesbian couples before and after the birth of their first child and found that lesbians' perceptions of support from their own and their partners' families increased across the transition to parenthood, although in general women reported the highest levels of support from friends. Similarly, Ben-Ari and Livni (2006) studied eight lesbian-parent families in Israel and observed that even family members who were openly disapproving of participants' sexual orientation tended to support women's decision to become parents, such that "grandchildren are perceived as 'compensation' for their daughters' sexual orientation" (p. 527). These data, taken together, suggest that family members may push their feelings about homosexuality aside in the interest of developing a relationship with a new grandchild or niece or nephew, particularly if the child is biogenetically related to them. Some lesbians and gay men, of course, inevitably confront hostility from family members upon announcing their intent to parent (Lassiter, Dew, Newton, Hays, & Yarbrough, 2006). As one participant in Lassiter et al.'s qualitative study of lesbian and gay parents noted, "Even those who are comfortable with you being gay may not be totally accepting of a gay person parenting" (p. 249). Such negative reactions by family members may be prompted by internalized myths that gay parents are more likely to molest their children and are psychologically unfit to parent (C. R. Matthews & Lease, 2000) or by concerns about the stigma that children raised by gay parents might experience (Johnson & O'Connor, 2002).

The transition to parenthood may also stimulate changes in the nature and pattern of lesbians' and gay men's friendships. In their 1999 follow-up, Gartrell et al. found that 38% of lesbian mothers considered close friends to be extended family (i.e., aunts and uncles to their children); however, 25% of lesbians felt that they had lost some close friendships, typically with women who were not mothers themselves. Indeed, 47% of women indicated that most of their current friends were parents. Other studies of lesbian mothers (Koepke, Hare, & Moran, 1992; Lewin, 1993) and gay fathers (Gianino, 2008; Mallon, 2004) also suggested that on becoming parents, some lesbian and gay parents find that they have more in common with heterosexual parents than with many of their childless gay friends. Becoming parents, then, may prompt changes in lifestyle and community that are somewhat bittersweet, as lesbians and gay men restructure their kinship networks in ways that reflect their changing families.

Division of Labor, Parenting Roles, and Equality
Across the Transition to Parenthood

Another domain that may change during the transition to parenthood is the division of labor. Among heterosexual couples, the transition to parenthood is marked by increasing role differentiation, with women spending more time in unpaid labor and men increasing their time in paid employment (Kluwer, Heesink, & van de Vliert, 2002). It is possible that same-sex couples may also experience increased differentiation in roles based on variables other than sex. For example, among lesbian couples that inseminate, role status (i.e., the fact that one woman carries, bears, and often nurses the child) may shape women's work–family roles, at least initially. Embodying differentiated family roles may be particularly hard for those lesbian couples that strongly value equality and equal power in their relationships (Blumstein

& Schwartz, 1983; C. J. Patterson, 1995). Alternatively, some lesbian couples may feel positively about embodying differentiated family roles (e.g., if they perceive this as an efficient and satisfactory means of dividing labor).

Goldberg and Perry-Jenkins (2007) interviewed lesbian inseminating couples during the last trimester and three months postnatally. They found that during the initial transition period, lesbian biological mothers were performing more child care, and nonbiological mothers (who typically received less parental leave) were performing more hours of paid work, although all women had decreased their hours in paid employment to juggle the demands of family life. Women contributed equally to housework. However, despite their unequal contributions to child care, the majority of women (60% of birth mothers and 80% of nonbirth mothers) considered both partners to be equal coparents. The remainder of women felt that the birth mother was more of the primary parent, a fact that they attributed to breastfeeding, the biological or genetic bond, and the fact that the birth mother spent more time with the child. Importantly, many nonbirth mothers used a number of strategies in an effort to compensate for the biological differential and their inability to breastfeed: For example, they contributed as much as possible to child care tasks, established a unique role or set of rituals with the baby (e.g., being the "bath-time mom"), and participated in feeding the child (e.g., through bottle-feeding). In this way, many couples actively worked to minimize potential inequity in their parental roles. Among those nonbiological mothers who perceived the birth mother as the primary parent, some women experienced feelings of jealousy and exclusion. Similarly, in their postbirth follow-up, Gartrell et al. (1999) found that although most couples (75%) considered themselves to be equal parents, 64% noted competitiveness and jealousy around bonding.

Contextual factors, such as work flexibility and supportive workplace policies, may facilitate equality in lesbian- and gay-parent families during the transition to parenthood. Gartrell et al. (1996) found that prebirth, 38% parents reported that they already had flexible work schedules which they could adapt to child care needs; post-birth, 53% of women had reduced their work hours to spend more time with their child (Gartrell et al., 1999). Furthermore, some couples may alternate their work schedules to reduce reliance on outside child care. For example, Reimann (1997) studied lesbian two-parent families and found that in 28% of families, partners took consecutive parental leaves to allow each partner solo bonding time with their child and to enable both partners to develop confidence in their competence as caregivers. In addition to facilitating equal bonding, and possibly preventing burnout, this arrangement also ensured that one woman did not assume disproportionate sacrifices with regard to her career. Thus, workplace factors and, more generally, social class can play an important role in the development and maintenance of equality in families. It is likely that low income- and working-class same-sex couples, who tend to have less flexibility in their jobs, may experience more challenges in balancing work and child care in the early months of parenthood and may consequently encounter greater barriers to maintaining equality (see also Carrington, 2002, as discussed in chap. 2, this volume).

Naming Practices: Communicating Parental Roles and (In)Equality

When lesbians and gay men become mothers and fathers, they do so in a societal context in which parental roles are clearly defined by gender. In turn, they must negotiate naming practices, which have been traditionally used to construct family and gender and to reinforce patriarchy. For example, children in heterosexual-parent families typically receive their father's last name (which in most cases is shared by their mothers), ensuring its preservation. Likewise, "Mommy" and "Daddy" are culturally understood labels that correspond to well-established parental roles. As they prepare to become parents, lesbians and gay men may increasingly consider how they will negotiate these complex naming practices. Indeed, same-sex couples may use naming to resist and transform traditional practices and to assert the child's relationship with the nonbiological and/or nonlegal parent. Some lesbian couples, for example, give their child(ren) the nonbiological mother's last name as a means of asserting and legitimating her parental role (Almack, 2005; Chabot & Ames, 2004), thereby creating for her a socially intelligible identity (Bergen, Suter, & Daas, 2006). Lesbian and gay adoptive parents may also adopt this practice in situations in which there is only one legal parent. That is, they may give their child the unofficial, nonlegal parent's last name as a means of asserting their relationship to one another. Other lesbian and gay couples choose hyphenation (Almack, 2005) to symbolize the child's equivalent connection to both parents. Still other lesbian couples choose to give the child the birth mother's surname (Almack, 2005; C. J. Patterson, 1998). In her study of lesbian mothers' naming practices, Almack (2005) found that this group of women typically offered very little explanation at all for their decision, which attests to the unstated power of biological motherhood. Indeed, the practice of assigning the child the birth mother's surname illustrates "how difficult it can be to escape the deeply conventional set of expectations and obligations attached to (biological) motherhood" (p. 249). Furthermore, even among couples who decided to give their children the nonbiological mother's surname, birth mothers sometimes experienced ambivalence about this decision. They agreed to it because it was "fair," but they nevertheless wanted to claim something "special and 'exclusive'" about birth motherhood and biological connections (p. 249). Thus, they held two desires—to maintain equality but to have something "special" with their child—that were ultimately at odds, thereby creating intrapersonal tension.

Similarly, lesbian and gay couples face decisions about what to have their children call them. In choosing their parental titles, lesbians and gay men are actively constructing and communicating their children's relationships to them. Address terms and referents are powerful communicators of identities, and the use of a term such as *Mama*, for example, functions to communicate the nonbiological mother's parental role to the child, to both parents, and to "generalized others" (Bergen et al., 2006, p. 208). Research results have suggested that some couples allow their children to establish their own names for them (Chabot & Ames, 2004), whereas others assign them (e.g., one mother is called "Mommy" and the other, "Mama"; or both are called "Mommy"). Sometimes a name other than Mommy/Mama or Daddy/Dad is chosen; for example, a name that is linked to a parent's cultural heritage may be selected (e.g., the Jewish term "Emah"). Some lesbian and gay parents may find that such gendered parental designations do not feel right to them, and they may therefore prefer a more unique title. Touroni and Coyle (2002) observed that some nonbiological lesbian mothers did not feel that the term *mother* accurately captured their relationship to their child, or they felt that there was something about the word that that they did not want to claim. Indeed, the mother identifier connotes images of self-sacrifice, hyperfemininity, and heterosexually defined roles that some women do not wish to embody. In turn, some women choose to be called by their first names (a decision that may have the unintended effect of communicating unequal parental roles to the outside world; Bergen et al., 2006) or seek to create new, innovative names for themselves (Pagenhart, 2006).

Notably, complex naming decisions are also encountered by transgender parents after they transition. As S. Hines (2006a) pointed out, the linguistic shifts that accompany changes in a parent's gender identity can be challenging for both parents and children to navigate. In her interviews with 30 transgender adults, 7 of whom were parents, Hines found that rather than reversing the parenting nouns of Mom and Dad, the parents typically suggested that their children call them by their new first name or a nickname, which was typically a variation of their pretransition name. More research is needed to explore the naming practices of transgender parents and their children, as well as the ways in which naming and language are used to construct, and deconstruct, gender.

Changes in Relational and Individual Adjustment Across the Transition to Parenthood

Becoming a parent is stressful (C. P. Cowan & Cowan, 1988). The process involves expanding one's repertoire of roles to include that of a parent, (re)negotiating issues of housework, child care, and paid work, and negotiating changes in social support. Furthermore, becoming a parent is often associated with increased fatigue, worries about finances, and, at least temporarily, the forgoing of previously enjoyed hobbies and routines. Given these demands, it is not surprising that researchers have been interested in how adults' relationship quality and mental health change during the transition to parenthood. While little research has as of yet addressed these issues longitudinally in lesbian and gay couples, some limited data are available.

The only known study of lesbian inseminating couples' relationship quality across the transition to parenthood found that, similar to heterosexual couples (Krieg, 2007), lesbians' relationship quality declined and the frequency of relationship conflict increased (Goldberg & Sayer, 2006). Goldberg and Sayer found that women with more neurotic personality styles tended to experience greater declines in relationship quality across the transition. Also, nonbiological mothers who expected high levels of support from their partners' families reported increases in conflict, which might be due to frustrated expectations: That is, they did not receive as much support as they thought they would. Alternatively, their partners' families may have met or exceeded their support expectations to such an extent that their involvement might be experienced as intrusive; for example, perhaps birth mothers' families tended to undermine the nonbiological mother's parental role.

Several qualitative studies have examined lesbians' retrospective reports about how their relationships changed upon becoming parents. McCandlish (1987) conducted in-depth interviews with five lesbian couples that revealed that, upon becoming parents (in these cases, by alternative insemination), the women felt that they needed more support and nurturance from their partners but found that they were giving and receiving less of both. Perhaps, given that lesbian couples tend to highly value psychological intimacy in their relationships (see chap. 2, this volume), declines in communication and nurturance are experienced as particularly upsetting to women. Similarly, in their postbirth follow-up, Gartrell et al. (1999) found that 55% of coupled lesbian mothers felt that child-rearing had been stressful to their relationships, 91% felt that they had less energy and time for their partner relationships, and 80% reported that sexual intimacy had ceased for many months after the birth. The demands of nursing may be partly to blame for this decline in intimacy: Reimann (1997) found that some birth mothers attributed their lack of interest in and energy for sex to the emotional and physical strain of breastfeeding.

However, nursing is certainly not the only factor responsible for decreased relationship satisfaction, as evidenced by the fact that gay men also appear to experience the dip in relationship quality that is characteristically associated with the transition to parenthood. Mallon's (2004) study of 20 gay fathers revealed that many men also recalled increased conflict in their relationships immediately following their transition to adoptive parenthood. Men attributed the increased strain in their relationships to the time and energy demands of parenting as well as sleep deprivation: There was little time to talk or communicate about anything other than day-to-day parenting issues. Indeed, men faced the very difficult challenge of balancing the demands of new parenthood with the need to maintain and nurture their relationships. Some men sought to accomplish that by setting aside specific times to talk, communicate, and work out conflicts, which often involved differences in parenting style and jealousy/competition. Similarly, the men in Gianino's 2008 study of 16 gay male adoptive parents (8 couples) recalled that exhaustion and sleep deprivation, as well as differing views on parenting, constituted significant stressors in their relationships during the early months of parenting. These men, like the fathers in Mallon's study, sought to collaboratively and directly deal with conflicts as they came up, as opposed to allowing tensions to build over time.

Very little research has explored same-sex couples' mental health across the transition to parenthood. One exception is a study by Goldberg and Smith (2008b). Using three waves of data (i.e., lesbian couples who conceived their child by insemination were interviewed during the last trimester, 3 months postnatally, and 3 years postnatally), the authors explored whether aspects of the child (temperament), the relationship (relationship quality, the division of labor), and the broader environment (extrafamilial support) were related to change in anxiety over time, for biological and nonbiological mothers. They found that on average, all mothers' anxiety tended to increase across the transition, particularly that of biological mothers, whose anxiety scores approached the clinical range by the time their child was 3 years old. (Interestingly, their scores were similar to those of heterosexual mothers of young children in the general population [McMahon, Barnett, Kowalenko, Tennant, & Don, 2001].) None of the examined predictors explained change in anxiety among biological mothers. Among nonbiological mothers, women who perceived high levels of outside instrumental social support (e.g., the presence of people to help babysit) prior to the birth, as well as women who perceived their children as more temperamentally difficult postnatally, experienced greater increases in anxiety. The authors speculated that nonbiological mothers, who were working more hours outside of the home than birth mothers, may be particularly sensitive to the availability of people to assist with (or compensate for their lesser involvement in) child care. Moreover, because of their lesser involvement in child care, it is possible that they are more sensitive to and affected by their child's negative behaviors (a finding that has also been found for fathers; Perren, von Wyl, Burgin, Simoni, & von Klitzing, 2005).

The Unique Contexts of Lesbian and Gay Parents

How is the transition to parenthood experience shaped by the route that lesbians and gay men choose (e.g., insemination, adoption, foster care, surrogacy)? How are the experiences of gay men who become parents different from those of lesbians who become parents? How do parents' social class and financial and social resources affect their transition to parenthood? How does the racial makeup of the family (i.e., one's own race, one's partner's race, one's child's race) shape the transition? How does relationship status (i.e., single, coupled) shape the transition to parenthood experience? These are important questions that have not yet been explored in depth. However, the data point to some potential ways in which the transition to parenthood experience may differ for individuals depending on their route to parenthood, as well as other factors such as parents' gender and parents' relationship status.

Route to Parenthood

Lesbian couples who inseminate are spared many of the complexities associated with adoption (e.g., a potentially long wait for a child). Additionally, one partner has the perhaps desired opportunity to experience pregnancy and give birth, and the child is genetically related to one of the partners. However, lesbian inseminating couples are also in the unique position of having to negotiate various asymmetries in their relationship: in the pregnancy experience, the breastfeeding experience, and in the partners' genetic relatedness to the child. This creates the potential for inequity in parental roles, feelings of jealousy on the part of the nonbiological mother, and questions and conflicts over who the child "belongs" to. Couples may also negotiate legal asymmetries, in that the birth mother may be the only partner legally related to the child.

Adoptive lesbian and gay couples, in contrast, start out on equal footing, more or less. While adoptive partners may differ in terms of their previous experience with children, desire to stay home, work flexibility, and many other factors that could create potential polarization or asymmetry in their parental roles, their lack of a genetic relationship to their child is equivalent. Of course, legal inequities, in couples in which only one partner is the legal parent, may create feelings of invisibility, anxiety, or jealousy in the nonlegal partner, or feelings of guilt and over-responsibility in the legal parent. When only one partner is legally recognized as the parent, the other partner has to go out of his or her way to assert a parental role, possibly creating stress for both members of the couple (Mallon, 2004). Coparent adoptions, then, can serve an important role in shaping both short-term and long-term couple and family dynamics in that they affirm both partners' equal commitment to parenting and serve to validate both partners' parental status.

Lesbians and gay men who adopt face a number of unique tasks. For example, lesbian couples may come to adoption after struggling with infertility, an experience that may have residual effects on their mental health and their adjustment to parenthood. Indeed, one study of lesbian and heterosexual couples during the preadoptive period found that having tried IVF and experiencing greater infertility-related stress were associated with higher levels of depression for both types of couples (Goldberg & Smith, 2008a). More research is needed to determine whether the stress of infertility carries over into the postadoption phase of parenthood.

Lesbians and gay men who adopt also face the task of negotiating relationships with individuals other than their own child during their transition to parenthood. These relationships may be symbolic, as in the case of closed adoptions (which most international adoptions are), or they may be quite real, as in the case of private open adoptions or adoptions through the child welfare system. For example, lesbians and gay men who choose to pursue open adoption may experience ongoing relationships with the birth parents of their children. Initiating, maintaining, and negotiating such relationships can be stressful, joyful, and complicated, particularly in the early (overwhelming, sleep-deprived, bonding-intensive) months of parenting. Indeed, lesbians and gay men who adopt sometimes feel that their children are strangers to them when they take them home; thus, intensive bonding is critical to the development of the parent-child relationship (Alexander, 2001; Lev, 2004). Furthermore, adoptive lesbian and gay parents' transition to parenthood may be complicated by navigating racial, ethnic, and cultural differences in their children. They may need to educate themselves about the racial and cultural needs of their children, including how to help their children develop a sense of pride in themselves. Parents may also face pragmatic issues such as how to address health, hair, or skin needs that may differ from their own (Lev, 2004). Finally, their decision to adopt a child who is racially, ethnically, or culturally different from themselves may be met with discomfort or lack of support from family members, friends, neighbors, and society at large (Johnson & O'Connor, 2002).

For lesbian and gay parents who foster or adopt children with special needs, the transition to parenthood will likely be complicated in additional ways. In one survey of lesbians and gay men who had adopted through foster care, 29% of children had prior exposure to physical neglect, 16% had confirmed incidents of physical abuse, and 11% had confirmed indications of sexual abuse at the time of their adoption (Ryan & Cash, 2004). Such experiences of trauma and abuse necessarily present unique issues, such as attachment difficulties, to be dealt with in the initial transitional period and beyond. Likewise, sexual minorities who adopt children with physical and cognitive difficulties, older children, and children who have experienced multiple foster care placements will also encounter unique challenges that may require significant time, energy, and attention. Thus, lesbians and gay men who foster or adopt children with special needs may experience particularly high levels of stress, especially in the initial adjustment phase. In the long term, however, there is some evidence that these families function remarkably well. Leung, Erich, and Kanenberg (2005) studied lesbian, gay, and heterosexual adoptive-parent families and found particularly high levels of family functioning in lesbian and gay adoptive-parent families with (a) older children and (b) children with higher numbers of foster care placements. More research is needed to explore the distinctive challenges and strengths of lesbian and gay adoptive-parent families, particularly those with special needs children.

Some lesbians and gay men become parents incidentally—that is, by partnering with individuals who already have children (e.g., who were conceived in the context of heterosexual relationships, or who were born or adopted into a prior same-sex relationship). As Lynch (2004a, 2004b) observed, the lesbian or gay stepparent's transition to parenthood is uniquely defined by the fact that they are alone in this transition, in contrast to planned lesbian- or gay-parent families, in which partners become parents together. Furthermore, in contrast to intentional lesbian- and gay-parent family arrangements, lesbian and gay stepparents and their partners tend to engage in very little preparation for stepfamily formation. Stepparents—heterosexual or gay—may have unrealistic expectations, believing that the transition to a parenting role will be relatively uncomplicated. As a result, they are often unprepared for the challenges associated with the stepparenting role (e.g., competition and tension between the stepparent and the children, challenges to asserting authority). For sexual minorities, these challenges may be further complicated by their invisible status as lesbian or gay stepparents. Indeed, this transition may be particularly challenging if a parent's coming out and the introduction of the stepparent into the family occur simultaneously. Children may experience great difficulty sorting out their feelings with regard to each of these events and may respond negatively to the stepparent's attempts to parent them (A. Martin, 1998). Some lesbian and gay stepparents may also confront resistance from the biological or legal parent when they attempt to exert decision-making power over the child or the household. For example, Moore (2008) interviewed members of 32 Black lesbian stepfamilies and found that biological mothers were often opposed to sharing decision-making authority with regard to child-rearing, viewing themselves as "the mother" and primary caregiver. Further, and interestingly, many biological mothers actively sought to assume greater responsibility for household chores, out of awareness that maintaining greater control over this domain would ultimately grant them a stronger say in other aspects of family life such as child-rearing.[13]

Perhaps it is not surprising that no research has examined the transition to parenthood for transgender persons, although some sources note that with the recent advancements in reproductive technology, more male-to-female transsexuals are freezing their sperm so that they can have birth children by insemination sometime later in their lives (Lev, 2004). Female-to-male transsexuals sometimes choose to give birth before their transition, or, in some cases, after their transition (Daily News, 2008; Lev, 2004; Lothstein,

---

[13]Thus, for Black biological lesbian mothers, being the primary caretaker (and household organizer) represented a source of power in their relationships, a finding that stands in contrast to the literature on heterosexual, White married couples, in which women's greater responsibility for domestic work has often been reported as unchosen and involuntary (Coltrane, 2000).

1988). Consideration of the transition to parenthood experience for transgender persons raises many fascinating questions about the negotiation of gender and family relationships, the blurry nature of "fixed" categories such as male and female, and the gendering and de-gendering of parenthood. Questions are also raised about the impact of societal transphobia on the development and maintenance of such families.

Male Versus Female

Of course, the context of gender necessarily shapes lesbians' and gay men's transition to parenthood, in that mothers and fathers are treated differently in society. Gay men who become parents do so in the context of powerful stereotypes of men as incapable of nurturance. Thus, they enact parenthood in a society that is poised to judge them for their failures—for what they presumably cannot provide (as men), for the stigma that they will inevitably lay upon their children (as gay), and for what they are, which is immoral and inadequate (as gay men). Going shopping for diapers, visiting the pediatrician, and walking in the park with one's child are all activities that invite questions from outsiders, such as, "Where is that child's mother?" "Are you sure you know what you're doing?" or "Do you need a hand?" Lesbians, of course, are also met with the cultural imperative that "every child needs a father" (Goldberg & Allen, 2007), but this imperative is perhaps not as great as the societal dictate that "every child needs a mother" (Berkowitz & Marsiglio, 2007; S. Hicks, 2005b). Women's solo mothering in the absence of men is more culturally accessible than solo fathering in the absence of women. Two women strolling in the park with their 1-month-old son may invite fewer stares and questions than a similar scenario with two men (Mallon, 2004). Of course, all gay parents, regardless of whether they are male or female, coupled or single, are aware of and must contend with societal judgments about the unfitness of gay persons to parent.

Coupled Versus Single

The transition to parenthood experience for lesbians and gay men (as well as bisexual women and men) who become parents in the context of same-sex committed relationships is necessarily different from that of single sexual minorities. Practically speaking, single lesbians and gay men have it harder in many ways: They must navigate sleep deprivation, time management, and emotional and physical exhaustion by themselves, without the extra hands of an active coparent. They also lack the emotional support and camaraderie of a partner. On the other hand, they are spared the daily negotiations and potential conflicts that may arise during the early coparenting stage, as well as the emotional work that it takes to maintain and nurture an intimate relationship. Also, the sexual orientation of single sexual minorities is invisible: They are able to pass as heterosexual single parents with very little effort. No research has systematically explored the transition to parenthood process for single sexual minorities, although they are sometimes included in larger studies (e.g., Gartrell et al., 1996, 1999; Mallon, 2004).

CONCLUSIONS AND RECOMMENDATIONS

The research on the transition to parenthood for same-sex couples suggests that while their experience of becoming parents is in many ways similar to that of heterosexual couples, their unique status as stigmatized and marginalized persons necessarily shapes their path to parenthood. Social, legal, and political barriers to becoming parents make the process of considering and then pursuing parenthood far more complex and labor-intensive for same-sex couples than it is for heterosexual couples. Another unique characteristic of same-sex couples is, of course, the fact that they consist of two men or two women. The same-sex nature of their unions permits them greater freedom with regard to creating their roles as parents; of course, in the absence of clearly defined guidelines about how to "do" same-sex parenthood, everything, in essence, must be negotiated, possibly creating conflict (discussed further in chap. 4, this volume).

Much more research is needed on lesbian and gay parents' transition to parenthood. In particular, longitudinal research that is initiated preparenthood is needed to understand how lesbian and gay parents' lives, relationships, and well-being change during this key life transition and what factors are associated with this transition (Gartrell et al., 1996, 1999; Goldberg, 2006; Goldberg & Perry-Jenkins, 2007; Goldberg & Smith, 2008b). Research on the transition to adoptive parenthood in is especially needed, as very little work in this area has been initiated (Goldberg & Smith, 2008a). In particular, research on the transition to parenthood among same-sex couples who adopt transracially and transculturally is needed to identify the sorts of unique challenges that these couples face in the early transitional phase. Also, given that gay men may encounter both sexism and heterosexism in the adoption process (e.g., in the form of social workers and adoption professionals who believe that men are incapable of nurturing; Gianino, 2008; McPheeters, Carmi, & Goldberg, 2008), research that addresses gay men's experiences and perceptions of this process is of particular importance.

The research reviewed in this chapter has a variety of practice-related implications. At the most basic level, adoption agencies, lawyers, prenatal educators, gynecologists, and other health care professionals who work with lesbian and gay parents and prospective parents should strive to communicate a philosophy of inclusion and acceptance. Ideally, this philosophy will be evident in their materials and the physical environment in which they work. For example, pink triangle or rainbow decals can be posted inconspicuously in hospitals, offices, and waiting rooms, where they will likely be noticed by parents and family members for whom they are meaningful (Perrin,

1998). Such symbols of acceptance may encourage sexual minority clients to disclose their sexual orientation, which will in turn enable them to obtain the support and services that they need and deserve. Such acceptance must also carry over into professionals' interactions with lesbian and gay prospective parents. For example, facilitators of prenatal education classes and adoption support groups can create a comfortable and accepting atmosphere by setting ground rules for the group that refer to accepting and valuing diversity and by actively challenging discriminatory comments and homophobia from group members if they arise (Mallon, 2007). The use of inclusive language (e.g., terms such as *partner*) in classes and groups will also help to communicate acceptance of varied situations and family forms (Goldberg, 2006; Ross et al., 2006). Adoption agency and hospital administrators who wish to promote an inclusive and respectful atmosphere for their sexual minority clients should consider seeking out specialized training for their staff. A study of 80 public child welfare workers in eight U.S. agencies found that attitudes toward lesbians and gay men as adoptive parents were in part influenced by professional socialization (Ryan, 2000). Specialized training was found to be highly effective in the formation of affirmative attitudes and behaviors related to adoption by lesbians and gay men.[14]

Health care providers and educators who work with lesbian couples in the prenatal and early postpartum period should be particularly mindful of the importance of treating both partners as equal parents, as opposed to assuming or inadvertently communicating that the birth mother is more of a parent than the partner. For example, providers can assist couples in designing a birth plan that is inclusive of the nonbiological mother; providers can also talk with couples about how to include both mothers in breastfeeding (e.g., by utilizing a breast pump and bottle-feeding).

Furthermore, clinicians and other practitioners who work with prospective lesbian and gay parents should assist these individuals and couples in their decision-making process with special attention to the areas that uniquely define their transition to parenthood experience (e.g., exposure to heterosexist systems and institutions). Moreover, they should aim to educate couples in advance about the legal barriers that they may face (e.g., in obtaining coparent or second-parent adoptions) and should seek to support them in (a) understanding the consequences of such barriers (e.g., the fact that their child will have one legal and one nonlegal parent); (b) considering whether to pursue alternative or additional legal safeguards (e.g., living wills, medical powers of

---

[14]For a list of gay-inclusive practice recommendations for adoption agencies and child welfare professionals, see the Evan B. Donaldson Adoption Institute's document "Expanding resources for children: Is adoption by gays and lesbians part of the answer for boys and girls who need homes?" at http://www.adoptioninstitute.org/publications/2006_Expanding_Resources_for_Children%20_March_.pdf. Also, in 2007 the Human Rights Campaign launched the All Children, All Families initiative, which is dedicated to promoting fairness for LGBT foster and adoptive parents. Their best practices guide for child welfare professionals can be found at http://www.hrc.org/issues/parenting/7609.htm.

attorney, financial powers of attorney, and hospital visitation authorizations); and (c) discussing, as a couple, how open to be about their unequal legal status with others (e.g., should adoptive couples tell friends and family which of them is their child's legal adoptive parent?). Finally, practitioners might also encourage sexual minorities to consider the potential risks and benefits of talking to their employers about their status as parents-to-be, particularly if they are not giving birth to a child and their impending parenthood status is thus invisible.

In the next chapter, I examine the research on lesbian and gay parenting in light of significant questions: How do lesbian and gay parents' relationships, roles, and identities continue to unfold past the transitional stage? How do lesbian and gay parents navigate and experience the unique aspects of their family structure? Specifically, how do they manage disclosure about their families to their children's schools, strangers, and so on? What are the implications of parents' routes to parenthood (e.g., alternative insemination versus adoption) with regard to their parenthood experience?

PRACTICAL RESOURCES

Becoming Parents

Book: Mallon, G. P. (2004). *Gay men choosing parenthood*. New York: Columbia University Press.

> *Summary:* Mallon examines the experiences of 20 gay men to explore issues such as the initial reactions to bringing a new child home, community responses to gay dads, and gender politics. He also provides insight into the emotions common to gay men who choose to become parents.

Book: Lev, A. I. (2004). *The complete lesbian and gay parenting guide*. New York: Berkeley Books.

> *Summary:* This book, geared toward potential LGBT parents, contains practical, useful advice as well as personal real-life stories.

Web site: http://www.familyequality.org (Family Equality Council)

> *Summary:* The Family Equality Council (formerly Family Pride) is the national advocacy organization committed to securing family equality for LGBT parents and allies. The Web site contains links to blogs and parenting support groups.

Web site: http://www.gayparentmag.com (*Gay Parent* magazine)

> *Summary: Gay Parent* magazine (GPM) is a newsprint magazine featuring the personal stories of LGBT parents from around the world. Parents speak candidly about their experiences with international and domestic

adoption, foster care, donor insemination, using a surrogate, and so on. GPM's Web site also provides resources on reproductive technology, adoption, and foster care agencies, as well as gay-friendly private schools and day and overnight camps, and gay-friendly family vacation ideas.

Film: Symons, J. (Director). (2002). *Daddy & Papa* [DVD]. Harriman, NY: New Day Films.

Summary: This documentary explores the growing phenomenon of gay fatherhood and its impact on American culture. Through the stories of four different families, *Daddy & Papa* delves into some of the particular challenges facing gay men who decide to become dads (e.g., surrogacy, interracial adoption, gay divorce).

4

LESBIANS AND GAY MEN
AS PARENTS

As detailed in chapter 3 of this volume, the transition to parenthood is a challenging time for families in general and for lesbian- and gay-parent families specifically. Seeking out and obtaining services in order to become a parent, securing legal protections once one has become a parent, and navigating one's parental identity in the context of potential nonsupport from family, friends, and the broader community are several aspects of the transition that are uniquely different, and potentially challenging, for sexual minorities. What happens next? How do lesbians and gay men manage the stigma associated with their families? How do lesbians and gay men navigate their dual identities as partners and parents? What are their experiences of balancing work and family? How do they negotiate the tensions that may arise in the context of sharing the role of father or mother? This chapter attempts to answer these and other questions by addressing the parenting experiences and parental adjustment of lesbians and gay men, from the perspective of lesbians and gay men themselves.

In the following section, I address some of the unique challenges of parenting in a heterosexist society, including the need to anticipate and respond to homophobic encounters and the need to anticipate and respond to societal concerns about father or mother absence. Then I address parents' perceptions of the possible benefits that their children might enjoy as a function of growing up in a lesbian- or gay-parent family.

PARENTING IN A HETEROSEXIST SOCIETY

Lesbians and gay men parent their children in a societal context that routinely scrutinizes and questions their parenting choices. In turn, lesbian and gay parents must anticipate, and respond to, their own and others' concerns regarding how homophobia will affect their children, as well as how not having a live-in, opposite sex parent may affect their children.

Managing and Responding to Concerns About Homophobia

As lesbian and gay parents raise their children, many of the concerns that may have initially held them back from pursuing parenthood may still exist, albeit to a lesser extent. Specifically, many lesbian and gay parents are troubled by the possibility that their children might be persecuted because of their family structure (Bennett, 2003a; Hare, 1994; Johnson & O'Connor, 2002; van Dam, 2004). Van Dam (2004) found that over 75% of lesbian mothers worried that their children might experience harassment or teasing related to their parents' sexual orientation. Similarly, Bennett (2003a) interviewed 15 lesbian couples who had adopted their children internationally and found that most women felt that their nontraditional family status would represent the greatest challenge for their children, even more so than their children's racial/cultural minority status or the fact that they were adopted. Such concerns reflect, and indeed stem from, the dominant cultural narrative, which portrays children of lesbian and gay parents as vulnerable to victimization and therefore at risk for problems in adjustment. This supposition (contested by, e.g., Clarke, Kitzinger, & Potter, 2004) is frequently invoked by opponents of gay parenting and is cited as grounds for denying sexual minorities the right to have or adopt children.

Aware of the realities of heterosexism, including the possibility that their child will be teased because of their family structure, lesbian and gay parents express concerns about how best to navigate the dual challenge of modeling a sense of acceptance and pride in one's family structure while also preparing their children for possible encounters with stigma (Gartrell et al., 2000). As their children grow older and therefore come into increasing contact with social institutions (e.g., schools, camps, religious institutions) and the broader society, lesbians and gay men are confronted with numerous opportunities to provide such socialization. Indeed, parents are highly aware that how they choose to respond to public inquiries regarding their sexual orientation and family structure (including mistaken assumptions of parental heterosexuality and homophobic remarks) may have implications for their children's sense of pride in their family structure and for how their children handle homophobic encounters themselves (Chabot & Ames, 2004; Dundas & Kaufman, 2000; Gartrell et al., 2000; Lassiter et al., 2006; Schacher, Auerbach, & Silverstein, 2005). For example, they are attentive to the possibility that in failing to confront homophobia, they may be communicating a message to their children that their families are shameful and must be kept secret. Thus, many parents purposefully strive to model openness and pride in their interactions with outsiders (Gartrell et al., 2000; Schacher et al., 2005). Similarly, parents may be sensitive to the fact that failing to correct a stranger's assumption of parental heterosexuality or single parenthood effectively erases the other parent, thereby suggesting to children that some family members are more legitimate than others (Dalton & Bielby, 2000).

Of course, in deciding how to respond in such situations, lesbian and gay parents may balance their desire to be good role models for their children with their own personal comfort with public disclosure of their sexuality and the practical realities of the situation (e.g., whether coming out would threaten their own or their child's safety; Chabot & Ames, 2004; Gartrell et al., 2000). Various social–contextual and psychological–internal factors will also determine whether lesbian and gay parents choose to come out in response to heterosexist remarks made in the presence of their children, such as the nature of the remark (e.g., a homophobic joke vs. a relatively innocuous assumption of parental heterosexuality), the nature of the relationship with the speaker (e.g., a stranger or someone with whom the family can expect to have ongoing contact), the immediate social pressures (e.g., time, opportunity to respond), and perceived importance (e.g., whether the child is paying attention and/or understands the nature of the remark). Parents' own general level of outness regarding their sexual orientation may also play a role: Parents who are not out in their communities (e.g., because they live in homophobic neighborhoods or neighborhoods in which homosexuality is invisible, because of their own internalized homophobia) will find it difficult to model comfort with and openness about their sexual orientation. Finally, in deciding whether to respond to homophobic encounters, parents will also consider their children's developmental level. Parents of adolescents, for example, may be particularly sensitive to their children's desire and need for privacy and hence may not come out in particular situations (Bozett, 1987).[1]

In addition to consciously modeling comfort with their sexual orientation and family structure, parents are also aware of the need to prepare their

---

[1]If the child in question is adopted (and the child's adoptive status is being raised because, e.g., he or she is racially different from the parents), the lesbian or gay parent may be particularly sensitive to the child's need for privacy (i.e., the parent may feel that the child's adoption story is the child's own story to tell) and may therefore be less likely to disclose details about the family's structure and family formation, at least without the child's permission.

children for heterosexism and stigma, even when their children are very young. Gartrell et al. (2000) interviewed lesbian mothers of 5-year-olds and found that most mothers reported ongoing efforts to prepare their children for the possibility of prejudice and discrimination. Preparation strategies included discussing different types of families, emphasizing the importance of appreciating diversity, and role playing responses to homophobic comments. Litovich and Langhout (2004) interviewed a small sample of lesbian mothers of children aged 7 to 16 years and found that women sought to prepare their children for bias by warning them about the possibility of heterosexist incidents. However, even as they emphasized the importance of preparing their children for bullying and bias, these parents also minimized its actual occurrence, claiming that their children were rarely teased. Similarly, Henrickson (2005) surveyed lesbian and gay parents in New Zealand and found that only 33.3% of parents reported that their children had encountered difficulties pertaining to their parents' sexual orientation; the remaining 66.7% denied that their children had encountered any problems. Acknowledging homophobic bullying can be painful for some parents: If they acknowledge it, "they will be held accountable and punished for making homophobia visible; on the other hand, denying bullying . . . will be dismissed as implausible" (Clarke et al., 2004, p. 536). Understandably resistant to being held accountable for such bullying, parents may therefore normalize homophobic taunting when it occurs, treating it as just one example of the many things (e.g., weight, height, race) that children are teased about (Clarke et al., 2004).

Of course, some parents may wish to help their children avoid homophobic bullying and harassment altogether, to the extent that they can. Toward this end, lesbian and gay parents may search out progressive and diverse schools, day care providers, neighborhoods, and communities (Kosciw & Diaz, 2008; Kranz & Daniluk, 2006; Mercier & Harold, 2003), particularly when they are the parents of children of color (Kosciw & Diaz, 2008). Obviously, these kinds of efforts are contingent on certain kinds of financial, social, and educational resources: Many families have few choices regarding the neighborhoods in which they reside or the schools that their children attend (Casper, Schultz, & Wickens, 1992). Lesbian and gay parents may also seek to promote a supportive school climate for their children by talking directly to their children's teachers about their family structure and suggesting ways to incorporate awareness of diverse families into the classroom curricula (Kranz & Daniluk, 2006; Lindsay et al., 2006; Mercier & Harold, 2003), efforts that are more likely among middle-class parents whose children attend private as opposed to public schools (Casper & Schultz, 1999).

To advocate on behalf of their children, however, lesbian and gay parents must come out to their children's schools and teachers. This decision is not always an easy one, as parents may realistically worry about the potential consequences of disclosure, for themselves and their children (Casper et al., 1992). A 2008 study conducted by the Gay, Lesbian, and Straight Education

Network (GLSEN),[2] which focused on LGBT-parent families' experiences in education, found that more than half (53%) of LGBT parents surveyed described various forms of exclusion from their children's school communities (e.g., being excluded or prevented from fully participating in school activities and events, being excluded by school policies and procedures, being ignored; Kosciw & Diaz, 2008). For example, parents were told that they could not be aides in their children's classrooms; that only one parent was allowed to attend a school event; and that their offers to assist with creating a more inclusive classroom (e.g., reading *Heather Has Two Mommies* to the class) were not welcome or needed. Furthermore, 26% of LGBT parents reported being mistreated by other parents (e.g., being stared at, whispered about, ignored). In this context, it is understandable that some LGBT parents may prefer to closet themselves out of concern for their own and their children's safety and comfort. Indeed, Lindsay et al. (2006) interviewed 13 lesbian-parent families and found that parents in 7 of the families tended to hide their family arrangements within the school setting, feeling that it simply was "not their business." These families tended to live in communities that they perceived as intolerant and conservative, and thus their secrecy was a realistic response designed to protect their children from social censure. At the same time, their secrecy inevitably inhibited their ability to respond to and protest the exclusion of lesbian-parent families from school curricula.

Parents who are out to their children's schools and teachers, then, experience both challenges and advantages compared with parents who are closeted: They are more vulnerable to discrimination, but they are also in a better position to confront unjust practices and to shield their children from exclusion and stigma in the classroom. Ideally, lesbian and gay parents should not have to advocate for their children's safety and well-being. Given the increasing presence and visibility of lesbian and gay parents, schools should institute comprehensive safe school policies that protect both students and their parents. Safe school policies prohibit harassment and discrimination based on actual or perceived sexual orientation and gender identity, require that school officials and staff respond to incidents of harassment and discrimination, and enumerate the appropriate consequences and remedies that should be pursued should such incidents take place. Such policies appear to benefit both adults and children: In the GLSEN survey, parents whose

---

[2]GLSEN obtained national samples of children of LGBT parents currently enrolled in middle school or high school (n = 154) and of LGBT parents of children currently enrolled in a K–12 school (n = 588). Participants were recruited through community groups and organizations for LGBT families, online bulletin boards and Listservs serving the LGBT community, summer events for LGBT families, and summer camp programs for children of LGBT families. In the parent group, most participants were women. The majority of parents had a child in elementary school. About 16% of the families had White parent(s) and a child of color, and about 14% of the families consisted of one White and one non-White parent. In the student group, participants' ages ranged from 13 to 20 (average age = 15 years), most respondents were female, and about two thirds of students were White.

children's schools had such policies reported lower levels of mistreatment than schools that did not have such policies (Kosciw & Diaz, 2008).

Managing and Responding to Concerns About Father or Mother Absence

In addition to managing concerns about heterosexism and homophobia, some lesbians and gay men also experience anxiety about how the absence of a female or male parent might affect their children's development (Berkowitz & Marsiglio, 2007; Bozett, 1987; Chrisp, 2001; Goldberg & Allen, 2007; Johnson & O'Connor, 2002; Mallon, 2004). In turn, they may worry about their ability to provide their children with enough male or female adults (i.e., for role modeling purposes; Goldberg & Allen, 2007) and may therefore respond to such fears by emphasizing the availability of men or women in their extended families and highlighting the presence of men and women in the broader society (Clarke & Kitzinger, 2005; Goldberg & Allen, 2007). Parents may also worry about the possibility of being judged by others should they choose not to seek out, or be unable to find, male or female role models for their children. Such concerns reflect, and are in response to, cultural anxieties about (a) the need for children to be exposed to both male and female influences, and (b) the potential negative consequences of mother or father absence on child development (Donovan, 2000; Silverstein & Auerbach, 1999). These anxieties are related specifically to beliefs about gender socialization: According to social learning theory, boys need adult male models to emulate and identify with, whereas girls need adult female models (Bandura & Walters, 1963). The belief that children of lesbian and gay parents are at particular risk of inadequate gender socialization is driven in part by the common but inaccurate perception that because sexual minorities are in sexual relationships with persons of the same sex, they therefore must only live with, socialize with, and interact with people of the same sex and sexuality (Clarke, 2001). Of course, anxieties about father or mother absence in lesbian- and gay-parent families are also related, more broadly, to ideological assumptions about the functional and moral superiority of the heterosexual nuclear family: Families that lack a father or mother are assumed to be deficient, and the children in these families are presumed to be at risk.[3]

Several studies have empirically examined concerns about father or mother absence among lesbian and gay parents, as well as parents' efforts to manage and respond to these concerns. It is important to highlight that the

---

[3]The fact that there are indeed two parents in many lesbian- and gay-parent households is often dismissed. For example, the risks associated with living in a single-mother home, which are often characterized by lower income and less parental monitoring compared with two-parent homes, are often assumed to apply to lesbian, two-mother households—an argument that is illogical and unwarranted (see Goldberg & Allen, 2007).

vast majority of these studies have focused on lesbians' concerns about and management of father absence; little work has explored these issues among gay fathers. Dundas and Kaufman (2000) found that many of the lesbian mothers in their study expressed some concern about lack of male role models, although they did not feel that this absence would negatively impact their children's development. Similarly, in a 2007 study, Goldberg and Allen explored 60 lesbian mothers' (30 couples') ideas and behaviors surrounding male contact and involvement. Lesbian couples were interviewed during the pregnancy and when their children were three months old. The authors found that the majority of women ($n = 40$) were highly conscious of the fact that their child would not grow up with a male parent and expressed some concern about the absence of a male figure. As a result, they were relatively systematic, planful, and deliberate in their attempts to secure male role models: They talked with brothers, fathers, friends, and male neighbors about the possibility of their involvement, even before their child was born. Other women, though, were relatively flexible in their approach. They assumed that the men that they already had in their lives would be enough, or they did not feel that male involvement would make or break their children's development. Notably, mothers of boys were particularly deliberate in their approach to male involvement; mothers of girls could "afford" to be more relaxed. This is consistent with Kane's (2006) finding that lesbian and gay parents sometimes felt accountable to others in relation to their sons' (but not their daughters') gender performance.

Women in Goldberg and Allen's (2007) study named a range of reasons for desiring male involvement. For some women, particularly mothers of boys, awareness of social norms and expectations had heightened their sensitivity to the issue of male involvement. Thus, they responded to cultural anxieties about the necessity of male role models by actively desiring and seeking out male role models. Other women sought out male role models out of a desire to be "fair" to their children: For example, they had wonderful relationships with their fathers and wanted their children to benefit from the kind of paternal nurturance that they had enjoyed as children. The pursuit of male role models in an effort to be fair to one's children echoes some women's reasons for seeking known donors: that is, some women feel that their child has the right to know who their biological father is (see Almack, 2006; chap. 3, this volume; Gartrell, Deck, Rodas, Peyser, & Banks, 2005; Touroni & Coyle, 2002). Some women explained their desire for male involvement in terms of their wish to have their children exposed to a diverse range of people: gay and straight, male and female, individuals of different racial/ethnic backgrounds, and so on. Indeed, women desired a wide range of male role models for their children, including gay men (who they hoped would serve as a challenge to heteronormative masculinity) and those they referred to as "good straight men." The fact that women explicitly named both types of men may "reflect a true valuing of diversity . . . and their sense that many types of men can be good role models, [but it] may also reflect the tension these women face in trying to create families that will not be targeted with criticism, while also honoring their own values and ideals" (Goldberg & Allen, 2007, p. 362).

Notably, Goldberg and Allen (2007) found that, even as infants, the children in this study were described by their mothers as being exposed to a broad range of men, including women's brothers, fathers, colleagues, and friends. As Clarke and Kitzinger (2005) pointed out, lesbian mothers often respond to societal concerns about male role models by emphasizing the presence of men in the world and in their kinship networks. In emphasizing both the quality and quantity of men in their support networks, then, these women effectively defend their families against criticism (e.g., by challenging the stereotype of the man-hating, separatist lesbian). Nevertheless, some scholars have argued that by readily providing such descriptions, these women fail to challenge or subvert—but rather serve to uphold—the necessity of male role models (Clarke & Kitzinger, 2005). For example, Clarke and Kitzinger described lesbian mothers' tendency to highlight the availability of the men in their networks as an "assimilationist" strategy, in that lesbians' resistance is structured around "the oppressor's discourse" (p. 149).

Regardless of the ideological roots of lesbian mothers' inclusion of male role models, it is notable that their children often appear to maintain these relationships—which are necessarily structured in part by their parents—as they grow older. Patterson, Hurt, and Mason (1998) found that 58% of children of lesbian mothers had regular contact with their biological mother's father, 24% with their nonbiological mother's father, and 62% with unrelated male adults, suggesting that both male friends and family members are important sources of support in children's lives. Known donors may also play a role: Gartrell et al. (2000) found that when the children of lesbian mothers were 5 years old, 29% of known donors had regular contact with the children and 71% of known donors saw the children occasionally.

It is significant that while lesbian mothers by and large appear to value men's involvement, many—and perhaps most—do not appear to desire men's involvement as fathers. Donors and friends are often described as having an "uncle-like" relationship to their children (Dunne, 2000; Goldberg, Downing, & Sauck, 2008; Haimes & Weiner, 2000); the word *father* is used less frequently. Indeed, lesbian mothers who decide to have children in the context of committed same-sex relationships are often dedicated to creating a very intentional kind of family, one that does not necessarily include a male coparent. Some women, though, do choose known donors precisely because they want their child to have a "father-like" relationship (Almack, 2006; Touroni & Coyle, 2002) or because they wish to shield their child from the stigma of not having a father (Touroni & Coyle, 2002). Lesbian mothers who became parents in the context of heterosexual relationships, of course, have a different relationship to the issue of father involvement. Their children's biogenetic fathers are also their social fathers; this fact does not change after they end their marriages and renounce their heterosexual identities (Kirkpatrick, Smith, & Roy, 1981).

Few data are available about how gay men feel about and structure their children's contact with female role models. However, some data suggest that gay fathers who pursue open adoption may do so in part because they wish to maintain a relationship with the child's birth mother, thereby ensuring the presence of at least one female role model (McPheeters, Carmi, & Goldberg, 2008). Indeed, some gay adoptive fathers consider the birth mothers of their children to be members of their families, at least symbolically (Berkowitz & Marsiglio, 2007). Research is needed that explores gay fathers' beliefs about the role of female adults in their children's lives and their strategies for managing the practical pressures related to female involvement.

Perceived Benefits of Growing Up in a Minority Family Structure

Whereas lesbian and gay parents often have realistic concerns about the challenges associated with growing up in a minority family structure, many parents also believe that their children may experience certain unique benefits as a function of growing up with sexual minority parents. Johnson and O'Connor (2002) interviewed over 400 lesbian and gay parents and found that 89% of lesbian mothers and 82% of gay fathers felt that their children would benefit in some way from having grown up with gay parents. The most commonly mentioned advantage was parents' belief that growing up in a family that is perceived as different would cause their children to be more tolerant and accepting of others (54% of mothers and 63% of fathers). Similarly, Lynch and Murray (2000) studied lesbian stepfamilies and found that many parents felt that their children would be more appreciative of human diversity as a function of their growing-up experience. Women also felt that although living in a heterosexist society was indeed stressful in certain ways, it also functioned to create a greater sense of openness and communication within the family. They viewed their children as more open to discussing their difficulties with them, given that their parents could naturally empathize with their experiences of feeling different or unacceptable. Hare (1994) also found that lesbian mothers perceived a range of benefits for their children as a function of growing up with gay parents, including a greater tolerance for diversity, a greater sensitivity to discrimination, and growing up in a loving environment. Finally, Muzio (1995) found that lesbian mothers believed that their own shared parenting represented an asset for their children in that they would witness and experience freedom from traditional models. That is, their children would be exposed to more equal parenting and would therefore develop less gender-stereotyped ideas about men's and women's roles.

It is notable that some of these perceived advantages are directly related to the experience of growing up as members of a marginalized family form; that is, children are not expected to benefit directly from their parents' sexual orientation per se but from the associated experience of living in a family in which one's parents' sexual orientation is stigmatized. By virtue of this exposure, children should theoretically learn to empathize with other minority groups and to recognize the commonalities across diverse groups of people. Other perceived advantages seem to be related to some unique combination of parents' gender and their gender combination. That is, sexual orientation and gender interact to create new kinds of family structures and processes such as egalitarian models of sharing paid and unpaid labor (Stacey & Biblarz, 2001) that should inspire children to embrace freedom from gendered roles.

In sum, it is clear that while lesbian and gay parents realistically anticipate that their children may encounter certain challenges associated with growing up in a minority family structure, they also believe that their children may demonstrate unique strengths. Balancing realism with optimism, they passionately describe numerous ways in which their children will be better people for their personal exposure to discrimination and their families' experiences of marginality.

LESBIAN AND GAY PARENTS: RELATIONSHIPS, ROLES, AND IDENTITIES

As I suggested in chapter 3, the relationships, roles, and identities of lesbians and gay men are permanently transformed once they become parents. Couples may experience a shift in the division of labor, such that lesbian birth mothers perform more unpaid work and nonbiological lesbian mothers perform more paid work, in the early months of parenthood. Birth mothers may, in turn, be perceived, at least initially, as the more primary parent. The nonbiological mother's role is less defined, less recognized, and less protected, so that family members, friends, and society may regard her as less of a parent or "not quite" a mother. Parents' intimate relationships also change during the transition to parenthood, with both partners' attention shifting dramatically from their relationship to the child. Lesbian and gay parents' relationships with family, friends, and the broader community may also shift as they become part of the parenthood culture. For example, they may develop new relationships (i.e., with other parents) while letting go of others (i.e., friendships with single nonparent friends).

Of interest is how couples' relationships and parental identities continue to evolve as their children develop. For example, how does the division of labor, and parents' corresponding parental roles, change as children grow older? How do lesbian and gay parents' child-rearing attitudes and practices compare with those of heterosexual parents? What kind of support do lesbian and gay parents receive from their families and communities? This chapter reviews some answers to these complex and interrelated questions from the research on various aspects of lesbian and gay parenting.

The Division of Labor: Child Care, Housework, and Paid Work

Dunne (2000) asserted that when lesbian couples, in particular, approach parenthood, they do so with a special awareness of issues of power and the importance of equality in relationships. Specifically, their parity in the gender hierarchy (as women and as lesbians) enables the development of more egalitarian approaches to work, parenting, and finances. Some scholars argue that as "family outlaws" (Calhoun, 1997), lesbians—and, theoretically, gay men—live outside of the traditional gender system and are therefore free to construct parental roles and labor arrangements that do not reflect and perpetuate the gender order. And yet lesbian and gay parents do exist within the broader social structure: Even as they pave their own way, they may also draw on, and may be shaped by, larger cultural, social, and legal institutions. For example, as highlighted in chapter 3 of this volume, the immediate practical demands of parenthood (e.g., the fact that lesbian birth mothers often breastfeed and are typically granted more time off from paid employment) combined with cultural and social forces (e.g., greater validation of the birth mother's role) may result in an arrangement in which birth mothers perform more unpaid work and nonbirth mothers perform more paid work, at least initially. This is not to say that lesbian mothers are reproducing gender relations along the lines of biology; rather, it suggests that they are shaped by (and also shape) broader social patterns and various structural and symbolic forces. As Dalton and Bielby (2000) stated: "For lesbian couples, guides to action may be proactively constructed and flexibly scripted, but they are by no means fully insulated from dominant institutional understandings of marital and parenting roles" (p. 39). Furthermore, while the division of labor is initially polarized, for some couples these dynamics may change as time unfolds. Indeed, a diverse range of arrangements has been described in the literature, with some couples showing relatively polarized labor arrangements and others demonstrating more fluid arrangements.

Goldberg, Downing, and Sauck (2008) conducted a follow-up study of the lesbian couples initially described by Goldberg and Perry-Jenkins (2007) (see chap. 3, this volume), all of whom had their children via alternative insemination. This follow-up occurred when the children were three years old. The authors found that birth mothers, on average, continued to do more of the child care, while nonbiological mothers tended to be engaged in more hours of paid work. Women shared housework relatively equally. Similar findings were obtained by Johnson and O'Connor (2002), who also surveyed lesbian parents of young children: Nonbiological mothers tended to perform more paid work and biological mothers tended to do more child care. There was also a tendency for birth mothers to do more housework; this finding approached statistical significance. Similar patterns (i.e., specialization along the lines of biology) have also been documented in several studies of lesbian mothers of school-aged children (e.g., Bos, van Balen, & van den Boom, 2007; C. J. Patterson, 1995) and one study of Black lesbian stepfamilies, in which biological mothers consistently performed more child care than lesbian stepmothers (Moore, 2008). In a rare study of lesbian inseminating couples, lesbian adoptive couples, and heterosexual adoptive couples, Ciano-Boyce and Shelley-Sireci (2002) compared the division of labor among these three groups and found that lesbian adoptive couples shared child care the most equally. In the absence of sex or biological difference to guide or stratify their roles, these couples succeeded in establishing remarkably egalitarian arrangements, although they also experienced more conflict about the division of child care. Thus, while freedom from stratification based on sex and biology may create the potential for greater equality, it may also force more intense deliberations surrounding the division of labor: In the absence of prescribed roles, both the practical and symbolic aspects of the division of labor must be negotiated. Thus, although same-sex couples may have "a unique potential for creating more democratic-egalitarian living arrangements" in that there are "fewer set patterns, expectations and assumptions in non-heterosexual households," the creation of these arrangements may require "considerable amounts of emotion work . . . in the form of discussions of and negotiations around who does what, when, how, and for whom" (Oerton, 1998, p. 72).

Other research, though, has not found evidence of labor divisions based on biology (Chan, Brooks, Raboy, & Patterson, 1998; C. J. Patterson, Sutfin, & Fulcher, 2004; Tasker & Golombok, 1998). For example, Chan, Brooks et al. (1998) interviewed lesbian-parent families and heterosexual-parent families with children aged 5 to 11 years who had been conceived via donor insemination. Lesbian couples were found to share child care tasks relatively equally—more so than their heterosexual counterparts—with heterosexual fathers doing less than lesbian nonbiological mothers. Furthermore, nonbiological mothers did not work longer hours outside the home than biological mothers. This finding is somewhat consistent with qualitative studies that describe a tendency for both lesbian partners to reduce their work hours to deal with child care demands or to take turns being the primary wage earner (e.g., Dunne, 2000). Furthermore, Gartrell, Deck, Rodas, Peyser, and Banks (2006) interviewed lesbian mothers of 10-year-olds and found that 74% of mothers worked full-time and 26% worked part-time; there were no differences between birth mothers and comothers in the number of years spent in part-time or full-time work. The tendency for both women to lower their commitment to their careers while their children are young might perhaps reflect both women's gendered socialization as women (Oerton, 1998);

that is, as women, they are influenced by particular ideologies that presume career sacrifices on the part of women in the service of caring for children. (Consistent with this notion, 12% of lesbian mothers in Gartrell et al.'s 2006 sample reported that less career advancement was due to their choice to prioritize parenting responsibilities.)

How does one reconcile these disparate findings regarding the role of biology in structuring the division of paid and unpaid labor? Notably, most quantitative research studies report averages, which may obscure the full range of distinct patterns that have been documented in the literature: namely, the fact that some couples divide labor along the lines of biology and others do not. For example, Gartrell et al. (2006), in her study of lesbian mothers of 10-year-olds, found that 14 of the 37 couples who were still together reported sharing child care and housework equally; 7 couples agreed that the birth mother did more; and 5 agreed that the comother did more. Similarly, in Sullivan's (1996) study of lesbian two-mother households, most women felt that they shared domestic labor relatively equally; five couples, however, adhered to a strict full-time-breadwinner–full-time-caregiver arrangement. Thus, there is significant variability within lesbian couples with regard to their labor arrangements, a fact that has often been overlooked and underemphasized (Downing & Goldberg, 2008).

What might lead to a deeper, richer understanding of how lesbian and gay couples enact and construct the division of labor? One possibility is greater use of ethnographic and observational research methods, such as those used by Carrington (2002), whose research on the division of labor among same-sex couples was discussed in chapter 2 of this volume. Carrington's research revealed that both lesbian and gay couples tended to describe the division of household labor in ways that functioned to actively construct gender identity—and in ways that sometimes deviated from the objective, or observed, distribution of tasks. For example, Carrington observed that gay couples sometimes described the division of household labor in ways that protected the gender identity of those men who were heavily engaged in domesticity. That is, gay men—as well as their partners, friends, and relatives—sometimes concealed the domestic labor that they did to protect them from the stigma of appearing feminine and unmasculine. Likewise, in lesbian couples, the partner who did more of the domestic labor sometimes emphasized the few domestic contributions made by her less domestically inclined partner, which Carrington interpreted as in part emerging from the need to destigmatize one's partner (Haddock, 2003). Explains Carrington:

> If your partner is a prosecuting attorney and she has to work 70 hours a week, her capacity to pull off a domestic regimen is quite limited. She will not be baking holiday gingerbread cookies, shopping for holiday gifts and other such things. So, when she does do a domestic task, she and her partner will really emphasize it to protect her gender identity . . . to keep people from thinking, "Oh my, she's a man. She's some kind of gender

anomaly." So, these myths are created to prevent threats to gender identity. (Haddock, 2003, p. 69)

Carrington (2002) observed lesbians and gay men in their homes, in addition to interviewing them individually. Thus, he used multiple forms of assessment that ultimately uncovered certain inconsistencies (i.e., between what he saw and what was described to him). In this way, he gained valuable insights into the ways in which lesbians and gay men self-consciously constructed their roles and identities. His data, then, caution us to remain conscious of the "identity work" that is happening when couples report on their division of labor and to consider the possibility that different sources of measurement might yield very different conclusions.

Furthermore, it is important to consider the possibility that researchers' perspectives and interpretations (e.g., the tendency to view shared labor divisions as egalitarian and therefore nongendered and the tendency to view unequal labor divisions as unegalitarian and therefore gendered) do not necessarily mirror the experiences and interpretations of lesbian and gay parents themselves. Indeed, some lesbian and gay parents may enact labor arrangements that appear similar to traditional heterosexual parenting arrangements (e.g., one woman does more paid work, one woman does more unpaid work), others may execute labor arrangements that look very different (e.g., both women contribute equally to paid and unpaid work), and some may enact arrangements that we likely have yet to imagine, conceptualize, or understand. And yet it is imperative to consider the possibility that although a particular role arrangement may appear gendered when seen through a traditional family lens, it may not be experienced or interpreted in this way by parents themselves (Goldberg, in press). For example, Oerton (1998) pointed out that, given that "housewife as [an] identity in the postmodern sense is dynamic, shifting, and unstable (as all identities are)" the meaning and identity of "housewife" may be very different in the same-sex couple context than in the heterosexual couple context, such that one or both women (or men) may claim this identity, and interpret it in ways that are shaped by their unique relational context (p. 78).

Negotiating Parental Roles and Constructing Parenthood

To the extent that lesbian and gay couples share paid and unpaid labor more equally than heterosexual couples, they are, some scholars have argued, redefining the meaning and content of parenthood, "extending its boundaries to incorporate the activities that are usually dichotomized as mother and father" (Dunne, 2000, p. 25). These scholars often emphasize the revisionist potentialities of lesbian and gay parenthood, pointing to ways in which lesbians and gay men transform and transgress traditional notions of mothering and fathering. Such ideas have also been expressed by lesbian and gay parents themselves. Schacher, Auerbach, and Silverstein (2005) found that gay fathers often observed that they were blending mother and father roles such that they created new, hybrid, degendered parenting roles. Likewise, Gianino's (2008) study of gay adoptive fathers revealed that participants often perceived their status as gay fathers as allowing them to break out of the traditional male breadwinner role and to create roles for themselves that were far more diverse and satisfying. Lesbian mothers have also expressed these ideas (Downing & Goldberg, 2008).

It is notable that the work and negotiation that are inevitably involved in sharing parenting tend to be the focus of little discussion: That is, scholars have typically focused on the achievement of shared parenting as opposed to the complex negotiations and feelings that presumably might precede or accompany such arrangements. Indeed, lesbian mothers and gay fathers construct their parental roles in a heterosexist context that assumes a primary mother and a complementary father (Heineman, 2004) and that considers biological ties to be fundamental to kin relations (Hargreaves, 2006). Furthermore, as women and men, they have been socialized to associate certain qualities and ways of being with the maternal and paternal role. Finally, they have not been socialized to share the parenting role with another woman or another man. Thus, negotiating one's parental role in a dyadic context may in fact be both liberating and challenging for lesbians and gay men.

Inseminating lesbian couples, for example, create their parenting roles in a societal context that systematically devalues the nonbiological mother and privileges the birth mother.[4] Should both women strive to embody typical notions of mothering, significant tensions may arise. For example, Gartrell et al. (1999) found that although most mothers of toddlers considered themselves to be equal parents, 70% noted competitiveness around bonding; in their 2000 follow-up, 48% reported such feelings. Although Gartrell et al. did not discuss whether these feelings were more common among nonbiological mothers than biological mothers, it appears likely that such feelings may be particularly salient for nonbiological mothers in lesbian inseminating couples as well as stepmothers in lesbian stepfamilies, whose parental statuses are often ignored, undervalued, and misunderstood. Indeed, lesbian stepmothers may experience a lack of role legitimacy both outside of the family and possibly within the family, in that their efforts to parent and discipline may be resisted by both their partners and the children (Baptiste, 1987; Moore, 2008). Even when couples are equally committed to child-rearing, they must constantly battle for equal recognition in a societal context that grants greater legitimacy to the biological mother (Morningstar, 1999). This can create stress for both partners, as they must constantly and publicly assert their parity as parents and resist others' attempts to classify them as primary and secondary, mother and "other" (Dalton & Bielby, 2000).

---

[4]Although, as DiLapi (1989) argued, all lesbian mothers are regarded as inferior to heterosexual mothers.

These stresses may be exacerbated when children demonstrate a greater preference for, or attachment to, their biological mothers. Goldberg, Downing, and Sauck (2008) examined 30 lesbian couples' perceptions of and feelings about their children's parental preferences when their children were 3 years old. They found that most women perceived their children as demonstrating a relatively equal preference for both parents, such that biological and nonbiological mothers might be preferred at different times or for different things but that it evened out in the end. A minority of women, however, reported that their children had maintained a relatively stable preference for the biological mother since birth. Nonbiological mothers whose children stably preferred their partners, or whose children preferred their partners for stereotypical mothering needs, sometimes reported feelings of insecurity, jealousy, and resentment: It was painful to be rejected by their children after investing so much work and love in them (see also Brown & Perlesz, 2007). Notably, in explaining their children's preference for the birth mother, both birth and nonbirth mothers often invoked biological determinism (e.g., the genetic tie between mother and child); additionally, some women attributed this preference to the greater amount of time their child spent with the birth mother, as well as to the birth mother's superior parenting skills.

Feelings of competition and jealousy can also arise in couples in which there is no biological differential, that is, in adoptive couples. Bennett (2003b) interviewed 15 lesbian adoptive couples and found that 12 couples reported that their child demonstrated a preferential bond to one of the mothers during the first few years following the adoption, despite the couples' reported tendency to share parenting and child care tasks relatively equally during this time. Like the nonbiological mothers in Goldberg, Downing, and Sauck's (2008) study, the nonpreferred mothers reported feelings of jealousy, competition, and sadness. In the absence of a biological explanation to fall back on, these women typically invoked parental personality factors and parenting skills to explain their children's preferences. Importantly, the preferred parent was often described as having many of the personality traits that are commonly associated with cultural definitions of the mother; that is, they were characterized as nurturing, maternal, and patient. The nonpreferred parents, on the other hand, were often described as outgoing, more playful, and active. In this way, women construed themselves as actively shaping their children's preferences by their own personalities and natural abilities.

Adoptive lesbian and gay couples' inability to fall back on sex-based or biology-based explanations may lead them to experience greater tension surrounding their children's preferences. In their study of lesbian adoptive parents, lesbian inseminating parents, and heterosexual adoptive parents, Ciano-Boyce and Shelley-Sireci (2002) found that lesbian adoptive parents, who were the most likely to share child care equally, were also the most likely to report that their children's parental preference was a source of occasional conflict. Socialized to occupy a primary role in relation to their children, these women may be unprepared to take on the role of, and be treated as, a secondary caregiver. The authors suggested that

> the nonpreferred mother, feeling rejected by being relegated to the "secondary" maternal role, may wish to distance from this and thus may emotionally detach to some extent from the dynamic, and subsequently from her partner. Contributing to the distress is the fact that the mother in the "secondary" caregiver role may feel shame at not meeting society's standard assumptions about the role of mother. This is the same society that denigrates her sexual orientation, her choice of partner, and her relationship. (p. 11)

The potential for stress and competition may be somewhat lessened should partners prefer or be comfortable with more differentiated parental roles. Some nonbiological mothers are not entirely comfortable claiming the identity or role of mother (Ben-Ari & Livni, 2006; Gabb, 2005; Pagenhart, 2006), in part because of the gendered associations and expectations that it seems to embody, and are therefore at ease assuming a different, possibly secondary parental role to the biological mother. (Indeed, it is possible that the birth mother may choose to carry and bear the child precisely because she desires the maternal role and the nonbiological mother does not.) In some cases, nonbiological mothers identify their role as more paternal—for example, in her personal essay titled "Confessions of a Lesbian Dad," Pagenhart (2006) articulated her preference for and comfort with a "lesbian daddy role." Pagenhart stated:

> Here I was now, looking at parenthood, feeling adrift, no parental prototype to steer by that didn't trigger some cognitive tension at this visceral, gendered level. Every time I conjured up images of parenthood (which I could only see through the lens of motherhood), I couldn't help picturing traditional icons: June Cleavers and Laura Petries and Carol Bradys. Where were the butch moms, I wondered? [So] that night at the dinner table I began, for the first time, to name (and defend) my parental self from a position slightly other than *mother*. Doing so helped me to realize how much my emotional access to parenthood was predicated on my feeling comfortable with the title mother and the femininity that presumably went along with it. (pp. 38–39)

Thus, some couples appear to be comfortable with and partially identify with opposite-gender parental roles (Gabb, 2005). This does not necessarily suggest that lesbian couples imitate or approximate heterosexual parenting but, rather, is evidence of the ways in which "gendered parental roles and family status are constantly reviewed and reworked within lesbian parent families" (Gabb, 2005, p. 599).

Of interest is how gay men experience and construct their parental roles in a sexist and heterosexist society. Gay men who become parents inevitably confront societal stereotypes of men as inept as nurturers and caretakers, not to mention distrust and suspicion toward gay men who wish to parent (S. Hicks, 2005b). Nurturance and caretaking are closely tied to the social construct of mothering, which has historically been viewed as essential to children's development. Indeed, theories that posit that mothers are best suited to meet their children's needs originate in developmental psychology (Bowlby, 1951). Fathering is seen as important but perhaps not compulsory, although some scholars have argued that conservative social scientists are increasingly replacing the earlier "essentializing" of mothers with claims about the necessity of fathers, in part in response to the increase in single-mother households (Donovan, 2000; Silverstein & Auerbach, 1999). Both mothering and fathering, then, tend to be regarded as distinct, noninterchangeable social roles that are closely tied to biological sex and that cannot be enacted by members of the opposite sex (Silverstein & Auerbach, 1999).

Of course, from a social constructionist standpoint, parenting activities and roles are not "natural" behaviors derived from the capacity to reproduce but are historically and socially constructed. Mothering—that is, the social practices of nurturing and caring for children—is associated with women because universally it is women who tend to do the work of mothering (Arendell, 2000). Furthermore, research on equally sharing heterosexual couples and single fathers suggests that men can mother, although in doing so they may encounter hostility or resistance from others (Ehrensaft, 1990; Risman, 1987). The act, experience, and meaning of mothering are further complicated when two men are parenting together. In this context, both men must cooperatively negotiate the actuality of engaging in both mothering and fathering, and they must navigate the realities of (co)constructing and sharing the parenting role without the societal support and guidance that heterosexual couples receive.

Schacher et al. (2005) conducted focus groups with 21 men who became fathers as openly gay men in an effort to understand how they constructed their parental roles and identities. The men in this study rejected the common notion that women are naturally adept at parenting and believed that men, too, could be nurturing and engage in mothering activities. They saw themselves as sharing both the mothering and fathering roles with their partners, as opposed to taking on differentiated roles. Their perspectives challenge the essentialist perspective of parenting, which assumes that the biologically different reproductive functions of men and women lead to fundamental differences in parenting behaviors (Silverstein & Auerbach, 1999). Yet, even as they proudly embodied both maternal and paternal roles, the men in Schacher et al.'s study were sensitive to the gendered meanings of various parenting activities, behaviors, and decisions, such as taking time off to stay home with one's child. Engaging in such mothering activities as a man is not culturally valued; furthermore, involvement in such activities may require sacrificing other more societally valued goals, such as work achievement and career advancement. Men in this sample sometimes struggled with giving up the centrality of the provider role, recognizing that "societally, men are considered the breadwinner . . . [and] that has a value—it gives you a value" while at the some time wanting to create "a special bond" with their children by taking time off from work to stay at home (Silverstein, Auerbach, & Levant, 2002, p. 365). Similarly, some men in Mallon's (2004) study of gay fathers reported struggling with asking for the sorts of accommodations that mothers typically requested. Said one father in Mallon's study: "I think I was the first man who was taking family leave time. This was usually something that women staff did, not men" (p. 86).

Men's work orientation may change upon their becoming parents. The gay men in Mallon's (2004) study often emphasized their changed commitment to work once they became fathers. They strived to manage their time at work more efficiently so that they could devote as much time as possible to their families. In this way, they balanced their love for their children with financial necessity and their desire to remain engaged in the workforce. In shifting the object of their devotion from career to child, then, they challenged powerful external and internal messages that proclaim their incompetence as nurturers. Similarly, some of the men in Lassiter et al.'s (2006) qualitative study of lesbian and gay parents felt that being gay men gave them permission to be nurturing fathers, in that it freed them from hegemonic role expectations (e.g., that of successful breadwinner). As gay men, they did not conform to societal ideals of masculinity and manhood, and their awareness of that allowed them to embody parenting roles that defied gendered stereotypes. In this way, gay men's active and involved fathering bolsters the argument that neither mothers nor fathers are "natural" parents; rather, both parents learn by doing (Silverstein, 1996). Indeed, the fact that heterosexual fathers are, on average, less competent and sensitive parents than heterosexual mothers (McGovern, 1990) is in part a function of the fact that they spend less time with their children. When fathers (e.g., gay fathers) assume a primary parenting role, they are capable of acquiring mothering skills (Silverstein, 1996).

Public Representations of Parenthood:
Communicating Parental Roles and Identities

Of course, the very positioning outside conventionality that permits the construction and evolution of creative parenting roles also raises challenges with respect to societal acknowledgment and understanding (Dunne, 2000). Lesbian and gay parents' (de)construction and (re)definition of family life occurs within a broader context in which gay-parent families are not socially intelligible. In particular, nonbiological lesbian mothers, lesbian and gay stepparents, and adoptive lesbian and gay parents who lack legally recognized relationships to their children all occupy roles that are often invisible, misunderstood, or minimized. Lacking legal and institutional support, as well as symbolic language through which to define and describe their relationships to their children, partners must consciously articulate and communicate their roles, including how their role definitions and statuses match up (or do not match up) with existing notions of parenting, mothering, fathering, and stepparenting.

In an effort to effectively communicate their parental status to the outside world, legally and socially vulnerable lesbian and gay parents may seek to secure second-parent adoptions or other legal safeguards, if these options are legally and financially possible (see chap. 3, this volume). Such actions may help to legitimate their parental status in the eyes of the public, as well as their families of origin (Oswald, 2002). Similarly, commitment ceremonies may also be used to "forge a space" for lesbian mothers and gay fathers within existing definitions of parenthood and family (Hequembourg & Farrell, 1999, p. 753) and to "signpost" family relationships (Short, 2007). Parents may also engage in public displays of parenthood as a means of conveying their parental status. For example, some lesbian nonbiological mothers report strategically holding their children in public in an effort to communicate their motherhood status (Reimann, 1997). Nonbiological mothers may also purposefully take on the role of the primary stay-at-home caregiver, which powerfully communicates their maternal status (Short, 2007). Finally, as discussed in chapter 3, naming is also a powerful strategy that couples use to communicate parent–child relationships. Couples may choose to give their children the last name of the less recognized parent (i.e., the nonbiological lesbian mother, the nonlegal adoptive parent) or they may encourage their children to call the less recognized parent by a common parent identifier (e.g., Mama, Daddy; Almack, 2005; Short, 2007).

In pursuing legitimization and recognition in the form of symbolic and legal supports such as commitment ceremonies and second-parent adoptions, lesbian and gay parents are sometimes described as being assimiliationist (Weston, 1992) and are accused of trying to "be like" heterosexual families (Lewin, 1993; Mallon, 2004). Gay-parent families by definition lie outside of hegemonic definitions and understandings of family; thus, their deviant status and their freedom from roles prescribed by gender lend themselves to flexible boundaries and radical role definitions (Weston, 1992). Some critics have wondered why lesbian and gay parents, given their freedom from traditional gender and family roles, would choose to mimic heterosexual parenting arrangements. For example, Hocquenghem (1978; as cited in Weston, 1992) argued that instead of trying to maintain hegemonic kinship structures, gay people should seek to form elaborate friendship networks, friendship networks being more democratic than kinship "and a welcome alternative to Freud's derivation of significant relationships from filiation" (Weston, 1992, p. 122). In this view, kinship is a symbol of assimilation, and sexual minorities should therefore cease referring to lovers, friends, and even children as *kin* and should develop their own terminology to describe their relationships and experiences as opposed to adopting heterosexual language and institutions. But as Weston (1991, 1992) and Lewin (1993) pointed out, lesbian and gay parents and their families are rarely, if ever, purely assimilationist: They adopt, adapt to, co-opt, and transform heterosexual relationship structures and symbols in ways that suggest that they are both assimilating to and transforming kinship and family relationships. Furthermore, consideration of both the meaning that they give to the strategies that they use (e.g., naming and legalizing practices) and the functions that these strategies are designed to fulfill (e.g., to create, solidify, and announce familial ties) is necessary to understand how lesbian and gay parents are constructing family relationships. As Weston (1992) stated,

> A lesbian can choose to bear a child in the hope of gaining acceptance from "society" and straight relatives, or she can embark on the same course with a sense of daring and radical innovation, knowing that children tend to be "protected" from lesbians and gay men in the United States. (p. 124)

Thus, the decision to have a child, to pursue a second-parent adoption, or to celebrate one's relationship with a commitment ceremony, for example, may be made for multiple reasons and may have diverse implications.

Weston (1992) also pointed out that because the family is not a static institution but a cultural category that, depending on the context, can represent assimilation or challenge, "there can be no definitive answer to the debate on assimilationism" (p. 123). Arguments that gay-parent families are "normal, just like every other family" and arguments that situate gay-parent families as "alternative" are both problematic in that they reinforce the naturalness and reality of the family as an institution (Gabb, 1999, p. 13). Furthermore, while many lesbian and gay parents seek to ensure the safety and well-being of their families by employing the methods that they have available to them, it is necessary to recognize that they are not, in doing so, inevitably conforming to heterosexual constructions of family. Rather, they are resisting their marginalized status as vulnerable nonfamily members and asserting their relationships to each other in the absence of widespread recognition and support. They are also responding practically to societal strictures. Using socially meaningful titles such as "Mom" and "Dad," for example, may encourage others (e.g., family members, neighbors, teachers) to recognize them as the families that they are.

PARENTING ABILITIES AND FAMILY FUNCTIONING

As discussed, concerns about the potential impact of parents' sexual orientation on children's development and mental health have dominated societal thinking for several decades. Specifically, concerns regarding the effects of mother or father absence on children, the effects of societal discrimination on children, and the mental health and stability of sexual minorities are prevalent in society (Editors of the *Harvard Law Review*, 1990) and perhaps most apparent in the courtroom: The judiciary system has historically questioned the fitness of lesbian and gay parents on the basis of their sexual orientation (McIntyre, 2004; Ricketts & Achtenberg, 1987). Consider the famous case of Sharon Bottoms, a lesbian living in Virginia with her son. In 1993, her mother, Kay Bottoms, who strongly disapproved of her daughter's sexual orientation, filed for custody of her grandson. She was awarded custody on the basis of the court's assumption that Sharon Bottoms's sexual orientation represented a threat to her son's well-being. This case served as a landmark example of the perilous legal situation that lesbian and gay parents face—reflected in the Romesburg (2001) article title as "the worst-case scenario for gay families."

Legal decisions such as this served as the catalyst for a steady wave of research studies that compared lesbian and gay parents with heterosexual parents to determine whether parental sexual orientation has implications for parent functioning (e.g., mental health, parenting competence) and child outcomes (e.g., mental health, self-esteem, gendered role behavior) such that it would be reasonable to deny lesbian and gay parents custody on the basis of their sexual orientation (C. J. Patterson, 2006). By countering myth and stereotype with actual data, these studies have been extremely important in literally setting the record straight about gay parenting; still, in spite of this research and the fact that a number of mainstream organizations have taken supportive stands in treating sexual minorities without prejudice in custody and adoption decisions, many courts continue to believe that children will be harmed by having lesbian or gay parents (Kendell, 1999).[5] As Kendell argued, "Ignorance about the reality of lesbian and gay parent families, longstanding antigay bias, ingrained stereotypes, and, in some case, partisan religious convictions, combine to create a hostile judicial climate for lesbian and gay litigants in some regions of this country" (p. 42).

Despite such resistance to lesbian and gay parenting, the findings of early studies are consistent in suggesting that sexual orientation is not relevant to men's and women's adjustment and parenting capacities, thereby challenging stereotypes of lesbian and gay parents as unfit for parenting, emotionally unstable, and unable to assume maternal and paternal roles. For example, in an early study, Rand, Graham, and Rawlings (1982) examined lesbian mothers' well-being and found that women's scores on various indi-

---

[5]These organizations include the Child Welfare League of America, the American Bar Association, the American Medical Association, the American Psychiatric Association, the American Psychological Association, the American Academy of Pediatrics, the National Association of Social Workers, and the North American Council on Adoptable Children.

ces of psychological health were similar to female norms.[6] In another early study, Miller, Jacobsen, and Bigner (1981) investigated the home environment of lesbian-mother families and heterosexual-mother families and found that lesbian mothers were more "child oriented" than heterosexual women. This finding defies stereotypes of lesbians as antifamily: that is, lesbians are often depicted as selfish and pleasure-seeking, in contrast to idealized notions of mothers, who embody the feminine qualities of altruism and sacrifice (Almack, 2006).

More recent studies have supported and extended earlier findings. Several studies have compared lesbian and gay parents and heterosexual parents in terms of parenting stress and family stress and have found few differences between the two groups (Bos, van Balen, & van den Boom, 2004; Erich, Leung, & Kindle, 2005; Leung, Erich, & Kanenberg, 2005; McNeill, Rienzi, & Kposowa, 1998; Tasker & Golombok, 1998). Other studies have examined parenting awareness (i.e., awareness of the skills necessary for effective parenting) and self-reported parenting skill among lesbian and heterosexual parents and have found few differences between the two types of families (Bos et al., 2007; Flaks, Ficher, Masterpasqua, & Joseph, 1995). Indeed, Bos et al. (2007) compared lesbian biological mothers with heterosexual mothers and lesbian nonbiological with heterosexual fathers and found that lesbian nonbiological mothers appeared to be more skilled at parenting and more involved with their children than fathers. The authors noted that this effect is likely due to gender, as opposed to sexual orientation: In general, mothers tend to invest more in and be more skilled at child-rearing, compared with fathers (Furstenberg & Cherlin, 1991). Several studies have also examined parental warmth and intimacy. Golombok, Spencer, and Rutter (1983) found that divorced lesbian mothers and divorced heterosexual mothers did not differ in their ratings of feelings of warmth toward their children. Similarly, Golombok and colleagues (2003) conducted a community study of lesbian and heterosexual mothers and found that the two groups did not differ in terms of maternal warmth toward their children. Finally, Bigner and Jacobsen

---

[6]Some research, though, suggests that lesbian and gay individuals may be more likely to suffer mental health problems than heterosexual individuals in the general population. A 2003 meta-analysis by Meyer found that lesbian and gay persons were 2.4 times as likely to report disorders related to mood, anxiety, and substance abuse than were heterosexuals; experiences of discrimination and heterosexism were postulated as potential factors that may explain these higher rates. It is important, however, that the studies in this meta-analysis are characterized by numerous limitations: All but one of the studies included in the meta-analysis either (a) used a nonprobability sample or (b) used a probability sample but categorized respondents by their sexual behavior rather than by their self-identified sexual orientation. Furthermore, it is important to point out that the majority of the individuals in these studies who were categorized as nonheterosexual did not manifest psychopathology. Thus, the fact that research on lesbian mothers has failed to find higher rates of psychological problems in this group as compared with heterosexual mothers may (a) reflect the fact that lesbians who become parents are the most well-adjusted in the population (e.g., perhaps they possess certain resiliency factors that help them to cope with general heterosexism and effectively negotiate the barriers to becoming parents) or (b) point to problems in the sampling and measurement of those studies that have found elevated rates of psychopathology among sexual minorities (e.g., such as those in Meyer's meta-analysis).

(1989a, 1989b) compared divorced gay fathers and divorced heterosexual fathers and found that the two groups did not differ on self-reported degree of involvement or level of intimacy with their children.

Some research has examined lesbian and gay parents' child-rearing orientation and parenting style. Golombok et al. (2003) compared heterosexual and lesbian mothers and found that compared with heterosexual mothers, lesbian mothers reported engaging in less frequent physical discipline (e.g., smacking) and engaging in more frequent domestic and imaginative play with their children. Examining differences in parenting style within lesbian couples, Bos et al. (2007) found that lesbian biological mothers scored higher on structure and limit-setting than did lesbian nonbiological mothers. The authors suggested that lesbian birth mothers may feel more responsible for their children as a function of carrying and birthing the child. (It is also possible that this difference may in part be related to the fact that birth mothers were more involved in child care than their partners. Alternatively, lesbian birth and nonbirth mothers may also differ in the reasons for wanting to become parents, or in terms of personality traits, which could also explain differences in their child-rearing styles.) In a study of gay and heterosexual fathers, Bigner and Jacobsen (1989a, 1989b) found that in comparison with heterosexual fathers, gay fathers tended to be stricter and to set more consistent limits for their children's behavior. They were also more likely to provide their children with explanations for the rules they established and to ask their children for their opinion in family decisions. They also appeared to be more sensitive and responsive to the perceived needs of their children than were heterosexual fathers. Perhaps gay fathers experience heightened pressures to demonstrate, or at least report, their proficiency at parenting. Alternatively, they may simply be more androgynous in terms of gendered role orientation than heterosexual fathers. That is, they may demonstrate a more even integration of feminine and masculine values and traits (Bigner & Bozett, 1989) and may in turn be less conventional in their parenting practices, values, and goals.

Several studies have suggested that lesbians and gay men may have less conventional parenting values than do heterosexual women and men. Bos et al. (2004) found that both lesbian and heterosexual mothers felt strongly about the value of fostering independence in their children. Lesbian mothers, however, were less invested in fostering conformity in their children. Similarly, an early study by Hoeffer (1981) found that while heterosexual single mothers tended to prefer that their sons engage in masculine activities and their daughters in feminine activities, lesbian mothers' preferences for their children's play were gender-neutral. As stated, these data may reflect greater androgyny on the part of parents (Bigner & Bozett, 1989); they may also reflect a greater interest in and acceptance of diversity: Some research suggests that lesbian mothers are more accepting of differences in their children than heterosexual mothers (e.g., they are more accepting of their children's sexuality, whatever it might be; Tasker & Golombok, 1997).

As discussed in chapter 3 of this volume, parenthood necessarily changes the intimate relationship dynamics of lesbian and gay parents. In the following discussion of research on lesbian and gay parents' relationship quality and relationship trajectories, I pay special attention to the unique context of relationship dissolution in lesbian and gay parents. Indeed, the lack of legal safeguards and protections for same-sex relationships poses unique challenges for families when couples break up.

LESBIAN AND GAY PARENTS' INTIMATE RELATIONSHIPS

There is evidence that lesbian couples, like heterosexual couples, tend to experience an initial decline in the quality of their relationships upon becoming parents (Goldberg & Sayer, 2006), although no studies have prospectively examined how lesbian and gay parents' relationship quality continues to unfold after the initial transition to parenthood. Some research, however, does point to how lesbian mothers view parenthood as having affected their relationships. Specifically, Gartrell et al. (2000) found that by the time the children in their sample were 5 years old, 94% of the lesbian couples who were still together felt that having children had significantly reduced their time and energy for each other (compared with 91% at the postbirth follow-up). Related to this, most women reported declines in sexual intimacy. Similarly, in a cross-sectional study of 31 lesbian-parent families and 26 heterosexual-parent families, Giammattei (2008) found that, compared with heterosexual mothers, lesbian mothers tended to report more nurturance but less physical intimacy in their partner relationships.[7] Thus, in addition to broadly impacting same-sex couples' time and energy for their relationships, parenthood may have specific effects on couples' sexual intimacy (at least for lesbian couples).

Some cross-sectional studies have compared lesbian and heterosexual parents in terms of relationship quality and satisfaction. These studies suggest similar relationship outcomes in the two groups. Flaks et al. (1995) compared lesbian and heterosexual parents of 3- to 10-year-old children and found that the two groups of parents did not differ significantly from each other in terms of perceived relationship quality. Bos et al. (2004) compared the relationship satisfaction of heterosexual parents and lesbian two-mother fami-

---

[7]These data are consistent with research by Blumstein and Schwartz (1983; see chap. 2, this volume), which indicated that of all couple types (lesbian, gay, and heterosexual), lesbians tend to have the lowest frequencies of sexual contact in general. Lesbians, however, are certainly not the only ones to experience declines in their sexual intimacy during the transition to parenthood. Similar patterns have also been reported in studies of heterosexual couples (e.g., Haugen, Schmutzer, & Wenzel, 2004).

lies of 4- to 8-year-olds and found no differences between the two groups. Finally, in a study of lesbian mothers of 4- to 9-year-olds, C. J. Patterson (1995) found that, overall, couples were very satisfied with their current relationship, and there were no differences in biological and nonbiological mothers' levels of satisfaction.

Relationship Dissolution and Divorce

Not all relationships survive, and even some of the best-intentioned couples will ultimately end their relationships. Whereas the research on heterosexual couples' divorce experiences is vast (Berscheid, 2006; M. Coleman, Ganong, & Leon, 2006), the research on lesbian and gay couples' relationship dissolution is quite slim. This is unsurprising given the practical challenges of studying same-sex couples' relationship dissolution: Compared with heterosexual couples, same-sex couples' relationships are less easily defined by an official starting point (e.g., an engagement, a wedding) or ending point (e.g., legal separation). The lack of research is also unsurprising in light of the fact that same-sex relationships tend to be regarded as less real, meaningful, and important than heterosexual relationships. Indeed, the lack of societal recognition of same-sex marriage and divorce and, in turn, the absence of adequate language to describe these events allow for their trivialization, both externally and internally (Morton, 1998). Lacking legitimization of their partner relationships, lesbians and gay men confront a lack of understanding and empathy from their family members, friends, and workplaces if they ultimately dissolve their relationships. They may also experience external or internal pressure to downplay the importance of their relationship or the pain of separation. Consequently, the emotional—and economic—impact of relationship dissolution among same-sex couples often goes unrecognized, thus perpetuating the invisibility of same-sex relationships in general.

Additional complexity is introduced when same-sex couples who dissolve their relationships are also parents. Lacking legal guidance, lesbian and gay parents are forced to creatively and independently manage the details of their separation and to agree upon the mutual roles and obligations of each partner to each other and to their children. In cases in which only one partner is legally and/or biologically connected to the child, the nonlegal partner must consider the potential jeopardy of his or her future relationship with his or her children (Morton, 1998); indeed, concerns about the future of one's relationship with one's children may influence the nonlegal partner's willingness to end the relationship. It is clear that inequity in partners' legal and biological relationships to their children can have significant implications in the event of separation or divorce. For example, the legal, and therefore more powerful, parent may seek to set certain restrictions on the nonlegal partner's time with his or her children after the separation. In situations in which each partner has biological children, there is rarely any question about what will happen in the wake of relationship dissolution: Each parent will take his or her own biological children, effectively displacing them from their other parent and sibling(s) (Dunne, 2000), with possibly devastating consequences. As Allen (2007) noted in her reflexive personal narrative about the dissolution of her own long-term lesbian relationship:

> Our carefully constructed "family of choice" (Weston, 1991) that we had nurtured and protected for 12 years was split into two biological dyads without legal or social relationship to one another; no law or social contract protected us. The four of us—two moms and two sons—became one mother and one son, times two. . . . Today, I cannot see our younger son, and our older son, who is now 19, does not want to see my former partner. The losses are compounded and ongoing—the mothers do not see each other's children and the children do not see each other. (p. 178)

Thus, although intact, stable lesbian and gay couples may understandably minimize the biological and legal inequities that exist between partners, the reality of such inequities, and their profound consequences, are inevitably realized in the wake of relational and often familial dissolution. In this context, the nonlegal parent is ultimately dependent on the legal parent's approval to continue his or her relationship with the child he or she has helped to raise. Hence, the biological or legal parent's power, and the hierarchy within the couple, is unfortunately often revealed after the time for drawing up coparenting agreements,[8] contracts, and so on has passed.

Gartrell et al.'s longitudinal study sheds some light on rates of dissolution among lesbian parents. By the time the children in this study were 2 years old, 8 couples of the original sample of 73 had separated. By the time the children were 5, 15 additional couples had split up; thus, 23 couples (31%) of the original sample of 73 couples had separated (Gartrell et al., 2000). By the time the children were 10, another 7 couples had dissolved their relationships. Thus, of the 73 couples who were together when the study began during pregnancy, 30 couples had split up by the time their children were 10 (Gartrell et al., 2005, 2006). (These rates are similar to rates for heterosexual couples: According to the 1995 National Survey of Family Growth, one fifth of heterosexual couples terminated their first marriages within 5 years, and one third terminated their first marriages within 10 years: Bramlett & Mosher, 2001.[9]) Custody was shared in 13 cases; in 15 cases, the birth mother retained sole or primary custody (Gartrell et al., 2005, 2006).[10] Nine of the 30 comothers had secured a second-parent adoption prior to the sepa-

---

[8]Although not legally enforceable, coparenting agreements can be useful in the event of relationship dissolution in that they are an important record of lesbian and gay couples' intentions to parent together and may therefore be taken into consideration by a court in resolving custody disputes. For sample coparenting agreements, see Gil de Lamadrid (1991).

[9]Again, relationship dissolution rates among same-sex couples and heterosexual couples are difficult to compare because of the difficulty in establishing a starting and ending date to same-sex relationships.

[10]Custody arrangements for the remaining two couples were not reported by the authors.

ration; of these 9, 7 were among the 13 families that shared custody. Thus, the presence of legal safeguards helped to ensure family stability postdissolution.

Women perceived a range of issues as having contributed to the dissolution of their relationships, including incompatibility and growing apart (47%) and differences in parenting style (20%). Difficulties in sharing domestic, financial, and child-rearing responsibilities were also perceived as contributing to separation among some couples. Additionally, problems with sexual intimacy and sexual dissatisfaction were named as factors by several couples (Gartrell et al., 2006). These findings are somewhat consistent with those of Turteltaub (2002), who interviewed 10 lesbian mothers who represented five former couples. These women were the mothers of seven children, all of whom had been conceived by donor insemination. Women in this sample reported that their relationships ended because they disagreed about how to parent and how to manage finances. Lack of support from extended family members and legal barriers to becoming equal coparents also contributed to intracouple conflict.

Importantly, 22 of the 30 separated couples in Gartrell et al.'s (2006) study stated that having a child delayed the dissolution of their relationship. This suggests that, at least in these couples' eyes, having a child was not the primary factor that led to their breakup; in fact, it actually functioned as a temporary deterrent to ending their unions. This is consistent with research on heterosexual couples: For example, in one study of long-term marriages in which at least one partner expressed unhappiness with the relationship, children were one of the most frequently cited reasons for staying together (Lauer & Lauer, 1987). Thus, children may have a similarly stabilizing effect on lesbians' and gay men's relationship quality, such that relationship longevity (but not necessarily quality) is enhanced by the presence of children. Indeed, in the absence of many of the institutional supports that contribute to the longevity of heterosexual relationships (so-called relationship constraints) such as marriage, religious support, and family support, same-sex relationships are more vulnerable to dissolution (D. G. Patterson, Ciabattari, & Schwartz, 1999). Children may function as a powerful relationship constraint, serving to offset some of the other factors that undermine or at least do not contribute to the stability of same-sex relationships.

LESBIAN AND GAY PARENTS' FAMILY, FRIEND, AND COMMUNITY RELATIONSHIPS

In addition to experiencing changes in their intimate relationships, lesbian and gay parents may also experience changes in their relationships with family, friends, and their larger communities. Of interest is how lesbian and gay parents' extended family relationships unfold as children develop. For example, to what extent do lesbian and gay parents perceive their family members as supportive and involved in their own lives and their children's lives? How do lesbians' and gay men's relationships with friends change as their children grow up? Given that social support is a consistent predictor of adjustment among parents in general (Mayes & Leckman, 2007) and has been linked to adjustment in lesbian parents specifically (Vyncke & Julien, 2007), lesbian and gay parents' sources of, level of, use of, and feelings about support are of interest. Social support may function as an important buffer against some of the stresses associated with parenting in general and parenting in a heterosexist society specifically (Lassiter et al., 2006).

Family Support

Research suggests that lesbian and gay parents may experience less support from family members than their heterosexual counterparts do. For example, Kindle and Erich (2005) compared lesbian and gay adoptive parents with heterosexual adopters (average age of children was 6 years old) and found that lesbian and gay adopters reported less support from family members than heterosexual adopters. As discussed in chapter 3, however, there is some evidence that even if lesbian and gay parents do not receive the same overall level of support as heterosexual parents, their families of origin may nevertheless become more supportive when they become parents (e.g., Goldberg, 2006). This pattern is also suggested by cross-sectional studies that compare lesbian parents and lesbian nonparents. For example, a 2007 study by DeMino, Appleby, and Fisk found that lesbian mothers perceived more social support from their families of origin than did lesbian non-mothers. The authors also found that lesbian mothers perceived less support from friends overall and from lesbian and gay friends specifically, compared with lesbian nonparents. The authors interpreted these findings as suggesting that after becoming parents, lesbian mothers may shift their source of support away from friends to their families of origin. Support for this interpretation comes from work by Dunne (2000), whose interviews with lesbian mothers revealed that women tended to view the arrival of their children as bringing them closer to their families or as helping them to repair challenging relationships with family members.

Gartrell et al.'s (1999, 2000, 2006) longitudinal study of lesbian-parent families provided indirect evidence that family support and involvement may increase gradually over time. For example, when their children were 2 years old, only 29% of lesbian mothers reported that their parents were "out" about their grandchild's lesbian-mother family (1999). By the time their children reached 5 years of age, however, 63% of grandparents were out, and by the time their children turned 10, 73% of grandparents were out (2000, 2006). Thus, lesbian mothers perceived their parents as becoming increasingly open about their sexual orientation over time. Having grandchildren, then, may make it very difficult to stay in the closet about a daughter's lesbianism. Perhaps, though, these changes reflect actual increases in tolerance, such that their parents have simply grown to care less about hiding their daughters' lesbianism from the world.

Some research has examined lesbian-mother families' actual contact with their extended family and friendship networks. In their study of 37 lesbian-mother families (children ranged from 4 to 9 years of age) C. J. Patterson, Hurt, and Mason (1998) found that, according to parents' reports, children were involved with a range of adults, including family members, parents' friends, and parents' ex-partners. Notably, parents reported more involvement by and contact with the biological mother's family members, including grandparents and other adult relatives, than the nonbiological mother's family of origin. Thus, nonbiological mothers' extended families were seemingly less invested in their grandchildren, nieces, and nephews, presumably because they felt less connected to a child who was not related to them biologically and/or legally. Similarly, Hequembourg and Farrell's (1999) in-depth analysis of lesbian motherhood revealed that because nonbiological mothers lacked both biological and legal ties to their children, their extended families were generally more resistant to viewing them as mothers. However, when nonbiological mothers secured second-parent adoption rights, their parents (who, by extension, became the legal grandparents of these children) often became more willing to acknowledge them as parents and to devote emotional energy to their grandchildren. Thus, the establishment of legal ties may help to engender greater investment among family members. Indeed, nonbiological lesbian mothers who have successfully obtained second-parent adoptions often regard such legal safeguards as instrumental in enhancing their personal sense of security as parents and as an important tool in reducing social stigma and prejudice (Connolly, 2002b; Short, 2007).

Lesbian and gay parents who adopt across racial lines may be particularly vulnerable to lack of support from family members. Johnson and O'Connor (2002), for example, found that lesbian and gay parents who adopted transracially sometimes confronted criticism on several fronts. Some family members expressed discomfort because of their own racism, whereas others were resistant because they felt strongly about the importance of passing on one's genes. Family members also hinted at the challenges and vulnerabilities that the children might be exposed to because of their multiple marginalized statuses. Similarly, in her study of lesbian mothers of internationally adopted children, Bennett (2003a) found that women sometimes perceived subtle racism from family members, although most of them were relatively welcoming of the child on the surface. In light of evidence that lesbian and gay parents often adopt transracially (Gianino, 2008; Goldberg, 2008; Leung et al., 2005) and transculturally (Gates, Badget, Macomber, & Chambers, 2007), such dynamics are deserving of future attention.

As described in chapter 2 of this volume, racial/ethnic minorities who are also sexual minorities may be particularly cautious about coming out to their families out of concern that they will lose a valuable source of support. Racial/ethnic-minority gay men and lesbians who do come out and who have children in the context of same-sex relationships, then, may be especially vulnerable to rejection and alienation from family members. Should these individuals also perceive racism within the lesbian and gay parent community, they may suffer particularly notable deficits in support (i.e., they may lack a sense of connection and belonging to any particular group or community). Alternatively, it is possible that parenting may serve to more fully integrate sexual minorities who are also racial/ethnic minorities into White gay communities as well as racial/ethnic-minority heterosexual communities (Cahill, Battle, & Meyer, 2003). Much more research is needed to explore the experiences and perceptions of support that these multiple-minority parents encounter within their families and communities.

Lesbians and gay men from working-class families may also find themselves without family support as they build their own families. Specifically, because greater awareness of and criticism of heterosexism and homophobia is associated with education level, lesbians and gay men with parents and relatives who possess limited education may encounter more familial resistance and disapproval than individuals in middle-class families (Haddock, 2003). Indeed, Carrington (2002) observed that lesbian and gay couples from middle-class families tended to be more successful in uniting their families of origin and their families of choice (i.e., their friendship communities) than their counterparts from working-class families.

Friend Support

In becoming parents, lesbians and gay men may worry that they will no longer "belong" in the gay community and that they will lose contact with their nonparent lesbian and gay friends. Such concerns are not entirely unrealistic: Research has suggested that when people—heterosexual or gay—become parents, their social networks may change to include more parents and fewer nonparents (Lewin, 1993; Mallon, 2004). Gartrell et al. (2005) found that by the time that their children were 10 years old, lesbian mothers' support networks included more parents than nonparents and that many of these parents were heterosexual. Such changes in friendship network configurations likely reflect changing interests and priorities, as well as the changing salience of various aspects of one's identities: Some research suggests that lesbian mothers tend to identify more closely with heterosexual mothers than with child-free lesbians (Koepke, Hare, & Moran, 1992; Lewin, 1993) and that motherhood, not one's sexual orientation, tends to be the source of the more salient identity for many lesbian mothers (Lewin, 1993; Turner, Scadden, & Harris, 1990).

Sexual minorities' decreased reliance on nonparent lesbian and gay friends may also be related to a perceived lack of support from the gay community for one's choice to parent (C. R. Matthews & Lease, 2000). Mallon's

(2004) qualitative study of gay fathers suggests that gay men in particular may experience resistance from the gay male community when they become parents. Specifically, the gay men in his sample sometimes encountered the criticism that in becoming parents, they had sold out to the straight community and were trying to be just like heterosexual people. Moreover, some men found that their friends simply did not want children in their social circle. The loss of long-term friendships was quite painful for these men, although in some cases it pushed them to form new friendships, often with heterosexual parents. Many men, though, did report continued support from some friends, whom they came to regard as wonderful "uncles" to their children. Such ongoing support may be particularly important for lesbian and gay parents who lack satisfactory support from family members and who may look to friends (or "chosen family") as key sources of support and strength (A. Martin, 1998).

CONCLUSIONS AND RECOMMENDATIONS

The research on lesbian and gay parents strongly indicates that they are no less equipped to raise children than their heterosexual counterparts. They possess the skills necessary to be good parents, and they enjoy healthy relationships with their children. They care deeply about protecting their children from harm while also preparing them for potential stigma. Nevertheless, critics of gay parenting (e.g., Cameron, 1999; Lerner & Nagai, 2001) have argued that the scholars who conduct research on lesbian and gay parents and their children are biased and politically or personally motivated, and that the findings from these studies are therefore not reliable. They argue further that these studies are methodologically flawed. From a feminist perspective, this first point is of questionable merit, in that personal, social, and political agendas and values implicitly or explicitly characterize much of the research in the social sciences (Jager, 1989; Llewelyn, 2007). Indeed, the mere fact that a researcher possesses a certain set of values does not render that researcher's research, or research findings, noncredible. Second, while it is true that the literature on lesbian and gay parenting is to some extent characterized by small, nonrepresentative samples, this is a limitation that characterizes much of the research in psychology, and, importantly, there are exceptions to this trend (e.g., Golombok et al., 2003; Wainright, Russell, & Patterson, 2004). Furthermore, the findings of recent community-based studies that have used more representative samples are remarkably consistent with the findings of earlier studies regarding lesbians' and gay men's parenting capacities (e.g., Golombok et al., 2003). Still, more studies that use representative, diverse samples are needed. In particular, studies that investigate the intersections among social class, sexual orientation, geographical location, race, and multiple other social locations will help to shed light on the diverse perspectives and experiences of lesbian mothers and gay fathers. Moreover, the paucity of research on bisexual and transgender parents is problematic and should be addressed. Indeed, bisexual persons are often stereotyped as polyamorous and fickle (Tye, 2003), whereas transgender persons are often regarded as mentally ill (Israel, 2004). Such stereotypes likely influence parents' experiences as they navigate relationships with their children, family members, their children's schools, other parents, and society at large.

Regarding practice implications, therapists, practitioners, and educators should be aware of the ways in which social inequities and institutional heterosexism shape the parenting practices and experiences of sexual minority parents. For example, therapists should be conscious of the biological and legal inequities that characterize same-sex couples' relationships and of the ways in which these inequities may directly or indirectly impact parenting and parent–child relationships. Therapists should also be aware of the powerful impact of societal stereotypes of lesbian and gay parents (e.g., as deficient, immoral, and inferior) on their clients and should seek to counter these stereotypes in their work with lesbian and gay parents.

Therapists and practitioners should support lesbian and gay parents in anticipating and handling disclosure issues and in exploring their feelings about disclosure, by asking them to consider, for example, what it will be like to come out to their children's teachers about their families. Lesbian and gay parents at different stages of the life cycle may have different concerns and priorities regarding disclosure, such that, for example, parents of adolescents may wish to respect their children's desire for privacy, and may therefore choose to be less out than they have been in the past. Practitioners should support their clients in recognizing the changing needs of their families but should also encourage them to remain cognizant of the ways in which semi-closeting themselves could be counterproductive and harmful for themselves and their families.

Practitioners also should be aware of the potential for stresses that are common among lesbian and gay parents. Even though awareness of gay parenting is growing, sexual minorities and their families continue to be vulnerable to social stigma. Thus, stigma-related stress may, for sexual minorities, exacerbate issues that can affect any family, such as stepfamily formation, partner relational difficulties, parent–child problems, and problems with extended family of origin. Therapists and practitioners should thus remain conscious of the ways in which lesbian and gay parents' unique social and relational context may create additional challenges that need to be navigated (Ariel & McPherson, 2000).

Workplaces can play a significant role in supporting lesbian and gay parents and their families and can be stressful for sexual minority workers. For example, one review of 11 studies of LGBT workers found ranges of 25% to 65% of workers reporting workplace discrimination and prejudice at some point in their careers (Croteau, 1996). Sexual minorities with children may be subjected to especially high levels of hostility, particularly from colleagues and supervisors who do not believe that sexual minorities should have or adopt children. Thus, workplace policies that prohibit discrimination on the basis of gender, sexual orientation, and gender identity and that explicitly promote a tolerant and inclusive workplace culture may help to minimize the stress that lesbian and gay parents experience at their workplaces. Furthermore, workplaces are encouraged to offer domestic partnership benefits to sexual minority employees. Such benefits can be crucial to families' survival; in their absence, sexual minorities are unable to carry their partners or children on their insurance, leaving many family members uninsured (Fassinger, 2008).

Finally, it is essential that policymakers and court officials rely on the existing research—as opposed to stereotypes and morally driven arguments—in making custody and adoption decisions that involve lesbian and gay parents. The data on lesbian and gay parents strongly suggest that there is no reason to deny a parent custody of his or her children on the basis of his or her sexual orientation alone. At the broader policy level, better protections are necessary for lesbian- and gay-parent families. Children deserve the security and comfort of knowing that their parents' relationship to one another is legally recognized and that their own relationships to their parents are legally protected. The absence of such laws serves to undermine the commitments that family members have made to each other. Moreover, the absence of laws that protect lesbian- and gay-parent families renders them vulnerable to stigma and unfair treatment. For example, children whose heterosexual parents separate or divorce because of a parent's sexual orientation are still at risk of not seeing the gay parent. Likewise, children born or adopted into lesbian- or gay-parent families are at risk of not seeing their nonbiological and/or nonlegal parent, should the couple dissolve their union (Goldhaber, 2007).

In chapter 5 of this volume, I address the experiences of children with lesbian and gay parents. Questions considered include: How do children experience and perceive their minority family structure (e.g., what do they perceive as challenging about growing up with sexual minority parents)?; and how (if at all) does their family structure impact their development and adjustment (i.e., their sexual and gender identity development, as well as their social and psychological functioning)?

PRACTICAL RESOURCES

Parenting

Book: Clunis, M., & Green, G. D. (2003). *The lesbian parenting book: A guide to creating families and raising children* (2nd ed.). New York: Seal Press.

Summary: This book presents information on each stage of parenthood and child development. The second edition contains new information on circumcision, legal hoops for noncustodial parents, late-in-life pregnancy, balancing work and family, and more.

Web site: http://www.proudparenting.com (Proud Parenting)

Summary: ProudParenting.com serves as an online portal for LGBT parents and their families worldwide. The Web site contains information on adoption, foster care, and parenting support groups.

Parenting and the Schools

Web site: http://www.glsen.org (The Gay, Lesbian, and Straight Education Network)

Summary: GLSEN is an organization dedicated to research, education and advocacy pertaining to the safety of LGBT students and children of LGBT parents. GLSEN has published several reports that are intended to inform educators, policymakers, and the public about the school-related experiences of LGBT parents and their children. These reports can be accessed on the Web site.

Film: Chasnoff, D., & Cohen, H. (Directors). (1996). *It's Elementary: Talking About Gay Issues in Schools* [video]. Harriman, NY: New Day Films.

Summary: This documentary explores whether and how gay issues should be discussed in schools. It features elementary and middle schools where (mainly heterosexual) teachers are challenging the prevailing political climate and its attempt to censor any dialogue in schools about gay people. Rather than focusing on the debate between adults, though, the film takes the point of view of the school children, starting as young as first grade.

5

CHILDREN OF LESBIAN AND GAY PARENTS: ADJUSTMENT AND EXPERIENCES

As detailed in chapter 4 of this volume, the research that has been conducted on lesbian and gay parents and their children has been shaped by the broader social, historical, and legal context. The American Psychological Association and the American Psychiatric Association have not considered homosexuality to be a mental illness since 1973 (and the time period during which it was classified as a pathology—from 1951 to 1973, or 22 years—was of considerably shorter duration than the 35-year period since 1973). And yet, some right-wing conservative activists (e.g., P. Cameron & Cameron, 1996, 1998; P. Cameron, 1999, 2006; http://www.familyresearchinst.org) nevertheless have regarded homosexuality as a form of social deviance (P. Cameron, 1999, p. 282) and contended that homosexual persons are emotionally unstable (P. Cameron, 1999, p. 317), of poor character (P. Cameron & Cameron, 1998, pp. 1155, 1190), and hypersexual (P. Cameron, 1999, pp. 282, 298). This assumptive belief system frames the work of several right-wing activists (e.g., P. Cameron, 1999; P. Cameron & Cameron, 2002; Dobson, 2004) and legal scientists (e.g., Wardle, 1997) who have continued to publish writings that warn of the ill effects of lesbian and gay parenting. They have argued that homosexual parenting poses "significant potential detriment" to children (e.g., Wardle, 1997, p. 844) and contended that children of homosexual parents are unfairly exposed to peer ostracism (P. Cameron, 1999, p. 317; P. Cameron & Cameron, 2002, p. 77) and are at elevated risk of emotional and relational instability (P. Cameron, 1999, p. 317; Wardle, 1997, p. 863).

These opponents of gay parenting also have relied on the controversial literature on father absence (e.g., Blankenhorn, 1995; Popenoe, 1993) to bolster their claims, arguing that children fare best when they are raised by a mother and father, and have extrapolated from research on single-mother families to argue that children of lesbian and gay parents are at risk of numerous negative outcomes (e.g., delinquency, substance abuse, teen pregnancy). For example, in his report titled "The Potential Impact of Homosexual Parenting on Children," Wardle (1997), quoting Popenoe (1993), stated, "Separation of children from their fathers is 'the leading cause of declining child well-being in our society. It is also the engine driving our most urgent social problems'" (p. 10). Wardle concluded that "the advantages of dual-gender parenting for children and for society justify society's legal preference for this type of parenting" (p. 12). Furthermore, these authors drew from aspects of social learning theory to hypothesize about the ill effects that these children will suffer with regard to their sexual identity; that is, in the absence of a same-sex role model (and in the presence of homosexual "modeling") these children are "at risk" of developing aberrant gender identities and gendered role behavior, and homosexual orientations.

These arguments have been thoroughly critiqued (Silverstein & Auerbach, 1999; Stacey & Biblarz, 2001). However, ideas concerning the ill effects of parental homosexuality continue to pervade the societal discourse about homosexuality and lesbian and gay parenting, prompting judicial concerns about the parenting capabilities of lesbian and gay parents and, consequently, about the psychological, emotional, and social development of children raised by lesbian and gay parents. The research design and foci of studies of lesbian and gay parents and their children have reflected such concerns. For example, early studies of lesbian- and gay-parent families typically compared the development of children with divorced lesbian mothers with that of children of divorced heterosexual mothers, the rationale being that the latter group also lacked a father in the home, making it the most appropriate comparison group (C. J. Patterson, 1997). Furthermore, the topics under investigation in these early studies clearly represented those areas that were presumed to be most affected by living with gay parents: sexual identity (gender identity, gendered role behavior, and sexual orientation), social functioning, and mental health. Some current research has continued to focus on these domains, but researchers have extended their scholarship to other areas, such as the experiences and characteristics that are unique to children of lesbian and gay parents. Furthermore, researchers have also increasingly studied children of lesbian and gay parents in their own right, without reference to a comparison group (e.g., Gabb, 2005; Gartrell, Deck, Rodas, Peyser, & Banks, 2005).

The next subject of this chapter is the scholarship on the sexual identity, social functioning, and well-being of children of lesbian and gay parents. Additionally, research on some of the experiences that are unique to children of lesbian and gay parents is addressed, such as their experiences negotiating symbolic and actual relationships with unknown and known donors and dealing with disclosure about their family structure. Thus, the current chapter is divided into two sections: one that addresses mainly comparative research (i.e., research comparing the outcomes and experiences of children raised by lesbian and gay parents with those of heterosexual parents) and one that concerns the unique experiences of children of lesbian and gay parents.

SEXUAL IDENTITY: GENDER IDENTITY, GENDERED ROLE BEHAVIOR, AND SEXUAL ORIENTATION

Sexual identity has three components: gender identity, gendered role behavior, and sexual orientation (R. Green, 1974; Money & Ehrhardt, 1972). *Gender identity* refers to one's self-identification as male or female—that is, one's sense of oneself as being either male or female. *Gendered role behavior* refers to the extent to which one's behaviors, activities, attitudes, conduct, occupations, and so on are culturally regarded as feminine or masculine, and therefore whether they are seen as appropriate or typical for the male or female societal role. *Sexual orientation* refers to whether an individual is more strongly sexually attracted to members of his or her own sex, the opposite sex, or both sexes (homosexual, heterosexual, and bisexual, respectively).

It has often been presumed that the development of "normal" gender identity (i.e., gender identification that corresponds to one's biological sex), gendered role behavior, and sexual orientation might be disturbed in children with nonheterosexual parents. For example, some scientists have posited that the gender identity in boys with lesbian mothers might be disturbed as a function of the fact that they lack a male live-in role model with whom to identify and that they might ultimately identify as female (see C. J. Patterson, 1993, for a discussion of this argument). However, research has not detected any significant differences in the gender identities of children raised by children of lesbian and gay parents compared with children raised by heterosexual parents.

In an early study, Kirkpatrick, Smith, and Roy (1981) compared 20 school-aged children of heterosexual mothers and 20 school-aged children of lesbian mothers (ages 5–12) and found that only 1 child of a lesbian mother and 2 children of heterosexual mothers demonstrated concerns regarding gender issues. Studies by Golombok, Spencer, and Rutter (1983) and R. Green,

Mandel, Hotvedt, Gray, and Smith (1986) also compared children of lesbian mothers to children of heterosexual mothers and found no evidence that children of lesbian mothers were more likely to demonstrate disturbances in gender identity. Thus, the absence of a live-in male parent and the presence of a lesbian mother do not seem to have singular or combined effects on gender identity problems in boys or girls. As R. Green et al. (1986) pointed out, the cues that children use to categorize themselves as male or female include comparisons of genitals, dress, and word labels, all of which are likely available to children of lesbian mothers. Indeed, most children, regardless of family structure, have contact with many individuals outside their immediate household.

Similar findings were obtained in several studies of children of transgender parents. R. Green (1978) interviewed 16 children (aged 3–20) of seven transgender parents and found that none of the children had gender identity problems and all children reported gender-typical activities and interests. Similarly, R. Green (1998) interviewed 18 children of nine transgender parents (six parents were male-to-female and three were female-to-male), aged 5 to 16 years. He found that none of the children met the *Diagnostic and Statistical Manual of Mental Disorders, Fourth Edition* (1994), criteria for gender identity disorder and that no clinically significant cross-gender behavior was reported. One boy and one girl thought briefly about changing sexes when informed about their respective parents' decision, but this short-lived curiosity did not evolve into a desire to change sex. Finally, Freedman, Tasker, and di Ceglie (2002) studied 18 children (ages 3–15) of 12 transgender parents (all but 1 of whom was male-to-female) and found that only 1 adolescent girl reported temporary concerns regarding her gender identity.

Some researchers have argued that the studies in this area are flawed in that most tend to sample children with divorced lesbian mothers (i.e., children who have fathers, albeit fathers who are not living in the household; Belcastro, Gramlich, Nicholson, Price, & Wilson, 1993). Different findings might be obtained in studies of children raised in intentional or planned lesbian- or gay-parent households, who lack access to an active male or female parent. More research is needed that explores children's gender identity development in this context.

The gendered role behavior of children with lesbian and gay parents has also been examined. However, before discussing the research findings in this area, it is important to address how gendered roles have been defined and how they are presumed to develop. Certain personality attributes and behaviors have been culturally defined as more appropriate and desirable for one sex than the other (Boldizar, 1991). For example, traits and behavioral qualities considered masculine (e.g., assertiveness, competitiveness, dominance) are presumed to be more common among boys than girls, and, in turn, define the traditional male gendered role, and supposedly feminine traits and behavioral qualities (e.g., the qualities of being yielding, compassionate, and childlike) are presumed to be more common among girls than boys and therefore constitute the traditional female gendered role. Although raising children to adopt traditional gendered roles was considered a desirable goal in the 1950s, currently many scholars, parents, and educators agree that the socialization of strict adherence to traditional gendered roles limits boys' and girls' (and men's and women's) development (Eisenberg, Martin, & Fabes, 1996). Furthermore, some research has found that psychologically androgynous individuals (i.e., individuals with a balanced repertoire of feminine and masculine interests and traits) have higher self-esteem and tend to be better adjusted psychologically than individuals who are highly masculine or feminine (Alpert-Gillis & Connell, 1989; Boldizar, 1991).

How gendered roles develop has been the subject of much theoretical and empirical interest. According to classic social learning theorists (Bandura, 1977), the two processes that are most important for gender development are *differential reinforcement* and *modeling*. Parents are known to treat their sons and daughters differently starting in early childhood (e.g., offering them different toys, clothes, and furnishings; engaging in different activities with them as a function of gender), although the degree to which they are responding to preexisting differences (e.g., preferences for dolls by girls, preferences for trucks by boys) is unclear (Lytton & Romney, 1991). Parents also are thought to reward their children for demonstrating gender-typical behavior and to punish them for demonstrating cross-gender or gender-atypical behavior. Boys, in particular, may receive harsh punishment for cross-gender behavior because such behavior in boys (e.g., playing with dolls) is often viewed by parents as a precursor or indication of homosexuality (Kane, 2006). Research indicates that differential reinforcement by parents tends to decline when their children reach school age, when peers, teachers, and the media begin to take over as more important agents of socialization (Hoeffer, 1981; Kane, 2006; Lytton & Romney, 1991).

According to classic learning theorists, observing and imitating models of the same sex, particularly a same-sex parent, is also important to children's acquisition of gender-typed behavior. Contemporary theorists, however, have emphasized that children learn from many models in addition to their own parents: Peers, teachers, relatives, and the media (e.g., television, movies) are all powerful influences on children's selection of toys, activities, and playmates (Wood & Eagly, 2002). Children learn what behaviors are typical of their sex by observing many adults and peers and imitating those behaviors that seem to be performed more often by members of the same sex (Hoeffer, 1981; Maccoby, 1988). Children's early awareness of gender stereotypes may also facilitate acquisition of gendered role behavior (C. L. Martin & Ruble, 2004; Signorella, Bigler, & Liben, 1993). Thus, parents are but one source of influence on children's gendered role development.

Of course, lesbian and gay parents may differ from their heterosexual counterparts in some important ways that may have implications for their children's gendered role development. To the extent that lesbians and gay men may hold less rigid gender stereotypes, may be more tolerant of cross-gender interests and behaviors, and may model less rigid conformity to gendered roles in their dress, behaviors, and overall comportment, they may also facilitate similar nonconformity in their children (Kweskin & Cook, 1982). Furthermore, because same-sex couples cannot divide up household chores and responsibilities according to gender (difference), they inevitably model gender nonconformity and challenge traditional gendered roles. (Indeed, heterosexual parents who hold strong egalitarian values and/or who are relatively androgynous in their interests and behaviors often have children who seek out activities that are not gender typed; Witt, 1997.) Thus, lesbian and gay parents may cultivate a social environment that is nonpunishing of, or even encouraging of, more flexibility in gendered role behavior.

Gendered role behavior in children of lesbian and gay parents has been studied. Hoeffer (1981) studied 6- to 9-year-old children (20 of whom had lesbian single mothers and 20 of whom had heterosexual single mothers) and found that regardless of their mothers' sexual orientation, both boys and girls tended to prefer toys that were traditionally associated with their own gender, and boys more than girls preferred gender-typed toys more often than neutral ones. Furthermore, mothers in this study rated peers as the most influential determinant of their children's toy preferences; adults such as parents and other adults were rated as only somewhat influential. Similarly, Fulcher, Sutfin, and Patterson (2008) found that children with lesbian or heterosexual parents were not significantly different from one another in their knowledge of gender stereotypes or in their preferences in toys and activities. Notably, though, children with lesbian parents considered gender transgressions committed by boys (e.g., the idea of a boy wearing nail polish) to be less serious than did children of heterosexual parents.

In another study, R. Green et al. (1986) examined the favorite television programs, games, and toys of children of lesbian and heterosexual mothers and found no differences in these domains as a function of family structure. However, the authors did find that daughters of lesbian mothers were more likely to engage in "rough-housing" and to play with male gender-typed toys such as trucks and cars than were daughters of heterosexual mothers. With regard to career aspirations, Green et al. found that 95% of all boys, regardless of parent sexual orientation, chose traditionally masculine jobs. Daughters of lesbians, however, were more likely to aspire to traditionally masculine jobs (e.g., doctor, lawyer) compared with daughters of heterosexual mothers; 52% of the daughters of lesbians compared with 21% of the daughters of heterosexual mothers desired such careers. As the authors noted, this finding appears to indicate higher career aspirations among daughters of lesbian mothers—an arguably positive and adaptive characteristic. Perhaps this is a result of modeling: Their mothers may have been engaged in higher-status, "masculine" occupations or demonstrated higher career aspirations, which in turn shaped their daughters' career goals. Or perhaps their mothers' own enjoyment of both female- and male-typed activities led them to encourage their children to develop certain nontraditional interests or to pursue ambitious goals. Indeed, Kweskin and Cook (1982) studied heterosexual and lesbian mothers and found that women's own gendered role behavior was a better predictor of their desired gendered role behavior for their children than their sexual orientation: Women who were relatively androgynous in their interests and behaviors preferred, and therefore likely facilitated, more androgynous behavior in their children. Furthermore, a 2008 study by Sutfin, Fulcher, Bowles, and Patterson found that lesbian mothers showed less traditional (conservative) gender attitudes than heterosexual parents (e.g., they were more likely than heterosexual parents to feel that active play is just as acceptable for girls as for boys), and children of lesbian mothers, in turn, showed less traditional gender attitudes than children of heterosexual parents.

Other research has found that boys from lesbian-mother families may demonstrate less gender-typed behavior—but this may be more a function of parent gender than parent sexual orientation. MacCallum and Golombok (2004) studied 12-year-old children from lesbian-mother families ($n = 25$), single heterosexual-mother families ($n = 38$), and heterosexual two-parent families ($n = 38$) and found that boys in father-absent families tended to score higher on a femininity scale than did boys in father-present (i.e., heterosexual two-parent) families. There were no differences between the femininity scores of boys in single heterosexual-mother families and boys in lesbian-mother families. Additionally, there were no differences among boys from any of the three family types in terms of masculinity. Girls in the study did not demonstrate any significant group differences with regard to femininity or masculinity. The authors suggested that the mothers in single heterosexual-mother families and lesbian-mother families may be explicitly encouraging their sons to act in a more caring and sensitive manner than the stereotypical male. Such socialization may, arguably, have positive long-term effects: Men who possess an androgynous or gender-balanced orientation often enjoy better mental health and adjustment (Shimonaka, Nakazato, Kawaai, & Sato, 1997), score higher on tests of emotional intelligence (Guastello & Guastello, 2003), and are more involved as fathers (Russell, 1978; Sanderson, 2000), although, notably, they may also be vulnerable to teasing (Savin-Williams, 1998).

These studies, then, have suggested that children of lesbian and gay parents generally demonstrate gendered role behavior that is within normal limits, although some children may espouse greater flexibility in their interests and activities. That girls and boys develop normally with regard to establishing their feminine and masculine selves is unsurprising for several reasons. First, while lesbian and gay parents may be more likely to model or be accepting of gender nonconformity than heterosexual parents, they balance this orientation with concerns about accountability to others—for example, they express fear about how their children, particularly their sons, might be assessed by others (Kane, 2006). Such concerns may lead some lesbian and gay parents to guide their children's gender performance in such a way that their behavior will not be considered radical or deviant. Second, children's normative development of gendered roles is unsurprising given the pervasiveness of gender stereotypes in society. Peers, families, schools, and the media all serve as powerful socializing agents, reflecting and perpetuating gendered roles—and gender inequities—that are present in the broader society (Wood & Eagly, 2002). To the extent that children in lesbian- and gay-parent families perceive mild inconsistencies between the behavior, attitudes, and norms that are modeled in their families and in the broader social environment (e.g., their parents embrace and accept a broader range of behaviors than their peers), children will likely not, as critics have maintained, be "confused" but, rather, will simply assume a more balanced and arguably more adaptive repertoire of male and female qualities.

The cited studies have indicated that girls and boys in lesbian-mother families who demonstrate atypical gendered role behavior typically do so within socially acceptable limits. Their behaviors, interests, and orientations are not strictly "opposite-gender" in nature but are simply more gender-neutral and gender-balanced than are those of children in heterosexual-parent families. Nevertheless, the same researchers' data have been misrepresented to suggest that children are gender deviants (e.g., Cameron, 1999). Because society is less tolerant of gender nonconformity in boys (e.g., because of the association between femininity in boys and homosexuality; Connell, 1995; Kane, 2006), gender fluidity in the sons of lesbian and gay parents, in particular, may be cast as evidence of harm and deficit. Rather than being regarded as gender-balanced and well-adjusted, boys—specifically, boys with lesbian and gay parents—who demonstrate emotional expressiveness and other supposedly feminine characteristics may be denigrated for failing to achieve the hegemonic masculine ideal. Indeed, research suggests that boys who exhibit gender atypicality or nonconformity—characteristics that, again, are often stereotyped as related to homosexuality—are often vulnerable to abuse and ridicule by peers and adults (Savin-Williams, 1998), a finding that hints at the complex interconnectedness of sexism and heterosexism: Societal intolerance for gender-atypical behavior is a key component of heterosexism (Herek, 1986; Kane, 2006).

The sexual orientation of children of lesbian and gay parents has also been a topic of great interest. The current dominant view of research is that sexual orientation is shaped by a range of potential influences, beginning in the prenatal period. First, genetics seems to play a role, as demonstrated by studies that have shown that monozygotic (identical) twins tend to be more similar in sexual orientation than dizygotic (nonidentical) twins (Kendler, Thornton, Gilman, & Kessler, 2000). From this perspective, gay parents might raise gay children simply because of shared genetic material. Second, the prenatal hormone environment may also impact the development of sexual orientation (M. Hines, 2004), although more research is needed before firm conclusions can be drawn (Byne, 1997). Third, the social environment may be operative in the development of sexual orientation. Thus, because children of lesbians and gay men grow up in an environment in which same-sex attractions and relationships are not stigmatized, it is possible that they may feel more comfortable acting upon same-sex attractions, should they have them (Golombok & Tasker, 1996). Indeed, although the majority of lesbian and gay parents might prefer that their children assume a heterosexual identification as adults "because it's easier," they tend to be open to the possibility that their children may assume a range of potential sexual orientations (Costello, 1997; Nungesser, 1980).

The research to date, however, has been fairly consistent in suggesting that the children of lesbian and gay parents do not seem to self-identify as nonheterosexual at significantly higher rates than children of heterosexual parents. Huggins (1989) studied 36 adolescents (ages 13–19), half of whom had lesbian mothers and half of whom had heterosexual mothers. Only one child, the son of a heterosexual mother, identified as gay. Bailey, Bobrow, Wolfe, and Mikach (1995) studied 55 gay and bisexual men with sons ($n = 72$) of at least 17 years of age.[1] The authors found that more than 90% of sons were rated by their fathers as heterosexual and suggested that the finding is evidence against an environmental influence of gay fathers on their sons' sexual orientation.

Tasker and Golombok (Golombok & Tasker, 1996; Tasker & Golombok, 1997) compared 25 young adults who were raised by lesbian mothers with 21 young adults who grew up with heterosexual single mothers. The authors found no significant differences between the two groups in rates of self-reported same-sex sexual attraction. Furthermore, the large majority of young adults with lesbian mothers identified as heterosexual: Only two women from lesbian-mother households identified as lesbians, compared with none from heterosexual mother households. However, a significantly larger number of young adults with lesbian mothers reported that they had thought about the future possibility of experiencing same-sex attraction or having a same-sex relationship, compared with young adults with heterosexual mothers. They were also more likely to have had a relationship with someone of the same sex than young adults with heterosexual mothers (one son and five daughters from lesbian-mother families, compared with no children from heterosexual-mother families). Interestingly, young adults whose mothers had reported greater openness in demonstrating physical affection toward their female partner when their children were school-aged, as well as young adults

[1]Inevitably, some children of lesbian and gay parents do identify as gay, lesbian, or bisexual. However, it is important to note that these numbers do not tend to exceed population-based estimates (C. J. Patterson, 1997).

whose mothers had reported a higher number of same-sex relationships when their children were school-aged, were more likely to report same-sex sexual interest. According to the authors, this suggests that sexual orientation is influenced, at least in part, by social norms and social environment. By creating a climate of acceptance or rejection of homosexuality, parents may have some impact on their children's sexual experimentation. This is not to say, as Cameron (1999) concluded from these findings, that "homosexuality is learned, and therefore homosexual parents will very likely teach it" (p. 290). Rather, what these data suggest is that daughters of lesbians may experience a familial environment that is less stigmatizing of nonheterosexual attractions than that of daughters of heterosexual parents, and that environment may influence the degree to which they accept, and perhaps act upon, their own same-sex desires.

Reporting on data from this sample in their full-length book, Tasker and Golombok (1997) observed that girls raised by lesbian mothers had a higher number of sexual partners in young adulthood than daughters of heterosexual parents, whereas boys with lesbian mothers had fewer partners. Thus, in contrast to the children of heterosexual mothers, who tended to conform to gender-based norms, the children of lesbian mothers challenged gender-based norms. Lesbian mothers may be particularly likely to encourage exploration of sexuality in their daughters, whereas their sons, raised in families of women, may experience heightened consciousness of their status as males, which may facilitate greater cautiousness in their approach to and treatment of women.

While interesting theoretical and empirical questions can be explored by examining the intergenerational transmission of sexual orientation, treating sexual orientation as a relevant indicator of children's well-being per se is inappropriate, given that homosexuality is no longer considered a mental illness.[2] Even so, scholars typically have included child sexual orientation as an outcome in their research in light of continued public interest in the question of whether, as critics maintain, "gay parents make gay kids." While inclusion of sexual orientation as a child outcome is arguably justified at this stage, it should be clearly distinguished from other true mental health and well-being outcomes and accurately identified as one aspect of sexual identity development.

SOCIAL FUNCTIONING

In addition to studying gender identity, gendered role behavior, and sexual orientation in children of lesbian and gay parents, researchers have

---

[2]See, for example, the American Psychological Association's amicus briefs pertaining to various same-sex marriage cases: http://www.apa.org/psyclaw/issues.html.

also focused their attention on social functioning. Concerns that children raised by lesbian and gay parents will experience peer ostracism related to their parents' sexual orientation have been raised by judges and used as a rationale for denying custody to lesbian and gay parents (Stacey & Biblarz, 2001). In response to such concerns, researchers have investigated various dimensions of children's social functioning, namely, their social skills, their popularity, and how often they are the targets of bullying.

Golombok et al. (1983) compared the social functioning of 37 children of lesbian mothers and 38 children of heterosexual mothers (aged 5–17) and found that, according to parent reports, the two groups did not differ in the quality of their peer relationships. Only two children in each group were described as having significant peer problems, whereas about a third of the children were described as having some difficulties with peers (e.g., shyness, above-average frequencies of arguing). Similarly, Golombok et al. (2003) examined 7-year-olds' perceptions of peer relations and found no evidence that children of lesbian mothers viewed their peer relationships more negatively than children of heterosexual parents. R. Green et al. (1986) found no differences in self-perceptions of popularity in school-aged children of lesbian mothers and children of heterosexual mothers. Furthermore, there were no differences in parents' ratings of their children's sociability and peer acceptance. In their study of intentional lesbian-mother households, Gartrell et al. (2005) found that parents' ratings of their 10-year-old children's social competence were in the normal range compared with national age and gender norms; according to their biological mothers, 81% of children related well to their peers.

Vanfraussen, Ponjaert-Kristoffersen, and Brewaeys (2002) compared school-aged children from 24 intentional lesbian-mother households with children from 24 heterosexual-parent families and found no differences in the rates of teasing between the two groups. Children in both groups reported being laughed at, excluded, and called names; clothing, physical appearance, and intelligence (being "too" smart or being "stupid") were among the reasons for teasing in both groups. Family-related reasons for teasing were mentioned only by children from lesbian-mother families; however, 10 of 41 children of lesbian mothers had been teased about having two mothers, having a lesbian mother, not having a father, or being gay themselves. Thus, while the frequency of teasing was equivalent in both groups, the content of the teasing differed somewhat. Indeed, in evaluating these data, it is essential to remember that the experience of being teased is not at all specific to children with lesbian or gay parents: any atypical aspect of one's background, identity, or appearance can be the target of teasing in childhood (Brubacker, 2002).

Social functioning in adolescents has also been studied. For example, using data from a large national sample of adolescents, Wainright and Patterson (2008) found that according to both self and peer reports, adolescents with female same-sex parents (*n* = 44) and adolescents with hetero-sexual parents (*n* = 44) did not differ in the quality of their relationships with peers. Regardless of family type, adolescents whose parents described closer relationships with them reported having more friends and higher quality relationships with their peers.

A number of studies have examined teasing and bullying experiences in adolescents with lesbian and gay parents. Using data from a school-based survey, Rivers, Poteat, and Noret (2008) found that adolescents (ages 12–16) raised in families led by female same-sex couples were no more likely to be victimized than adolescents raised in families led by heterosexual couples. Similarly, MacCallum and Golombok (2004) examined 12-year-old children from lesbian-mother families, single heterosexual-mother families, and heterosexual two-parent families and found no differences among the groups in terms of mothers' worries about children's relationships at school or children's self-reported experiences of bullying.

Tasker and Golombok (1997) interviewed their sample of young adults (some of whom grew up with lesbian divorced mothers and some of whom grew up with heterosexual divorced mothers) about their bullying experiences in childhood and found that adult children from lesbian-mother families were no more likely to recall peer hostility or teasing than were adult children from heterosexual mother families. Within the group of individuals who were teased, however, the sons of lesbian mothers were more likely to remember having been teased about their own sexuality than were the sons of heterosexual mothers (mirroring Vanfraussen et al.'s 2002 findings that the content but not the frequency of teasing may differ for children of lesbian and gay parents). Given that hegemonic masculinity norms strongly prohibit male homosexuality in particular (Connell, 1992), perhaps boys with lesbian mothers are more likely to experience teasing about their sexuality than girls.

Some research has suggested higher frequencies of teasing and bullying than the above studies describe. The Gay, Lesbian, and Straight Education Network's (GLSEN's) 2008 study of LGBT-parent families' experiences in education found that 40% of the 154 students surveyed reported being verbally harassed in school because of their families (e.g., being called names such as "fag," "lesbo," and "devil's daughter"). Furthermore, although the vast majority of the students in the study identified as heterosexual, 38% of students reported being verbally harassed at school because of their real or perceived sexual orientation (i.e., they were assumed to be gay because their parents were gay; Kosciw & Diaz, 2008).

Importantly, studies have suggested that peer stigma and teasing among children of lesbian and gay parents may be more prominent at certain developmental periods and relatively minimal at others. Gartrell et al. (2000) found that 18% of mothers reported that their 5-year-old children had experienced some type of homophobia from peers or teachers. By the age of 10, almost half of the children had experienced some form of homophobia (e.g., teasing), suggesting that as children grow older, they may come into contact with teasing on a more frequent basis (Gartrell et al., 2005). Similarly, Ray and Gregory (2001) studied lesbian and gay parents and their children in Australia and found that no children in kindergarten through second grade had experienced bullying related to their parents' sexual orientation; 44% of the children in Grades 3 through 6 had experienced bullying (e.g., disparaging remarks, taunts); 45% of the children in Grades 7 through 10 had experienced bullying (typically, harsh put-downs); and 14% of the children in Grades 11 through 12 had experienced bullying. Children who did not encounter bullying typically attributed the absence of it to the geographical area that they lived in or the type of school that they attended (e.g., progressive private schools). Thus, as discussed in chapter 4 of this volume, middle-class and upper middle-class lesbian and gay parents may be at an advantage with regard to protecting their children from bullying. That is, education, socioeconomic status, and professional status can serve to mitigate lesbian and gay parents' oppression by enabling them to choose places to live that are safe from sexual orientation–related discrimination and to send their children to schools at which harassment related to their family structure is unlikely to occur. From the perspective of lesbian and gay parents, though, socioeconomic privilege serves to mitigate oppression more for White people than for people of color, who are vulnerable to harassment for reasons other than their presumed sexual orientation (Croteau, Talbot, Lance, & Evans, 2002).

Children's coping response to bullying may also vary as a function of developmental stage. In Ray and Gregory's (2001) study, younger children coped with bullying by talking with an older sibling or parent, getting other children to help, or telling a teacher. Children in secondary school also relied on these strategies; they also coped by ignoring their peers or fighting (some of the boys believed that fighting would help to fend off future attacks). In secondary school and beyond, children increasingly attempted to protect themselves from unwanted attention and bullying by hiding their parents' sexuality (e.g., not inviting friends over) and becoming more selective about whom they told about their families. Children in 11th and 12th grades also became increasingly likely to confront insulting language (e.g., words like "fag") directly by addressing the underlying issues at hand (e.g., pointing out that this is a degrading term to homosexual persons and not merely a general insult).

Ray and Gregory's (2001) study pointed to the importance of attending to developmental patterns in understanding rates of and responses to bullying. Their study provided some evidence that elementary school and junior high school (which coincides with preadolescence and early adolescence) may be the most difficult for children of lesbian and gay parents, but that by the later years of high school (mid-adolescence), fewer youth continue to experience bullying. Indeed, the rare(r) occurrence of bullying during the later years of high school in this study was consistent with general research on bullying suggesting that youths' self-reported victimization tends to decrease during the transition to adolescence (Pellegrini & Long, 2002; Sourander, Helstela, Helenius, & Piha, 2000). Such declines may in part reflect adolescents' greater maturity and independence (Pellegrini & Long, 2002). By mid-adolescence, youth are less susceptible to peer influence (Steinberg & Monahan, 2007). Notably, these developmental patterns in bullying parallel the reported concerns of sexual minority parents: LGBT parents of high school students tend to be less concerned about bullying than LGBT parents of elementary school and middle school students (Kosciw & Diaz, 2008).

More research is needed that clearly differentiates between victimization experiences in general and victimization specifically about one's parent's and/or one's own sexuality, because this distinction appears to be important (Tasker & Golombok, 1997; Vanfraussen et al., 2002). Furthermore, Ray and Gregory's study (2001), which considered children of varying ages, suggested that longitudinal research on children's experiences with bullying and victimization is needed. Such research will provide valuable insights into children's victimization experiences and coping responses at various developmental stages, which may in turn have implications for prevention and intervention efforts.

PSYCHOLOGICAL ADJUSTMENT

The psychological well-being of children of lesbian and gay parents has also been highlighted as an area of potential concern by some scientists and activists. The argument that children who are raised by lesbian and gay parents may be vulnerable to problems in psychological adjustment typically rests on several assumptions. First, children of lesbian or gay parents are assumed to experience greater peer victimization as a result of society's stigmatization of sexual minority families, which in turn may lead to lower self-esteem and increased risk of emotional and behavioral difficulties. Indeed, an association between peer victimization and mental health difficulties has been documented in the general population (Soulander et al., 2007). Thus, according to this claim, children are exposed to teasing as a result of societal heterosexism, and such experiences of victimization may in turn cause other difficulties. A second, very different type of claim is that children are at risk of higher levels of emotional distress simply as a function of living with lesbian or gay parents—that is, the experience of growing up with lesbian or gay parents is presumed to be inherently stressful (see C. J. Patterson, 1993). A third type of claim is that children raised by lesbian or gay parents are at risk of psychopathology by virtue of the fact that they lack a live-in male or female parent (Popenoe, 1993); such environments are regarded as deficient (indeed, the value of another same-sex parent in the home is often disregarded). Underlying the second and third types of claims, then, is the presumption that lesbian or gay parenting is inherently bad for children.

Such concerns have stimulated a number of studies aimed at exploring the mental health of children raised in lesbian- or gay-parent families. For example, in a study by Flaks and colleagues (1995), the psychological adjustment of children in lesbian two-mother households and children in heterosexual two-parent households (aged 3–9) was rated by their biological mothers and their teachers. Adults' ratings of children's emotional and behavioral adjustment did not differ by family type. Similarly, Erich, Leung, and Kindle (2005) examined the psychological adjustment of children (average age = 6.5 years) in lesbian adoptive-parent families, gay adoptive-parent families, and heterosexual adoptive-parent families, and they found no differences in emotional and behavioral adjustment, as rated by their parents, as a function of family type. Golombok et al. (2003) used a community sample to examine the social and emotional development of 7-year-old children and found that children in lesbian-mother families were no more likely to be classified as having a psychiatric disorder than children in heterosexual two-parent families and children in single heterosexual-mother families.

Studies of older children have also been conducted. Gartrell et al. (2005) found that 10-year-old children with lesbian mothers did not differ from population-based norms in terms of rates of emotional and behavioral problems; in fact, girls had somewhat fewer behavioral problems than would be expected. MacCallum and Golombok (2004) compared 12-year-old children in lesbian-mother families, single heterosexual-mother families, and heterosexual two-parent families and found that the groups did not differ in rates of emotional and behavioral problems. Finally, Rivers et al. (2008) found that 12- to 16-year-old children in families led by female same-sex couples did not differ from their same-age peers in families led by heterosexual couples in terms of their psychological functioning (e.g., depression, anxiety).

Some scholars have explored the factors that are associated with better adjustment among children of lesbian and gay parents. Chan, Raboy, and Patterson (1998) compared 7-year-old children conceived by donor insemination in lesbian-parent families and 7-year-old children in heterosexual-parent families and found that parents' sexual orientation was not associated with children's psychosocial adjustment: Children of lesbian mothers and children of heterosexual parents were equally well-adjusted. Rather, process-level factors were associated with children's adjustment, such that children in both types of families had more behavioral problems when parents reported higher levels of parenting distress and more dysfunctional partner interactions (e.g., more conflict in their relationships). Similar findings were also noted by Bos, van Balen, and van den Boom (2007), who studied school-aged children in intentional lesbian-mother households and heterosexual-parent households and found that family structure was not related to children's adjustment. Rather, parents—regardless of sexual orientation—who were highly satisfied with their partners as coparents rated their children as having fewer externalizing and internalizing problem behaviors. Again, these data suggest that sexual orientation does not moderate the relationship between parental relationship stability and child outcomes. That is, family processes may be more important than family structure in determining adjustment. Furthermore, these findings are consistent with the broader literature on heterosexual-parent families, which generally has found that children in unhappy, stressful, and conflict-ridden households experience poorer adjustment than children in stable homes (Abidin, Jenkins, & McGaughey, 1992; Erel & Burman, 1995).

Studies have also examined the factors that are associated with better adjustment among adolescents. Wainright, Russell, and Patterson (2004) used a large national sample (the Adolescent Health database) to examine psychosocial adjustment in adolescents in female same-sex and heterosexual-parent households and found that adolescents living with female same-sex parents did not differ from adolescents living with different-sex parents in terms of self-esteem, psychological adjustment (depressive symptoms and anxiety), academic achievement, or aspects of family relationships (e.g., parental warmth). Rather, teens' adjustment in both types of families was linked to relationship characteristics within the family, such as satisfying parent–adolescent relationships. Wainright and Patterson (2006) also used the Adolescent Health database to examine rates of delinquency and substance use among adolescents with female same-sex and different-sex parents and found no differences in these domains as a function of family type. Across the board, adolescents with closer relationships to their parents reported less delinquent behavior and substance use, underscoring the importance of process variables as opposed to structural variables in determining youths' mental health outcomes.

Other studies have focused on processes related to well-being that may be specific to lesbian-mother households. For example, Patterson (1995) examined 26 children (average age = 6 years) who had been born or adopted into lesbian two-mother households and found that children demonstrated better adjustment when biological and nonbiological mothers shared child care tasks evenly. In a study of 30 lesbian couples and their children, Chan, Brooks, Raboy, and Patterson (1998) found that it was nonbiological mothers' satisfaction with the division of labor, specifically, that was related to children's adjustment. Thus, their findings suggest that parents' subjective perceptions of the division of labor may be as important or more important than the actual division of labor in affecting children's well-being. Patterson's and Chan et al.'s findings are notable in light of prior research that suggests that lesbians are particularly likely to value and emphasize egalitarianism in their relationships (chaps. 2, 3, and 4, this volume). Thus, it is possible that the achievement of egalitarianism by lesbians who desire it may have an indirect positive effect on their children (e.g., by positively enhancing parents' well-being and satisfaction).

Children's peer relationships may also affect their well-being. In particular, perceptions and experiences of stigma in the environment have been linked to compromised well-being in children of lesbian and gay parents. For example, Bos and van Balen (2008) interviewed 8- to 12-year-old children in planned lesbian-mother families and found that children who perceived higher levels of stigmatization by peers experienced lower well-being (although, in general, children reported low levels of stigma). Specifically, girls who perceived high levels of stigma reported lower self-esteem, and boys who perceived high levels of stigma were rated as more hyperactive by their parents. Gartrell and colleagues (2005) interviewed 10-year-olds in planned lesbian-mother families and found that experiencing homophobia was associated with more emotional and behavioral problems, although on average these children did not experience more problems than would be expected in the general population. Similarly, Gershon, Tschann, and Jemerin (1999) conducted interviews with 76 adolescents with lesbian mothers (25 were born to self-identified lesbians; 51 were born in the context of a prior heterosexual relationship) and found that adolescents who perceived greater stigma related to having a lesbian mother had lower self-esteem.

Huggins (1989) also examined self-esteem in a small sample of adolescents, some of whom lived with their divorced lesbian mothers and some of whom lived with their divorced heterosexual mothers. She noted a tendency for children of lesbian mothers whose fathers were more rejecting of their mothers' lesbianism to report lower self-esteem than adolescents whose fathers had neutral or positive attitudes about their mothers' sexual orientation. Huggins also found that children who learned of their mothers' sexual orientation in adolescence tended to have lower self-esteem than those who found it out in childhood. Adolescence can be a particularly difficult time to learn of a parent's homosexuality or bisexuality (Baptiste, 1987), in that it is a key developmental transition during which youth experience significant biological, social, and psychological changes, as well as a time when peer acceptance is experienced as paramount. Of course, in the context of healthy, ongoing communication, parents and adolescents have an excellent chance of navigating this crisis of disclosure fairly smoothly.

Findings from the 2008 GLSEN survey suggest that perceived stigma and experiences of bullying may have deleterious effects on the academic functioning of adolescents with sexual minority parents. Specifically, the survey data indicated that students with LGBT parents who reported high levels of harassment at school were much more likely to report that they missed school because of feeling unsafe (Kosciw & Diaz, 2008). Thus, in addition to directly impairing adolescents' psychosocial well-being, being bullied may have indirect effects on academic achievement and educational outcomes, as when, e.g., a child stays home because of fear or anxiety, falls behind in school, and fails to advance academically.

CRITIQUE AND RECOMMENDATIONS

There are a number of problems—both methodological and conceptual—that characterize the research on children's sexual identity and social–emotional adjustment. Before reviewing these problems, however, it is necessary to emphasize that virtually all areas of psychological and sociological research are plagued by methodological and conceptual flaws: Many of the limitations that characterize the research on the children of lesbian and gay parents are not at all unique to this research area (Meezan & Rauch, 2005). Furthermore, studies on the sexual identity and adjustment of children with lesbian and gay parents are increasingly numerous and span several decades; thus, the extent to which researchers' findings are similar across studies and generations should inspire confidence in their validity.

The studies that have been reviewed were conducted largely with children of heterosexual divorced and lesbian divorced mothers; thus, household composition and parental sexual orientation variables are conflated (C. J. Patterson, 1997; Stacey & Biblarz, 2001), thereby precluding meaningful conclusions. In other words, study findings pertaining to child outcomes might be erroneously attributed to parental sexual orientation when in fact they could be a function of having endured parental divorce. Few studies have examined sexual identity and adjustment outcomes among children raised in intentional lesbian-parent families, or have compared the outcomes of children raised in intentional lesbian two-parent families with those of children raised in heterosexual two-parent families (e.g., Chan, Brooks, et al., 1998; Chan, Raboy, et al., 1998; Flaks et al., 1995). Such studies are necessary to isolate effects due to sexual orientation from effects due to parental divorce.

Moreover, few of these studies are longitudinal in nature. One exception is Tasker and Golombok's (1997) study of heterosexual-mother families and lesbian-mother families. The families in this study were interviewed when the children were age 10 and 24, on average. Another exception is Gartrell et al.'s (2000, 2005, 2006) longitudinal study of intentional lesbian-mother families. Gartrell and her colleagues have thus far completed assessments of these families prenatally and when the children were 2 years, 5 years, and 10 years old; additional follow-ups are planned. These longitudinal studies have provided unique insights into the developmental nature of family life; indeed, cross-sectional studies of children and families are limited in that they necessarily treat dimensions such as sexuality as if they were static entities that can be reliably measured at one point in time. More research that examines both lesbian and gay parents and their children over time is needed to (a) more fully describe the developmental trajectories of sexual identity, social functioning, and mental health, and (b) more fully elaborate the impact of changing parental behaviors, roles, and attitudes, as well as changes in family structure (e.g., the entrance or exit of a lesbian or gay stepparent) on changes in children's self-concept, identity, and well-being.

Another task for scholars is to tease apart the independent and combined effects of gender, sexual orientation, and heterosexism and to theorize more explicitly about all three, as opposed to just one or two, in their research on lesbian- and gay-parent families and their children. To more fully examine the effects of gender, much more research that includes children with gay fathers (especially intentional gay-father households) is needed, as demonstrated by the majority of studies reviewed in this chapter, which concern the experiences and adjustment of children raised by lesbian mothers. Ideally, studies will increasingly include children in both lesbian-mother and gay-father households, in order to more richly describe the unique and similar experiences of children raised in these two types of families. Furthermore, by including measures of perceived stigma and perceived community, neighborhood, and school climate, the effects of heterosexism (as distinct from the effects of parental sexual orientation per se) on child outcomes can be established. More specifically, by observing lesbian- and gay-parent families and children within their geographical context (e.g., attending to the laws, policies, and practices that govern adoption and marriage in their region), the role of broader social structures in perpetuating or countering heterosexism can be examined.

Qualitative research may play a key role in delineating in what ways children experience their parents' sexual orientation, their parents' gender, and heterosexism as having an impact on them, and which of these dimensions, alone or in combination, are perceived as shaping their lives, development, and identity. Specifically, where do children at various developmental stages perceive or experience the impact of their family structure? Do they perceive their own gender development as being affected? What about their political sensibilities? Furthermore, where do they locate the source of this impact? Do they locate it in their parents' sexual orientation, specifically? their parent's gender? their parents' values? (Goldberg, 2007a).

Greater consideration of how parents' sexual orientation and gender interact with other aspects of children's identity is also needed. For example, how do adopted children of lesbian and gay parents, particularly children not of their parents' race, negotiate their multiple minority statuses? Also of interest is how experiences of heterosexism, racism, and adoptism affect children's coping and mental health.

Finally, while comparative studies (i.e., those that include members of both lesbian- and heterosexual-parent households) are appropriate for answering particular types of questions, they may serve to either inadvertently or deliberately support heterocentric values and assumptions by suggesting that the heterosexual-parent family is the gold standard against which lesbian- and gay-parent families should be considered and evaluated. Studies that go beyond this framework to explore children's perceptions and experiences in their own right are needed. Toward this end, the next section of this chapter explores some of the experiences that are unique to children who grow up in lesbian- or gay-parent families. First, I discuss children's responses to and ways of coping with their parents' coming out. Second, I consider children's ideas about their family structure and their relationships with their family members and donors.

WHEN PARENTS COME OUT: CHILDREN'S EXPERIENCES AND REACTIONS

Children who grow up in planned lesbian- or gay-parent families often do not recall any single moment or event in which they learned of their parents' sexual orientation (Harris & Turner, 1986; Tasker & Golombok, 1997); rather, they experience a gradually increasing awareness and understanding of their parents' sexual orientation over time. This awareness is acquired through living in an environment in which parents and other members of the child's social network may openly discuss or allude to the parents' sexual orientation or the alternative nature of their family. Obviously, the depth and accuracy of children's understanding of what it means to be gay and to have gay parents varies as a function of developmental stage; thus, even if their parents never officially come out to them, many children will nevertheless have an aha experience about their parents' sexuality (e.g., suddenly realizing what it means to be gay, in a sexual way; suddenly realizing that their parents' gayness is the same gayness that is ridiculed on the playground).

For many children, however, their parents' sexual orientation is not a fact of life that they have lived with since birth or early childhood. Children who were born or adopted in the context of a heterosexual relationship, whose parents later come to identify as nonheterosexual (e.g., in the context of or after a divorce), may come to learn of their parents' sexual orientation in one of several different ways. First, some children are directly told by their parents: "I am gay." The timing of their parents' disclosure may be influenced by a variety of factors. For example, parents may come out to their children (a) when they feel their child is finally old enough to grasp the information; (b) in response to their child's request for information; (c) because they believe that their child might find out from another source, such as an ex-spouse; or (d) to explain or clarify a particular event such as a divorce (and related custody issues) or the beginning of a serious same-sex relationship (H. Barrett & Tasker, 2001; Lynch & Murray, 2000; West & Turner, 1995). Second, parents may disclose their sexual orientation to their children indirectly (e.g., by taking them to a gay social event, e.g., a family-oriented gay pride parade; Bigner & Bozett, 1990). Finally, other children may gradually come to grasp their parents' sexual orientation via clues in their environment (e.g., books on lesbian and gay issues) or in their parent's behavior (e.g., frequent outings with a close "friend"; Tasker & Golombok, 1997).

How do children react upon learning that a parent is gay? A range of reactions have been reported in the literature. Turner, Scadden, and Harris (1990) interviewed 10 gay fathers and 11 lesbian mothers about their children's responses to their coming out and found that 6 of 11 mothers reported that their children responded as though it was "no big deal," 4 reported that their child responded with confusion, and 1 reported a response of anger and shame. According to the gay fathers in the study, five of the eight children who knew of their fathers' homosexuality reacted "mildly," two were confused, and one responded with anger and confusion. Thus, slightly more than half of children had mild or neutral reactions. Harris and Turner (1986), however, interviewed 23 lesbian and gay parents about their children's reactions to their coming out and found that while initial reactions were varied, few were especially positive. According to parents, some of whom had multiple children, eight children showed confusion; six did not understand; five said they knew all along; three were worried; three expressed feelings of shame; two showed disbelief; two were overtly angry and displayed shock, guilt, and enhanced closeness to their parent, respectively. As the authors noted, "None showed sympathy, pleasure, relief, pity, or sadness" (p. 109). Children's current feelings, however, were perceived as less varied and were primarily neutral or positive: 11 were perceived as being indifferent, 8 were perceived as supportive, 5 were seen as confused, and 4 were viewed by their parents as angry, hostile, ashamed, and proud, respectively (1 each). Of course, given that parents do not always directly come out to their children, children's reactions are not always easily gauged. Rather, children may come to understand their parents' sexual orientation gradually over time, and thus their reactions may be unknown to their parents and may shift subtly over time (Tasker & Golombok, 1997).

Studies that examine the coming-out processes of transgender parents and, in turn, their children's reactions are beginning to emerge. In a rare study, S. Hines (2006a) interviewed 30 transgender persons, 7 of whom were parents, and noted that parents described their own coming out about their gender identity and their children's reactions in ways that were similar to lesbian and gay parents' descriptions. Parents told their children out of a desire to be honest and have a closer and more authentic relationship with them, and children tended to respond to their parents' coming out with initial distress, followed by gradual acceptance. Children of parents who transitioned from female to male were perceived by their parents as adapting more easily, perhaps because of greater cultural acceptance of female androgyny than male femininity.

Some children, then, do struggle with their parents' coming out. They may wonder what it means for them—for example, they may wonder whether their parents' gayness means that they will eventually be gay. They may also worry about peer discovery of their parents' sexual orientation and about potential harassment (Bigner & Bozett, 1990). Broadly speaking, they may struggle with reconciling the fact of their parents' homosexuality with the negative attitudes that they have internalized, or are at least aware of, by virtue of living in a heterosexist society. Notably, some studies have found that younger children tend to have the least difficulty accepting their parents' sexual orientation, whereas adolescents have the most difficulty (e.g., K. G. Lewis, 1980; Lynch & Murray, 2000), indicating that older children may have already absorbed more negative beliefs about homosexuality from the broader culture and are more aware of the social stigma surrounding same-sex relationships. Additionally, adolescents understand more about the sexuality involved in same-sex relationships and may be dealing with their own questions about their sexuality (A. Martin, 1998). Notably, some children and adolescents may not experience entirely negative or positive feelings about their parents' sexual orientation, but, rather, may regard it with mixed or ambivalent feelings. For example, children may be intellectually and overtly accepting of their parents' sexual orientation but may struggle on a deeper, more visceral level, because of their own emerging sexuality or because of their awareness of the stigma that surrounds nonheterosexual sexualities.

Regardless of how and when their parents came out, all children must negotiate whether and how to disclose to others about their families. Drawing from clinical experience as well as their own research findings (e.g., Bozett, 1980, 1987), Bigner and Bozett (1990) developed a framework for understanding how children of lesbian and gay parents seek to protect themselves from stigma related to their parents' sexual orientation. Bigner and Bozett suggested that children of lesbian and gay parents may use a number of controlling strategies to protect themselves from stigma. For example, children may use *boundary control* as a strategy for avoiding stigma. Boundary control consists of three components: (a) controlling the parent's behavior (e.g., asking the parent to behave in certain ways so as to conceal his or her sexual orientation); (b) controlling one's own behavior (e.g., refusing to appear in public with the gay parent and his or her partner); and (c) controlling others (e.g., not inviting friends over in order to keep them from discovering one's parent's sexuality). A second strategy that children may employ is *nondisclosure*: that is, children choose not to share the fact of their parent's sexual orientation with others. A final strategy is *selective disclosure*, or controlled disclosure to selected persons. The degree to which children use these controlling strategies depends on the child's developmental stage, how obvious they perceive their parent's sexual orientation to be, and whether they live with their gay parent (Bigner & Bozett, 1990).

Consistent with this framework, a number of studies suggest that upon finding out that a parent is gay, one of children's greatest concerns is that they will be ostracized if their parents' sexual orientation becomes widely known (Gabb, 2004b; Javaid, 1993; Lynch & Murray, 2000; Pennington, 1987; West & Turner, 1995); a related worry for them is that other people may assume that they are gay or will become gay (Pennington, 1987). Such concerns may in turn lead children to employ controlling strategies. For example, in their interviews with a small sample of lesbian and gay parents, West and Turner (1995) found that parents reported that their children rarely had friends over, and they speculated that this was due to concerns about how friends would respond to their parents' homosexuality (boundary control). Similarly, Ray and Gregory (2001) found that some adolescents attempted to protect their reputation and friendships by controlling where they saw their friends. Indeed, children whose gay parent lives with a same-sex partner or who have two gay parents may be especially cautious about bringing friends and dates home for fear of being discovered (Baptiste, 1987). When they do have friends over, they may lie about the identity of their parent's partner (e.g., referring to him or her as an uncle or aunt, roommate, best friend, godparent, nanny, or some other identifier) or avoid answering their friends' queries directly (Gabb, 2005; Javaid, 1993; Lynch & Murray, 2000).

Some studies have found examples of children using selective disclosure (Javaid, 1993; Ray & Gregory, 2001; Vanfraussen et al., 2002; West & Turner, 1995). The parents in West and Turner's (1995) study reported that their children sometimes told only a few close friends about their parents' sexual orientation, if they told anyone at all. Similarly, Vanfraussen et al. (2002) interviewed children aged 7 to 17 years from intentional lesbian-mother families and found that most children tended to share the fact that they had two mothers with their close friends but explained their family structure to other peers only if they were explicitly asked about it. Ray and Gregory (2001) also observed a tendency for some adolescents in their sample to engage in selective disclosure, particularly if they had had experiences with harassment in the past. Indeed, children may look for clues that peers are supportive before deciding whom they can safely tell about their parents' sexuality (Bozett, 1987). Selective disclosure also has been found in children with transgender parents. R. Green (1998) observed that children with transgender parents tended to be very careful regarding whom to tell about their parent's transition, telling only those friends who they felt were trustworthy and would not spread the information.

Of course, children who grow up with openly lesbian and gay parents will likely have less choice about whether or not to come out about their families, compared with children whose parents came out after having children in the context of a heterosexual relationship or children whose parents are closeted about their sexual orientation. For example, Gartrell et al. (2006) studied 10-year-olds raised in intentional lesbian-mother households and found that 57% of children reported that they were completely out about their families with peers, 39% were out to some of their peers, and 4% actively concealed information about their families from their classmates.

The Consequences of Secrecy for Children and Families

Because of the strong social stigma attached to homosexuality, children in lesbian- or gay-parent families may perceive the need for secrecy, to protect either themselves or their parents (Baptiste, 1987; Bigner & Bozett, 1990). Such secrecy, however, can negatively affect children and their families. Concealing fundamental aspects of one's family can lead to feelings of isolation and stress. Moreover, children's desire to keep their parents in a sense "hidden" may create tension among family members. Children may ask their parents not to hold hands in public, to avoid wearing gay-affirmative clothing, to come separately from each other to school events, and to sleep in separate rooms from each other when their friends come over. Parents, in turn, may be hurt or feel that they are being asked to compromise their integrity (James, 2002; Lynch & Murray, 2000; A. Martin, 1998). Ideally, parents will find a way to balance their own needs with sensitivity to their children's fears. For example, some parents, particularly parents of adolescents, may respect their children's preferences and may accommodate them, within reason (Lynch & Murray, 2000). Other parents, however, may resist hiding aspects of themselves, preferring to strategize with their children about how best to face various social pressures (James, 2002). They may also choose to frankly share their conflicted feelings with their children (James, 2002). Some sensitivity to how one's behaviors affect one's children, however, is optimal. Tasker and Golombok (1997) noted a tendency for young adults who felt that their mothers had been too open about their sexual orientation in front of their school friends to report more negative feelings about their family identity during their high school years. Young adults who felt that their mothers were sensitive to their need for discretion felt more positive about their family identity, likely because they felt that their mothers allowed them some control over the information.

Although a parent's coming out may be met with surprise, worry, and concerns about privacy from their children, this fact by itself should not be taken to suggest that (a) lesbians and gay men are placing an unfair burden on their children by coming out; (b) parents should avoid or delay their coming out in order to spare their children distress; or (c) children are destined to experience considerable and ongoing stress about their parents' coming out. Parents who foster honest and empathic communication with their children about their sexual orientation and who locate the source of the children's perceived "problem" in societal heterosexism and homophobia (rather than in their own nonheterosexual orientation) can help their children to accept and perhaps even embrace the changes that follow a parent's coming out.

CHILDREN'S IDEAS ABOUT FAMILY AND RELATIONSHIPS WITH FAMILY

Lesbian- and gay-parent families challenge heteronormative assumptions about the family as institution: namely, that the family is both heterosexual and patriarchal (Gabb, 2005; Perlesz et al., 2006). Furthermore, that members of lesbian- and gay-parent families are often not biologically related violates societal beliefs about the necessity of biological connections to family and kinship relations (Weston, 1991). Thus, their positioning outside of traditional norms and social structures may lead members of lesbian- and gay-parent families to think about and "do" family in ways that are creative, innovative, and fluid and which thereby shed new light on the nature and meaning of family (or, in Oswald, Blume, and Marks' [2005] language, they may "queer" the family). Even so, at the same time that they enact family in creative, novel, and complex ways that call attention to the distinction between family as institution and family as experience(d), members of lesbian- or gay-parent families are inevitably aware of and influenced by heteronormative discourses about family structure and relationships.

Given that children of lesbian and gay parents grow up within, and are therefore shaped by, the norms and influences of both their immediate family context and the broader social context, researchers are interested in how such children think about, define, and describe the meaning of *family* as well as their own personal family relationships. Several qualitative studies have explored this topic.[3] Perlesz et al. (2006) interviewed lesbian mothers and their children, some of whom had been born in the context of their parents' lesbian relationships and some of whom had been conceived in heterosexual relationships. Children expressed frustration with the lack of accepted and universally understood language to describe and define their family relationships. The absence of language was particularly challenging in the public domain, as children attempted to explain their families to school personnel, peers, and the like. Children encountered "semantic confusion over definitions of social and biological parenthood, donorhood and fatherhood" (p. 184) as they attempted to describe and represent their families. For example, one 5-year-old child was met with resistance as she attempted to explain her family to her school principal, who insisted that she must have a father, thus reinforcing dominant discourses about what constitutes a "real" family.

In presuming that all children have a father (even if absent or dead), adults like this principal are experienced by children as challenging the in-

---

[3]Many of the qualitative studies discussed in this section, as well as other sections of this chapter, were based on very small samples. These studies are extremely important in that they have provided rich descriptions of the perspectives and lived experiences of lesbian- and gay-parent family members, have shed light on potential interpretations of quantitative data, and have raised many ideas to be pursued in future research. However, it is inappropriate to generalize the data in these studies to the larger population of lesbian- and gay-parent families.

tegrity of their family units (S. E. Barrett, 1997). Such challenges create tensions that children negotiate in a variety of ways as they struggle to balance "dominant and subjugated discourses" about what it means to be a family (Perlesz et al., 2006, p. 187). For example, some children in Perlesz et al.'s (2006) study tended to define *family* in idealized and dominant terms (e.g., families are biologically related; families are headed by two adults) despite their lived experience in an alternative family form. This tension manifested itself in other ways as well. For example, some children easily defined their parents' partners as family; however, their awareness of normative conceptions of family constrained how they publicly described their families, such that their parents' relationships were sometimes rendered invisible. Adolescents in particular were highly aware of the social consequences of accurately naming their families, and thus they were particularly strategic and planful in how they defined their families. For example, the authors described a 14-year-old girl who, when filling out school forms, used an abbreviated form of her mother's partner's name (Rob, instead of Robyn) to make it appear that her mother was in a heterosexual and therefore more socially acceptable relationship.

Gabb (2005) also interviewed lesbian mothers and their children regarding their ideas about public representations of family. Like Perlesz et al. (2006), Gabb found that children struggled with the absence of language to describe their family relationships (e.g., the nonbiological mother or stepparent relationship). Interestingly, Gabb noted a tendency for children to resort to terms of friendship, as opposed to family, in describing their nonbiological mothers or their mothers' partners, thus avoiding the struggle of trying to fit these relationships into the heterosexual familial lexicon. Children who did define their nonbiological mothers as family relied on awkward terminology such as "second mother," or described them as "like a dad." Such reliance on hierarchical orderings and familiar parental identifiers illustrates that children structure their family relationships in ways that are constrained by but also expand on traditional gendered notions of parenthood. Furthermore, children's use of such language reveals the power of language in creating, perpetuating, and legitimating social inequalities: In the absence of language to describe their relationships, lesbian- and gay-parent families are diminished and rendered as "not real" families.

In addition to understanding how children of lesbian and gay parents think about their families and familial relationships, it is also important to gain insight into how they enact their family relationships as well as the dynamics that characterize these relationships. Several empirical studies have examined children's and adolescents' perceptions of their family relationships. In one study, 8- to 16-year-old children in intentional lesbian-mother families and heterosexual two-parent families were interviewed about various aspects of their family relationships (Vanfraussen, Ponjaert-Kristoffersen, & Brewaeys, 2003a). The authors found that in heterosexual-parent families, most children preferred to talk about emotional issues with their (biological) mothers as opposed to their fathers; however, no differences were found in lesbian-parent families, such that children were no more likely to talk with their biological mothers about emotional topics than with their nonbiological mothers. Regarding expressions of affection, 84% of children in heterosexual-parent families and 76% of children in lesbian-mother families showed equal affection (e.g., hugs, kisses) to both parents; the remaining children in both types of families were somewhat more affectionate toward the (biological) mother. The fact that approximately a quarter of children of lesbian mothers tended to demonstrate more affection toward their biological mother is intriguing and warrants further research. In some ways, it mirrors the findings of Goldberg, Downing, and Sauck's (2008) study on parents' perceptions of their toddler-aged children's parental preferences (see chap. 4, this volume). In Goldberg et al.'s study, a minority of children continued to prefer the biological mother during early childhood, which was typically interpreted as related to the biological mother's greater time spent with the child or to some aspect of the biological bond. These preferences sometimes caused interparental tension and jealousy. It would be useful to know how the mothers and children in Vanfraussen et al.'s (2003a) study might interpret and explain such differences in affection (i.e., do they understand them in terms of the biological connection between parent and child?) and, in addition, whether these differences are the source of conflict between parents.

Some research has also been conducted on the family relationships of adolescents in lesbian stepfamilies. In their longitudinal study of lesbian-mother and heterosexual-mother families, Tasker and Golombok (1997) found that young adults who spent time living in lesbian-mother stepfamilies tended to report better relationships with their mothers' new partners during adolescence than young adults living in heterosexual stepfamilies. Tasker and Golombok (1997) found that lesbian mothers' adolescent children tended to report better relationships with their mothers' new lesbian partners than heterosexual mothers' teenagers in regards to their mothers' new husbands or boyfriends. They were also more likely to view their mothers' partners as another parent, as opposed to just their mothers' girlfriend or a stepparent. Most of the lesbian mothers in the study had previously been married to men, and apparently it was easier for their children to incorporate female parental figures into their families because these women were not regarded as competing with or acting as replacements for their absent fathers.

Donor Relationships

Although biogenetically related to their offspring, sperm donors may have only symbolic relationships to the children whom they sired and to the lesbians who parent these children. Thus, donors occupy an interesting and ironic space within the lesbian-parent family: They are partly responsible for the child's existence but may have little to no social relationship to the child, a fact that both parents and children must negotiate throughout the child's development.

Research suggests that lesbian mothers who choose known donors for their children often do so with the awareness or desire that their child may have a relationship with the donor as he or she grows older (see chap. 3, this volume). However, only a few studies have explored how children in intentional lesbian-mother households think about and relate to their donors as they develop. Gartrell et al. (2006) interviewed lesbian mothers of 10-year-olds and found that among the 27 children with known donors, about half saw their donors regularly and half saw them occasionally. Thirteen of these children considered their donors to be fathers and therefore referred to them as "Dad." Twelve other children had "yes" donors—that is, they knew that they could eventually learn the identity of and possibly meet their donors when they were 18. These children were nearly evenly divided between regretting that they had to wait until they were 18 ($n = 5$) and not caring about the potential meeting ($n = 7$). Of children with unknown donors ($n = 48$), 70% had no regrets about not having a father.

Vanfraussen, Ponjaert-Kristoffersen, and Brewaeys (2003b) interviewed 41 children aged 7 to 17 years (average age 10 years) who were born into lesbian-parent households by means of unknown donor insemination. Children were questioned about whether they wanted to know more about their donors, as well as their motivations for wanting or not wanting more information. The authors found that 54% of the sample was satisfied with donor anonymity and did not have any desire to know more; 19% wished for nonidentifying information only; and the remaining 27% wished for identifying information (e.g., they wished to find out more about the donor by personally meeting him). Children who showed no interest in gaining more information about the donor often expressed their concerns with regard to their nonbiological mothers; that is, the idea of gaining more information was seen as disloyal or unnecessary. It is possible that such concerns may reflect children's sensitivity to parental ambivalence about the role of the donor; indeed, parents sometimes prefer less contact by the donor than the donor himself prefers (Hertz, 2002). Children who expressed a desire for more information (identifying or nonidentifying) were motivated primarily by curiosity. No differences in terms of adjustment, self-esteem, or relationships with parents were found between children who sought donor information and children who did not.

Some researchers have recently begun to examine whether having a known or unknown donor has an impact on children's developmental outcomes. Gartrell et al.'s (2006) study of intentional lesbian-mother households found that children with known donors were no different from children with unknown donors in terms of social and behavioral adjustment or outness about their families. Bos and Hakvoort (2007) also conducted a study of children (aged 4–8) raised in intentional lesbian-mother households, 42 of whom had a known donor and 58 of whom had an unknown donor. The authors found that donor type did not affect children's overall level of behavior problems. However, boys and girls in families with known donors had more social problems as reported by their mothers. Bos and Hakvoort suggested that, to the extent that donors are involved in the children's lives, it may be confusing for children to spend time in more than one home. Alternatively, the presence of a third party might be difficult for the nonbiological mother of the child; the effect on parenting satisfaction might, in turn, affect child adjustment. Similarly, parents may directly or indirectly communicate ambivalence or discomfort with the donor's role, causing children to experience distress over their conflicting loyalties (Vanfraussen et al., 2003b). The authors also found that mothers of children with unknown donors reported higher levels of stigmatization based on their family structure (e.g., annoying questions, feeling excluded). They suggested that this finding may reflect and arise from societal notions that it is better to have a mother and a father than two mothers.

CONCLUSIONS AND RECOMMENDATIONS

The research in this area has suggested that children and adolescents with sexual minority parents develop normally. Children with lesbian and gay parents may have more expansive and more flexible notions of gender; they also may be more open to the possibility of a same-sex relationship. Furthermore, they may be more likely to be teased because of their family structure at certain points in their development, although this research is inconclusive. Nevertheless, P. Cameron (1999), P. Cameron and Cameron (2002), and other critics of lesbian and gay parenting have argued that children of lesbian and gay parents are unfairly exposed to negative experiences (e.g., bullying) as a function of their parents' sexual orientation and that these experiences are so severe as to warrant denying lesbian and gay parents adoption, custody, and visitation rights. However, as Brubaker (2002) pointed out, most of the negative experiences that children of lesbian and gay parents encounter "may be interpreted as secondary consequences of living in an atypical household" (p. 331). That is, experiences of being teased, and a resultant desire to conceal some aspect of one's family, are not specific to children with nonheterosexual parents. "At any point in childhood, having a clearly atypical background can lead to teasing or bullying. . . . [T]his pattern . . . seems to be universal" (p. 332). Indeed, children of divorce, children of single parents, children with mixed-race parents, and children with disabled parents may also be exposed to social censure. Thus, the fact that children may be teased as a result of social intolerance is not sufficient justification to deny sexual minorities the option of parenting. As Clarke (2001) pointed out, the responsibility for stigma lies not with lesbian and gay parents but with the individuals and social institutions that legitimate and perpetuate it.

Much of the research in this area reflects the experiences of children with lesbian mothers. In part, this trend reflects actual demographics: There are more children living with lesbian mothers than with gay fathers (Gates, Badgett, Macomber, & Chambers, 2007). That said, there are likely other reasons for the paucity of data on children of gay fathers and transgender parents. One reason might be that accessing these populations may be more challenging, in that they are smaller in number and may therefore be more hidden. Researcher biases and assumptions may also play a role; for example, the notion of gay men parenting may be even more foreign than the notion of lesbians parenting. However, the absence of research on children of gay fathers in part reflects a larger problem, namely, that researchers have rarely studied adoptive lesbian- and gay-parent families, relying more often on samples of children who have been conceived by insemination and children who were born in the context of heterosexual relationships. Thus, more research on adopted children with lesbian and gay parents is also needed.

Child care workers, school personnel, social workers, family therapists, and human service professionals are encouraged to take steps to reduce stigmatization of lesbian- and gay-parent families and to actively create a climate of acceptance and inclusion of these families. School educators and administrators, for example, are encouraged to seek out ongoing training and education about diverse families (e.g., through the GLSEN). They can become advocates of diverse families and can actively fight prejudice against children resulting from their parents' sexual orientations.

Educators can create "safe spaces" at their schools by visibly marking places and people that are "safe" for children with lesbian or gay parents (as well as sexual minority students themselves). This is usually accomplished via with a pink triangle sticker or some other easily identifiable gay-affirmative symbol. When students, staff members, and teachers place these stickers on their bags, offices, or lockers, it indicates that they are safe to approach for support or guidance. Educators can also train student allies who wish to be involved in building safe spaces and creating a more affirmative school climate. School personnel may also wish to educate the larger school community about the importance of maintaining safe spaces for all students affected by antigay bias.

Pediatricians and other medical professionals who work with lesbian- and gay-parent families should be prepared for potential challenges faced by these families during key life transitions (e.g., when children enter day care or preschool) and can talk with parents about how to discuss their family constellation with their child's teacher or day care providers (Perrin, 1998). Indeed, entry into the school setting may bring new challenges. It may also be helpful for pediatricians to be knowledgeable about parenting books, resources, and groups specifically for lesbian- and gay-parent families.

In chapter 6, I explore the perspectives of adults with lesbian and gay parents. Although few studies have addressed the experiences of these adults, the research that does exist provides important insights into questions such as these, among others: How do adults with lesbian and gay parents come out about their families, and what factors do they consider in doing so? How do adults with lesbian and gay parents perceive themselves as having been impacted by their family structure? What benefits and disadvantages, if any, do adults believe they have experienced as a function of growing up with lesbian and gay parents?

PRACTICAL RESOURCES

Young Children

Book: Aldrich, A. R. (2003). *How my family came to be—Daddy, papa, and me.* Oakland, CA: New Family Press.

Summary: Narrated from the perspective of a school-aged child, the book shows how his family was created and that families are made up of people who love each other. Ages 3 to 6.

Book: Wilhoite, M. (1991). *Daddy's roommate.* Boston: Alyson Books.

Summary: A young boy discusses his divorced father's new living situation, in which the father and his gay roommate share eating, doing chores, playing, and living. Ages 2 to 8. Winner of the Lambda Literary Award.

Book: Newman, L. (1990). *Heather has two mommies.* Boston: Alyson Publications.

Summary: This book is about a child, Heather, raised by two lesbian mothers: her biological mother, Jane, who gave birth to her by alternative insemination and her nonbiological mother, Kate. At Heather's playgroup, her family situation is discussed in simple and positive terms, as are those of other children in nontraditional family units (e.g., children with single parents).

School-Aged Children and Adolescents

Book: Snow, J. (2004). *How it feels to have a gay or lesbian parent: A book by kids for kids of all ages.* Binghamton, NY: Harrington Park Press.

Summary: In this book, 32 individuals, ranging in age from 7 to 31, reflect on the experience of having a gay or lesbian parent (e.g., their initial reactions to their parent's coming out; dealing with the combined issues of parental divorce and a parent's coming out).

Web site: http://www.colage.org (Children of Lesbians and Gays Everywhere)

Summary: Children of Lesbians and Gays Everywhere (COLAGE) is a San Francisco–based organization that has weekly programs and activities for local individuals. There are 51 COLAGE chapters in 30 states, the District of Columbia, and Canada, which serve multiple functions, including providing safe spaces and peer-based opportunities for learning and advocacy. Many youth access COLAGE via the Web site, which provides advice and resources, and via the listservs, which are maintained by the site (e.g., there is one for children of LGBT parents who identify as LGBT themselves, there are several for various age groups).

Film: Spadola, M. (Director). (1999). *Our house* [video]. New York: First Run Features.

Summary: This documentary explores what it's like to grow up with gay or lesbian parents, by profiling the sons and daughters of five families with varied racial and religious backgrounds (e.g., African American, Latino, and White; Mormon, Christian, and Jewish) who illustrate some of the diversity of America's gay- and lesbian-parent families.

6

YOUNG ADULTS AND ADULTS
WITH LESBIAN AND GAY
PARENTS SPEAK OUT

As illustrated in chapter 5, the most common source of information about children of lesbian and gay parents is parents themselves. Children may provide information about themselves, their experiences, and their perspectives (e.g., Gabb, 2005; Vanfraussen, Ponjaert-Kristoffersen, & Brewaeys, 2003a, 2003b), but more commonly it is their parents who provide data on their functioning. This is largely because young children lack the emotional and cognitive maturity to respond accurately to questions about their behaviors, well-being, and adjustment. Furthermore, when children of lesbian and gay parents are interviewed, their responses may be constrained not only by their developmental level but also by concerns about the implications of what they say. For example, they may shy away from difficult topics (e.g., being teased about their parents' sexual orientation) or experience real or perceived pressure to paint an overly positive picture of their lives as the son or daughter of an lesbian or gay parent (Garner, 2004), for fear that the researcher, the media, or society will draw unfair conclusions about the negative impact of gay parenting on children. This burden, while heavy, may be lifted somewhat when these children reach adulthood and perhaps feel freer to speak about their experiences and opinions regarding their past and present. Furthermore, as adults, they possess greater emotional and intellectual maturity and may therefore have particularly valuable insights to share.

Thus, while studies that explore the perspectives of lesbian and gay parents and their children are clearly of great value, such studies are ideally supplemented by research on adults raised by lesbian and gay parents, whose viewpoints have rarely been considered. Indeed, although there are potential problems with the use of retrospective reports in research (e.g., memory errors; Hardt & Rutter, 2004), exploration of adults' reflections on their experiences in growing up with lesbian or gay parents is arguably worthwhile in that the purpose of such studies is not to supplant the data provided by children and their parents but to supplement them. Such studies may not only provide important insights into how adults reflect on their youth but may also shed important light on the reality of these individuals' lives as adults—that is, how they, as adults, continue to relate to and be affected by their families of origin. Life course theory, which emphasizes the lifelong interaction of individuals and their social contexts, considers the social networks in which individuals live and develop (e.g., one's family, one's spouse) to be contexts in and of themselves (Elder, 1998a). Families of origin, then, continue to represent relevant contexts of development and identity, even as individuals age, move away, and establish independent lives and relationships. Of interest is how adults view their families as influencing and having influenced them as they move into adulthood and beyond.

The current chapter, then, privileges the voices and perspectives of young adults and adults with sexual minority parents. Very few studies have explored adults' perspectives. Specifically, Goldberg (2007a, 2007b), Joos and Broad (2007), Kuvalanka (2007), O'Connell (1993), and Saffron (1998) have conducted studies on adults raised by lesbian, gay, and/or bisexual (LGB) parents. In a study of 46 adults (36 women, 10 men) with at least one LGB parent, Goldberg (2007a) explored adults' perceptions of how their membership in a nontraditional family structure influenced them in adulthood—in particular, with respect to their attitudes and behaviors regarding gender, sexuality, kinship, and community. Goldberg (2007b) interviewed 42 adults (33 women, 9 men) with at least one LGB parent.[1] The goal of this study was to understand the context and predictors of adults' disclosure regarding their parents' sexual orientation. Joos and Broad (2007) conducted e-mail interviews with 26 adult women, whose parents all had experienced heterosexual divorce and then had come out as nonheterosexual. Their study focused on these women's coming-out stories and their experiences in negotiating "family closets" (p. 287) as children. Kuvalanka (2007) interviewed 30 young adults between the ages of 18 and 25 who lived with at least one lesbian

---

[1]The sample in Goldberg 2007a overlaps with the sample in Goldberg 2007b.

parent during adolescence, with the goal of understanding participants' experiences in navigating heterosexism and homophobia in adolescence. Half of her participants were from divorced families (their lesbian mother had come out in the context of or after a divorce), and half were from intentional, planned lesbian-mother families. O'Connell (1993) interviewed 11 individuals (6 women, 5 men), ages 16 to 23, with lesbian mothers, in an effort to explore "the impact of a divorced mother's lesbian orientation on her children" (p. 281). Finally, Saffron (1998) interviewed 17 adults with lesbian mothers in an effort to understand what benefits or advantages participants associated with growing up with lesbian mothers. The findings of these studies form the basis of much of this chapter. An effort is made here to highlight participants' reflections on their childhood experiences as well as their current experiences. Additionally, questions are raised and future research directions are proposed throughout.

COPING WITH HETEROSEXISM

As the previous chapter details, some children of lesbian and gay parents report experiences of teasing and rejection related to their family structure. Importantly, research with adults suggests that they also recall incidents of heterosexism and homophobia during childhood and adolescence (Goldberg, 2007a, 2007b; Joos & Broad, 2007; Kuvalanka, 2007). However, adults' distance from these events, as well as their greater maturity, permit new and important reflections and insights regarding their experiences of these events, as well as their strategies for coping with heterosexism. Kuvalanka (2007) found that many of the participants in her study recalled incidents of heterosexism and homophobia. Specifically, more than three fourths of participants reported witnessing or experiencing heterosexism and homophobia at the institutional level (e.g., in their schools; in the local, state, or federal government; in religious institutions). For example, participants felt that school curricula regularly reinforced institutional heterosexism by avoiding any reference to same-sex relationships or sexuality (e.g., in health education classes) as well as any mention of alternative families (notably, these participants' experiences are consistent with the finding of the Gay, Lesbian, and Straight Education Network [GLSEN] study (2008) that less than a third each of students and parents reported that the school curriculum included representations of lesbian, gay, bisexual, and transgender [LGBT] people, families, history, or events; Kosciw & Diaz, 2008). Participants in Kuvalanka's study also recalled teachers and school staff who were explicitly tolerant of homophobic slurs (e.g., failing to reprimand students who made gay jokes and at times even making homophobic comments themselves). Participants who witnessed such acts by staff and teachers recalled a growing awareness of the reality that adults—who were supposed to be protecting the children in their care and in their classrooms—were often the engineers and enforcers of institutionalized heterosexism and homophobia. In turn, this awareness led some participants to closet their families out of fear of harassment and censure.

In addition to institutionalized heterosexism and homophobia, the vast majority of Kuvalanka's (2007) participants also reported witnessing or experiencing heterosexism and homophobia on the part of peers. Most participants recalled overhearing general homophobic slurs and negative comments about gay people. Additionally, more than half of participants confronted heterosexism more directly. Some recalled peers making heterosexist assumptions about their family structures or relationships, and others recalled teasing or harassment during their childhoods. Such incidents caused participants to experience feelings of vulnerability and marginalization and, in turn, to limit disclosures about their family structure. Interestingly, and consistent with the findings of Ray and Gregory (2001), participants who experienced significant feelings of vulnerability related to their family structure during middle school often reported feeling less fear later in their adolescence, that is, during high school, although a minority actually reported feeling more exposed and vulnerable (e.g., because of their increasing involvement in political activism, or their involvement in student activities and organizations that related to gay issues).

Kuvalanka (2007) found that experiences of heterosexism were not limited to interactions with peers. More than half of participants recalled heterosexist treatment from members of their extended family. Some participants recalled hearing family members (e.g., among adults with divorced lesbian mothers, their heterosexual fathers) make disparaging remarks about their lesbian mothers. Others simply recalled being aware of family members' disapproval of their mothers' sexual identity or lesbian partnerships. Some participants in Goldberg's (2007b) study, in recalling similar incidents, wondered whether such negative reactions from family members might have influenced their own initial reactions to their parents' sexual orientation. For example, in explaining his early shame about his gay father, one man in Goldberg's study emphasized that his stepfather had a "very negative attitude about homosexuals" (p. 113).

Studies of adults' perspectives suggest a range of factors that may facilitate resilience in the face of stigma and heterosexist discrimination. For example, Goldberg (2007b) observed that participants who grew up in intentional lesbian-mother families, as well as families in which their parents came out to them when they were very young, often recalled an atmosphere of open communication about their parents' sexual orientation and their "unique" family structure. The fact that their parents were LGB was constructed as normal and healthy, but at the same time their parents warned them about the stigma attached to these identities, thereby helping them to prepare for the questions that they would ultimately face from peers, teachers, and neighbors. Thus, an environment that simultaneously emphasized openness and realism was recalled as instrumental in helping them to cope effectively with heterosexism.

Perceived social support from family members is likely also important in fostering strength and resilience in the face of heterosexism. Many participants in Kuvalanka's (2007) study expressed gratitude toward their biological kin (parents, siblings, adult relatives) as well as nonbiological kin (e.g., "aunties," lesbian friends of participants' mothers) for the support that they provided during trying times. Some family members, such as their mothers and their mothers' partners, served as models of resilience and empowerment, whereas other family members simply distinguished themselves by "being there" for participants when they experienced fears of or actual victimization. Relationships with good friends were also cited as important in buffering the stress associated with heterosexism. In particular, relationships with other children of lesbian and gay parents helped participants to feel less vulnerable and alone. In the presence of other children with lesbian and gay parents, participants could talk openly about their families without fear of negative reactions or consequences. Awareness of sexual minorities in general (e.g., among their teachers or parents' friends) also helped participants in Kuvalanka's study to feel less isolated during childhood and adolescence. Similarly, Goldberg (2007b) found that knowing other sexual minorities and living in a progressive or gay-friendly community were perceived by participants as offsetting potential feelings of shame and stigma surrounding their parents' sexual orientation.

Indeed, factors such as geographical location, urbanicity, and the presence or absence of a gay community may all play powerful roles in shaping the experiences of children (and adults) with lesbian and gay parents. In particular, the degree to which children are aware of other families like their own, have opportunities to meet and interact with children with sexual minority parents, and are aware of a gay presence in their communities may shape their own feelings about having lesbian or gay parents and their ability to be resilient in the face of homophobic encounters.

COMING OUT ABOUT FAMILY: ADULT EXPERIENCES AND PERSPECTIVES

As highlighted in chapter 5 of this volume, coming out about one's family is often challenging for children and adolescents because doing so may invite unwanted attention, teasing, and rejection. Consequently, some youth prefer to conceal their parents' sexual orientation out of concern for their own and their families' privacy and social standing. How the disclosure practices of children of lesbian and gay parents continue to unfold past young adulthood merits exploration. Adults possess more control over whether, who, and when they tell others about their parents' sexual orientation; moreover, their motivations for disclosure or nondisclosure may differ from those of children. Even though most adults no longer live with their lesbian or gay parents (and therefore no longer feel required to come out), they may not feel comfortable allowing others to maintain the heteronormative assumption that everyone has a mother and a father, and they may therefore feel compelled to make "political disclosures," that is, disclosures to promote social change through education and consciousness raising (Cain, 1991a, 1991b). Alternatively, some adults might simply be motivated to disclose in the context of more intimate relationships, in that self-disclosure is itself an act of intimacy and functions to both deepen and maintain relationships (Sprecher & Hendrick, 2004). Of course, some adults may choose not to tell anyone about their family structure because of their own internalized homophobia or the homophobia of those around them.

To explore these possibilities, Goldberg (2007b) conducted a study of 42 adults with one or more LGB parents in an effort to explore adults' prior and current disclosure patterns and their subjective motivations for disclosure or nondisclosure. Several themes emerged concerning participants' perceived motivations for disclosing about their families in adulthood. Almost half of the sample reported that they were open about their families in part because they felt a sense of duty or obligation to educate others about LGB-parent families, family diversity, and sexual diversity. They often disclosed about their family structure in the context of confronting homophobic remarks and speaking up about current events or political matters such as same-sex marriage and gay adoption. Such purposeful disclosures may function to foster a sense of power over their situation (Corrigan, 2005). Other participants noted that coming out about their families functioned as a litmus test in that it allowed them to gauge whether a person was someone they wanted to get to know better or not. That is, they sometimes came out about their families in order to determine whether the individual at hand was a true ally. Also, for some adults, being open and honest about their family structure was experienced as important in light of how closeted their families were when they were children. Although such closeting was often perceived by participants as necessary (e.g., to ensure their own or their family's safety), growing up in a culture of secrecy had made them intolerant of dishonesty, and now, as adults, they required truthfulness in their interpersonal relationships. Just as sexual minorities often come out because of a psychological need for authenticity (and a need for relief from hiding; Herek, 1996), these individuals felt compelled to own their difference and make up for years of hiding. Said one woman in Goldberg's (2007b) study:

> I realized how damaging it was for me to have to hold, as a young girl, that much secrecy. I felt afraid to tell men I was dating about my family. Because I was afraid they would probably think I'm going to be a lesbian. Or I might, if they marry me, I might be that. There was a lot of fear

around that. Now it feels like something that I don't want to keep secret. It's definitely an up front kind of thing. I don't know, maybe it's my way of announcing to the world what I wasn't able to when I was younger. (p. 120)

Finally, several participants reported feeling that their parents' sexual orientation was irrelevant and said that they preferred to keep it to themselves unless absolutely necessary. They did not appear to avoid disclosure out of fear of a negative reaction, but, rather, they simply did not view their parents' sexual orientation as a central or defining feature of their own identity. These individuals disclosed only in situations in which they anticipated that someone might find out (i.e., preemptive disclosure), or they did not disclose at all.

Thus, for some adults with sexual minority parents, their parents' sexual orientation may cease to feel relevant, either because they do not experience it as a salient aspect of who they are or they may simply live far away from or not have a close relationship with their parent(s). But many adults do inevitably continue to encounter situations and contexts that prompt them to deliberate about whether to come out about their parents. Sometimes these situations are quickly and easily negotiated, and sometimes they are more complex. For example, in planning a wedding, adults must consider the reality and implications of their parent's sexual orientation. Should they include their parent's partner in the program? How should they handle seating? What about pictures? Is it "safe" to invite colleagues? How will one's fiancé/fiancée's parents, family members, and friends handle the situation? This is just one of many situations that may require careful thinking about how to handle the ifs, whens, and hows of coming out about a lesbian or gay family member.

Notably, both Goldberg (2007b) and Joos and Broad (2007) documented a pattern whereby many participants "move[d] from younger days of fear, harassment, and secrecy to more adult experiences of independence and openness about their parent(s)' identity" (Joos & Broad, 2007, p. 286). This movement from silence to openness may in part reflect these individuals' developmental status, such that, as adults, the possibility of rejection is perhaps not as feared or as likely. Furthermore, some adults may also purposefully surround themselves with like-minded, "progressive" individuals, a strategy that may further reduce the chance of negative reactions to their coming out (Goldberg, 2007a, 2007b). Such increased openness on the part of these adults may also reflect historical factors: Most of the adults in these studies (who, in the early years of the 21st century, when they were interviewed, ranged in age from 20 to 50) grew up in the 1960s, 1970s, and 1980s, a time when gay parenthood and nonheterosexuality were arguably less visible and less accepted in mainstream society than they are today.

More research is obviously needed to explore how adults with sexual minority parents handle coming out at different stages of the life cycle. For example, situations that bring together family of origin with members of one's friendship network, members of one's partner's family, and so on (e.g., weddings, graduations) may prompt disclosure about one's family structure. Additionally, having or adopting children may also prompt adults to be more out about their families (e.g., as their parents become grandparents and perhaps take on an active child care role). Of course, many factors will shape the degree to which adults are out about their parents, regardless of their stage in the life course. For example, if a person's parents are unpartnered or in a heterosexual relationship (e.g., for those with bisexual parents), it may seem irrelevant or even strange to announce their sexual orientation to friends and colleagues. Similarly, parents' preference to remain closeted might inhibit disclosure by their adult children to the latter's social network.

(HOW) DOES IT MAKE A DIFFERENCE? PERCEIVED INFLUENCES OF GROWING UP WITH LESBIAN OR GAY PARENTS

From a social constructionist perspective, it is difficult to believe that having sexual minority parents would fail to have any impact on individuals' perceptions of themselves, their relationships, and the world that they live in (Oswald, Blume, & Marks, 2005). Several studies have examined the broad question of how growing up with LGB parents shapes individuals' identities, choices, and values, both as children and as adults. Both Saffron (1998) and Goldberg (2007a) addressed adults' perceptions of how they had been influenced by growing up with sexual minority parents. Saffron was specifically focused on adults' perceptions of the advantages of being raised by a lesbian mother, whereas Goldberg was interested in adults' general reflections about how growing up in an LGB-parent family had affected them as children and as adults. Several other studies (e.g., Kuvalanka, 2007; O'Connell, 1993) also addressed aspects of adults' perceptions of their parents' influence, to a limited extent. Findings from these studies, taken together, form the basis for the next section.

Tolerance of Differences

Participants in Goldberg's (2007a), Kuvalanka's (2007), O'Connell's (1993), and Saffron's (1998) studies emphasized that growing up with sexual minority parents had facilitated their capacity to tolerate differences among peoples and to embrace diversity. Specifically, many participants in these studies described themselves as open-minded, nonjudgmental, and accepting of differences. They highlighted their acceptance of a range of lifestyles, types of families, cultures, religious beliefs, and political standpoints, and they viewed these characteristics in the context of growing up in a society that judged their parents, their families, and them. That is, the experience of being in families that were marginalized and that challenged societal norms facilitated their openness and empathy toward people who were different from them. Stated one woman in Goldberg's (2007a) study:

> I think knowing from a very early age what it is to be different or not, to be like the mainstream or not accepted . . . that gives me an understanding that people just come from so many different walks of life and that respect and an open mind and encountering the world with love and flexibility is definitely how I live my life. I just don't judge. Well—that's not true. I have biases and I make assumptions, but I work very hard to try and be honest about those and try and be reflexive about who I am. This is what my mother taught me. (p. 555)

In addition to sensitizing individuals to general issues of difference and discrimination, growing up with sexual minority parents also affected some participants on a more personal level, heightening their sensitivity to and awareness of homophobia and heterosexism (Goldberg, 2007a; Saffron, 1998). These men and women were highly aware of the ways in which their families were misrepresented or simply not acknowledged in the news and media, and they took note of the assumptions made by friends, acquaintances, and strangers with regard to families, homosexuality, and LGBT issues (Goldberg, 2007a).

Yet to be examined is how such tolerant attitudes with regard to homosexuality and other forms of difference shape adults' life choices and trajectories across the life course. For example, do they motivate adults to pursue careers that are oriented toward reducing social inequities and promoting social justice? Do these sorts of attitudes have intergenerational impact— that is, do adults with sexual minority parents teach their children similar values of tolerating differences and appreciating diversity? In support of this possibility, a rare qualitative study of 16 lesbian grandmothers found that women who perceived their children as being accepting and supportive of their sexual orientation described fewer concerns about their grandchildren's comfort with their sexuality (Orel & Fruhauf, 2006). These grandmothers trusted that their children had appropriately educated their own children about sexual diversity (or would do so, when the time was right), such that learning of their grandmothers' lesbianism would be a relative nonissue. More research that privileges the voices of members of multiple generations is clearly needed to more fully describe and understand the intergenerational relationships of sexual minority family members.

Transforming Enactments of Family and Community

In addition to espousing particularly tolerant attitudes concerning diversity and diverse groups, adult children of sexual minority parents may also perceive themselves as having broad ideas about and definitions of family and community. For example, participants in both Kuvalanka's (2007) and

Saffron's (1998) studies explicitly named nonbiological kin (e.g., lesbian step-parents) as family, thereby rejecting the notion that genetic or legal ties are necessary or sufficient criteria of family membership. Some participants in Goldberg's (2007a) study articulated their sense that their very definitions of family had been "queered" or transformed by their growing up experiences: That is, they spoke of a "queer orientation" to families and community, feeling that, for example—echoing terminology introduced by Weston (1991)—"chosen family is what matters" (Goldberg, 2007a, p. 557). By recognizing the power of both biolegal and chosen kin, these individuals created families and communities that challenged conventional notions of kinship and family relatedness.

Individuals' experiences growing up in a lesbian- or gay-parent family, then, may continue to shape their ideas about and behavioral enactment of family as adults. These experiences may also influence individuals' perceptions and enactment of community. Although adult children of sexual minority parents have the freedom to disidentify with LGBT issues and the gay community, they may nevertheless continue to see themselves as members of this community. For example, about half of the adults in Goldberg's (2007a) study continued to view themselves as part of the gay community. These individuals were what Garner (2004) labeled *culturally queer*: Having been shaped by the gay cultural context in which they grew up (i.e., a context defined by shared values and beliefs and community gatherings), they sought to maintain this sense of belonging as adults. This was particularly evident in their friendship networks (which often included nonheterosexual people) and their jobs and hobbies (which often included LGBT activist organizations and activities). And yet, because their family background and personal history were not transparent, some participants found that their interest in and identification with the gay community was sometimes questioned on the basis of their heterosexual identification. This caused them to wonder whether they really belonged and were entitled to claim a culturally queer identification and to experience feelings of uncertainty or tension about their true place within the community. One woman talked about her partial membership in the gay community:

> I have been trying to become more a part of the gay community, like participating on a Pride planning committee, but that is hard. I go to a meeting, and I have to out that I am straight. I just have a gay mom, but I grew up in a gay culture. I feel like I belong, but over and over I can't and I don't. I feel like I have to both apologize for my privilege and meekly ask to participate, when I have 32 years of participation in the gay community! (Goldberg, 2007a, p. 557)

More research is needed that explores how adults with sexual minority parents negotiate their membership in multiple and sometimes contradictory communities. That is, what does it mean to be heterosexual and to possess heterosexual privilege but to have invisible roots to the gay community? What are the effects of being ousted from a community that one has participated in since childhood? For example, to what extent does this precipitate feelings of "cultural homelessness" (Garner, 2004)? Indeed, heterosexual adults with sexual minority parents may feel marginalized and excluded from both mainstream and gay communities. More research is needed to explore individuals' experiences in negotiating these tensions.

Transforming Sexuality and Gender

Another area that may be transformed or "queered" by virtue of having sexual minority parents is adults' attitudes about sexuality and gender. Consistent with the findings on children and adolescents (e.g., R. Green, Mandel, Hotvedt, Gray, & Smith, 1986; Tasker & Golombok, 1997), Goldberg (2007a) found that many adults felt that having sexual minority parents had led them to develop less rigid and more flexible notions and ideas about sexuality and gender. Specifically, almost a third of the participants in this study noted that as adults, they enjoyed relatively fluid ideas about sexuality (e.g., they viewed sexuality as on a continuum and viewed a range of attractions as normal), which they attributed to their experiences growing up with nonheterosexual parent(s). Similar findings were observed by Saffron (1998), who found that participants often held the view that there was more than one acceptable sexual identity and expressed discomfort with sexual binaries and labels. Furthermore, in both Goldberg's and Saffron's studies, several participants voiced their sense that having nonheterosexual parents had influenced their ability and willingness to think deeply about their own sexuality and to understand it in more complex and nuanced ways.

Regarding gender, Goldberg (2007a) observed that about half of the sample emphasized the impact that having nonheterosexual parents had on their attitudes about gender and relationships. As adults, they felt that they were more comfortable with gender nonconformity than they might have been if they had been raised in a more traditional family environment. It is important that most of these individuals had grown up with lesbian mothers; in turn, their responses indicated that they viewed their freedom from gendered roles in the context of growing up with strong, feminist women, as opposed to lesbian women, specifically. For example, sons of lesbians observed that growing up with strong female parents encouraged them to be more sensitive, to feel free to pursue stereotypically unmasculine interests (e.g., dancing), and to value capability in female partners. Daughters noted that having strong women as mothers encouraged them be self-confident and independent and to pursue stereotypically unfeminine careers and interests, thereby extending R. Green et al.'s (1986) finding that daughters of lesbian mothers tended to have higher (more masculine) career aspirations than daughters of heterosexual mothers. Furthermore, participants also indicated that growing up with nonheterosexual parents had led them to emphasize egalitarianism in their own adult relationships. They engaged in what Oswald et al. (2005) called *complex gendering*, in that they resisted gender stereotypes and strove for relationships in which both members were free to be who they were without gendered role constraints.

Here, again, it is interesting to consider potential intergenerational effects. Individuals raised by sexual minority parents who espouse more expansive definitions and embodiment of gender and sexuality may raise children with more complex ideas about gender, sexuality, and family (Goldberg, 2007a; Oswald et al., 2005). Specifically, they may be vigilant about introducing their children to a full range of activities and interests, modeling gender nonconformity in their approach to housework and paid work, teaching their children about family diversity, and ensuring that their children are exposed to a range of family types. Research is needed to examine how adults with sexual minority parents aim to socialize their own children with respect to gender and sexuality.

TOUGH ISSUES:
UNDERSTUDIED AREAS, IMPORTANT INSIGHTS

The limited work on adults with sexual minority parents has exposed several important and somewhat controversial topics. While scientific inquiry has generally steered clear of these issues, their salience in the lives of children of sexual minority parents suggests the need for more research in these areas.

"Protecting Our Families"

Several authors have observed that adult children of sexual minority parents, in recollecting their youth, often describe their heightened awareness of societal scrutiny of their families (Garner, 2004; Goldberg, 2007a; Kuvalanka, 2007; O'Connell, 1993). Some adults recall feeling as though they grew up under a microscope, with the media lens carefully poised to capture any sign that they or their families were dysfunctional or maladjusted. For example, some participants in Goldberg's (2007a) study recalled that as children, they were sensitive to the fact that when lesbian and gay parent families were featured in the news or other media, considerable attention was paid to the children in these families. Specifically, the adjustment and well-being of these children was treated as a barometer for how the parents were doing, and, in turn, as an indicator of whether they deserved to be parents. Consequently, these participants recalled feeling some pressure to succeed as children of lesbian or gay parents, in order to discredit homophobic and antifamily stereotypes of sexual minorities. Such pressure sometimes made them cautious about acknowledging areas of difficulty (e.g., in interactions with teachers and guidance counselors, in interviews with reporters) out of concern that any admission of normative child or adolescent struggles might be framed as pathological and attributed to their parents' sexual orientation.

Children, of course, are not the only ones who are sensitive to media depictions of lesbian- and gay-parent families. Their parents are also sensitive to such issues, a fact that children may be highly attuned to. Indeed, some children may be particularly reticent to talk to their parents about difficulties that they are experiencing if these difficulties (e.g., teasing at school) are related to their parents' sexual orientation (Garner, 2004). They may not wish to upset their parents by suggesting that their peers are not nearly as tolerant as their parents may believe or hope them to be. Such concerns may lead children, as Garner (2004) observed, to present one reality to their parents (things are fine) while they are living another (they are being teased at school). Children may do this out of a desire to protect their parents from their experiences, because they do not wish to appear unsupportive. However, youth who internalize the need to present their lives as "normal" both outside of and within their own families carry a heavy burden. This burden may be particularly heavy during adolescence, when, as Garner (2004) pointed out, many youth—regardless of their parents' sexual orientation—just do not like their parents very much.

Children of lesbian or gay parents, then, understand that being seen as "well-adjusted" involves emotional stability and normal social functioning. They are also likely sensitive to the notion that the term *well-adjusted* itself implies a heterosexual identification. This sensitivity may lead the minority of youth with nonheterosexual sexualities to "play it straight" during their adolescence and early adulthood (Garner, 2004). For example, several participants in Goldberg's (2007a) study delayed their own coming out because of concerns about how this might be received by family members, friends, and the public. They were hesitant, even fearful, about the possibility of confirming the "gay parents raise gay kids" stereotype. In a few cases, these anxieties were exacerbated by their parents' reactions to their coming out: that is, their parents directly or indirectly expressed concern about the possibility of confirming right-wing ideological arguments that gay parents raise nonheterosexual children.

Thus, aware of the potential implications of their self-presentation, children with sexual minority parents may consciously or unconsciously strive to represent themselves as successful, psychologically healthy, and heterosexual. Of concern is whether these individuals hide or minimize personal struggles and challenges (e.g., depression, anger at their parents) because of the pressures of proving how normal they are. Alternatively, children with sexual minority parents may resist the real or perceived pressure to be poster children and respond by acting out (Kuvalanka, Teper, & Morrison, 2006).

Sexual Minority Young Adults With Sexual Minority Parents

As indicated in chapter 5, there is not a great deal of evidence to suggest that children of lesbian and gay parents are more likely than children of heterosexual parents to identify as lesbian or gay themselves. However, some children of nonheterosexual parents do inevitably come to identify as nonheterosexual. While researchers tend to acknowledge and perhaps briefly comment on these individuals, their experiences have not been subject to in-depth exploration. Indeed, Stacey and Biblarz (2001) argued that researchers have "deflected analytic attention" from the differences in sexual attitudes and behaviors between children of lesbian and gay parents and children of heterosexual parents (p. 171).

There are several possible reasons why scholarship has not focused on nonheterosexually identified children of lesbian and gay parents. Relatively little research has been done with children of lesbian and gay parents in general, and even less research on children of bisexual and transgender parents exists. Researchers are therefore only beginning to conduct studies that examine the lives of the majority of children with lesbian and gay parents (i.e., heterosexual-identified children). Moreover, some researchers may be wary of highlighting the experiences of "queer children of queer parents" for fear that critics of lesbian- and gay-parent families will use the research as evidence for the argument against gay parenting (i.e., gay parents make their children gay; Stacey & Biblarz, 2001). As a result, however, the experiences of this perhaps doubly marginalized group of children with nonheterosexual parents who identify as nonheterosexual themselves are overlooked, and many questions are left unanswered. For example, what is it like to identify as nonheterosexual when one's parents are also nonheterosexual? What is it like to come out to one's parents, friends, extended family, and community? How do nonheterosexual individuals with nonheterosexual parents experience heterosexism and homophobia in relation to both themselves and their parents?

The research that has explored these issues from the perspectives of adults with sexual minority parents is very limited. Kuvalanka and Goldberg (in press) explored the perspectives of 18 adults (ages 18–35) with LGB parents who ultimately identified as LGBT. Both authors independently conducted studies (discussed and referenced earlier) on the experiences and perspectives of adults with sexual minority parents. In conducting their research, they noted that several of their participants identified as nonheterosexual. Specifically, of the 46 individuals whom Goldberg (2007a) interviewed, 8 identified as lesbian, bisexual, transgender, or queer,[2] and of the 30 participants in Kuvalanka's sample, 13 identified as gay, bisexual, transgender, gen-

---

[2]Two participants were ultimately dropped from the analysis because they were much older than the majority of participants.

der-ambiguous, or queer.[3] The two authors collaboratively examined the narratives of these participants and identified a number of themes and experiences that were present in both sets of data, despite the fact that participants in the two studies were asked very different questions and neither study was explicitly designed to explore the perspectives of nonheterosexual adults with nonheterosexual parents. These themes were primarily oriented around experiences of coming out and being out and coping with heterosexism and homophobia.

About half of the adults in the combined sample expressed their sense that they had discovered their own sexual orientation and sexual identity earlier than they would have if they had grown up with heterosexual parents. They were careful to note that their parents did not make them gay; rather, they emphasized, it was their parents' acceptance of nonheterosexuality that made it possible for them to come out earlier. They felt that they would have identified as LGBT regardless of who their parents were. Having LGB parents, though, helped them to avoid the feelings of shame and confusion that they might have experienced if they had not been exposed to the notion that a range of sexual orientations can be considered normal and acceptable. As one woman noted, "We grew up with it being normal for some people to be gay. If I hadn't had queer moms, it might have taken me a lot longer to come out as queer." And yet, as discussed previously, some adults did delay their own coming out, not wishing to validate or confirm critics' "worst fears," namely, that gay parents produce gay children.

Most adults recalled expecting that it would be easy to come out to their parents, because they themselves were gay. Consistent with these expectations, most parents reportedly expressed acceptance and understanding when their children came out to them. However, several adults voiced unhappiness about how their parents had responded to their coming out. For example, the parents of several participants were described as seeming disappointed or concerned (e.g., they asked if they had done anything to cause their child's homosexuality or transgender identification), in this way revealing their own internalized homophobia as well as their concerns about negative reactions from friends, family members, and society. Participants who ultimately came out as transgender were particularly likely to report unsatisfying reactions from their parents, feeling that their lesbian mothers simply did not really understand or feel comfortable with the idea of transgender identification. Finally, some parents expressed concerns that their

---

[3]It is important to emphasize that these two samples are likely not representative of the broader population. That is, the relatively large proportion of participants in these studies who identified as LGBT likely reflects the methodology used to recruit participants. Namely, individuals who are more identified with the LGBT community—because of their parents, and possibly themselves—are more likely to be affiliated with organizations such as COLAGE. In turn, sampling strategies that rely on such organizations for participants will likely yield samples of adults with LGBT parents that are more open about their parents' sexual orientation and, possibly, who are more likely to identify as LGBT themselves.

children would experience the same challenges that they had endured as a result of homophobia, and for that reason they couldn't help wishing that their children were heterosexual, as it would be easier for them.

In some cases, parents' fears about social censure and stigma were realized. Participants did experience homophobia and heterosexism as a function of both their parents' sexuality, and their own. Furthermore, some participants recalled that extended family and friends often responded to their coming out by suggesting that their homosexuality, bisexuality, or transgender identification might be attributed to or blamed on their parents. This kind of feedback caused participants to feel a range of mixed emotions, including increased feelings of protectiveness for their parents, anger and frustration, and disempowerment and marginalization.

Some participants purposefully did not come out until they reached adulthood, despite their own growing awareness of their sexuality (Kuvalanka, 2007; Kuvalanka & Goldberg, 2008). Acutely aware of the heterosexism and homophobia that they faced because of their parents, they did not wish to commit social suicide by announcing their own nonheterosexual sexual orientation. Indeed, several adults came out about their parents as a means of deflecting attention away from their own sexual identity. Others joined organizations such as their schools' gay–straight alliances, where they could claim an interest by association while safely and privately exploring what it might be like to come out. Importantly, LGBT young adults with LGBT parents who are open about both their sexual orientation and their family structure may be particularly vulnerable to harassment: In the GLSEN survey, students with LGBT parents who also identified as LGBT experienced higher levels of victimization at school than youth with LGBT parents who did not identify as LGBT (Kosciw & Diaz, 2008).

Transracially Adopted Young Adults With Sexual Minority Parents

As discussed in previous chapters, there is little research on adoptive lesbian- and gay-parent families. Furthermore, almost no published data to date explore adopted young adults' perspectives on growing up with lesbian or gay parents. One exception is a study being conducted by Drs. Mark Gianino and Abbie Goldberg. This ongoing exploratory study focuses on the perspectives and experiences of young adults (ages 15–21) who are the adoptive children of lesbian or gay parents and who are of a race different from that of one or both of their parents. The study richly documents the complex nexus of identities that characterize transracially adopted young adults with lesbian or gay parents and points to many important new areas for future research.

As of this writing, 14 in-depth interviews have been conducted. These interviews have generated a number of initial themes. One particularly interesting theme that emerged is the changing salience of race in these youths' lives over time. In their descriptions of their younger school years (e.g., elementary, junior high), youth tend to recall less identification with their race and also less attention to or understanding of the difference between their race and that of their parents. This period of less identification is often followed by a period of wishing that their parents were of the same race as they (which parallels the tendency for some adopted children to wish that their adoptive mother had in fact given birth to them; D. Brodzinsky, personal communication, June 16, 2008). Similarly, in middle school and junior high school, youth often wished that their parents were of a different sexual orientation, or at least struggled with this wish. In late high school, college, and beyond, participants recall feeling more identified with their race and more aware of the challenges of having parents of a different racial identity. Furthermore, as they grew older, they became more comfortable with their parents' sexual orientation and more proud of them.

Most of the youth who were interviewed reported that their parents had involved them in the gay community when they were younger (e.g., gay parent support groups, gay parent family picnics). From youths' perspective, their parents could more easily identify with and engage in gay-oriented support networks than they could transracial adoption- and adoption-oriented support networks, although the latter were often found within the gay community. Some youth, however, did recall that their parents made active efforts to incorporate their racial background into their activities and lifestyle (e.g., through food, music, and festivals). As these youth grew older, they recalled struggling with feeling connected to their racial background, in spite of or in the absence of such activities, although most said they felt their parents supported their racial identity.

Importantly, participants recalled much more teasing regarding their parents' sexual orientation than regarding their adoptive status or racial background. In particular, boys with little exposure to lesbian or gay supports seemed to experience the most harassment, mainly in the form of teasing from peers (e.g., being called names such as "faggot" and "homo") and negative treatment (e.g., "weird looks" by teachers). This finding is consistent with data obtained by Ryan and Cash (2004), who surveyed lesbian and gay adoptive parents (whose children varied significantly in age) and found that according to parents, children were more likely to have been teased because of their parents' sexual orientation than their adoptive status.

CONCLUSIONS AND FUTURE DIRECTIONS

The research reviewed in this chapter suggests that privileging the voices of adults with sexual minority parents may reveal important insights regarding the experiences of both youth and adults with LGB parents. Furthermore, the research indicates that as adults, individuals with LGB parents continue to have experiences that are unique to their family structure (e.g., they must debate the practical and relational consequences of coming out about their families—and, sometimes, themselves). And finally, the research points to ways in which individuals' ideas about gender, sexuality, and family have been queered, or transformed by virtue of having LGB parents. In turn, there is the possibility that this queering may reverberate in individuals' social networks, such that their friends,' partners,' and children's ideas and attitudes are also queered.

The research in this area is largely qualitative in nature, permitting in-depth exploration of understudied aspects of adults' experiences. Nevertheless, more quantitative studies are needed. Studies that compare adults raised by sexual minority parents with adults raised by heterosexual parents should use matched samples: That is, participants should be matched for age, race, and geographical location. Additionally, samples should be matched on the basis of the age of participants when their parents divorced; or, if adults raised in planned two-mother families are studied, these individuals should be matched to adults who grew up in heterosexual two-parent households.

As in many studies, all of the studies discussed here used nonprobability (convenience) samples, rather than probability samples such as those used in large-scale national opinion surveys. This fact must be considered in evaluating the findings presented in this chapter. It is likely that the adults in these studies did not speak for the population of adults with LGB parents as a whole. There is clearly a need for a broader range of participants in this area. For example, there is a need to consider the perspectives of adults who do not necessarily identify as an "adult child of an LGB parent"—that is, adults who do not view this aspect of their family structure as a key aspect of their core identity. These adults would be unlikely to volunteer for such studies even if they happened to hear about them. Thus, the perspectives of these adults might be obtained in the context of larger, more general studies (e.g., those that aim to investigate adults' relationships with their parents and families of origin).

The existing research in this area (as well as the research discussed in chap. 5, this volume) suggests that youth and adults with sexual minority parents often possess unique strengths and adaptations. Nevertheless, they are vulnerable to the effects of societal heterosexism. In childhood, they are inevitably more vulnerable to teasing and harassment. Moreover, adults with sexual minority parents also face societal heterosexism. They risk alienation from friends, supervisors, and colleagues when they disclose details about their family structure. They may be told that talking about their families is inappropriate in the workplace (thereby revealing the power of heteronormativity). Practitioners who work with adults with sexual minority parents should be sensitive to the ways in which their clients' growing-up experiences may have shaped their identities; at the same time, they must be careful not to assume that having sexual minority parents is inevitably tied to or responsible for every challenge (or strength) that clients report. Also, more generally, practitioners will benefit from considering broader and more inclusive notions of family and community. Adults with sexual minority parents may not initially present as such; thus, given that they are a relatively invisible minority group, it is important that professionals avoid making assumptions about family structure or implying that certain family forms are more legitimate than others.

PRACTICAL RESOURCES

Adults with LGBT Parents

Book: Garner, A. (2004). *Families like mine: Children of gay parents tell it like it is.* New York: HarperCollins.

Summary: This book draws from Garner's experience as the daughter of a gay man and as an activist in the gay community, as well as her interviews with more than 50 adult sons and daughters of LGBT parents. It describes the ways in which the experiences of children with LGBT parents are both similar to and different from those of children with heterosexual parents.

Film: Gilomen, J. (Director). (2007). *In my shoes: Stories of youth with LGBT parents* [video/DVD]. San Francisco: Frameline.

Summary: This documentary was produced by the Children of Lesbian and Gay Parents Everywhere (COLAGE, Youth Leadership and Action Program) and provides first-person narratives of five young people whose parents are LGBT. In this film, they share their views on topics ranging from same-sex marriage to what it means to be a family.

7

CONCLUSIONS AND
FUTURE DIRECTIONS

This volume has thus far reviewed the research and contemporary issues concerning lesbian and gay parenting. In this final chapter, I briefly (a) summarize the major research findings on this topic; (b) highlight the major content areas that are in need of further research; (c) revisit some of the major methodological problems and challenges in the research that were discussed in chapter 1 and offer suggestions for how to improve future research; and (d) offer some concluding thoughts.

SUMMARY OF MAJOR RESEARCH FINDINGS

Although most same-sex couples lack access to the many rights and benefits that accompany legal relationship recognition, many female and male same-sex couples appear to enjoy satisfying long-term committed relationships. The strength and endurance of these relationships is particularly notable in light of the many challenges that same-sex couples continue to face in society. Currently, institutionalized forms of heterosexism continue to deny lesbians and gay men legal recognition of their partner relationships, legal recognition of their relationships with their children, equal access to job opportunities, and many other basic rights. But social change is occurring, as evidenced by recent legislation concerning same-sex couples' right to relationship recognition. Given such change, how will access to the rights and benefits that accompany legal relationship recognition influence sexual minorities' relationships and the gay community at large? Will lesbians and gay men in committed, legally sanctioned relationships enjoy measurable benefits with regard to their emotional, psychological, and physical well-being, compared with lesbians and gay men in committed but legally invisible relationships? How will sexual minorities who believe that marriage is a patriarchal, outdated, and undesirable institution respond to sexual minorities who choose marriage for themselves? That is, will marriage ultimately create schisms within the gay community? These are important and interesting questions that future researchers can and should pursue.

Also of interest is how legal relationship recognition might impact lesbians and gay men who choose to become parents. The research on the transition to parenthood for same-sex couples indicates that while their experience of becoming parents is in many ways similar to that of heterosexual couples, they face unique social, legal, and political barriers that make the process more stressful. For example, they confront the possibility of heterosexist treatment by health care providers, the potential inability to protect both partners' legal relationship to their child, and widespread resistance to and disapproval of their desire to parent. Marriage would provide same-sex couples with greater emotional and financial security and, in theory, require institutions such as hospitals, fertility and medical centers, and adoption agencies to treat them the same as married heterosexual couples. More widespread access to coparent and second parent adoption rights would also likely have a tremendous effect on lesbians' and gay men's transition to parenthood. Specifically, in granting both partners legal parentage, such legislation might indirectly impact same-sex couples' psychological and relational well-being during a key life transition, specifically by validating and protecting both partners' equivalent relationship to their child. This possibility can be empirically studied, for example, by comparing same-sex couples who have access to such rights with those who do not, on a variety of indicators of perceived equality and well-being, across the transition to parenthood.

The research suggests that lesbians and gay men possess numerous strengths as parents. For example, they have greater freedom with regard to creating their roles as parents, as well as the potential for greater equality with regard to dividing up paid work and family work. Similarly, the research has been consistent in suggesting that they are no less equipped to raise children than their heterosexual counterparts. They appear to possess the skills necessary to be good parents, and they describe positive relationships with their children. Furthermore, they recognize that their children may face stigma as a function of their family structure and are deeply committed to minimizing their children's experiences of rejection and discrimination. Many questions still remain, however, regarding the experiences of lesbians and gay men as parents. For example, how do lesbian and gay parents balance their awareness of societal scrutiny of their families and children with their personal ideals and values regarding parenting? Also, how does access to and contact with other lesbians and gay men with children shape the parenting experiences and adjustment of lesbian and gay parents? Finally, how do parents' relationships with their children's donors (in the case of families formed through alternative insemination) and their children's birth parents (in the case of families formed through open adoption) unfold and change over time?

Notably, the research has suggested that children and adolescents with sexual minority parents, despite their vulnerability to heterosexism, are developing normally. Specifically, while there is some (inconclusive) evidence that the children of lesbian and gay parents may be more likely to be teased at certain points in their development because of their family structure, their overall mental health does not appear to differ on average from that of children of heterosexual parents.

Children of lesbian and gay parents may differ in some interesting and important ways from the children of heterosexual parents, however. First, there is some evidence that they may have more expansive and flexible notions of gender. However, the implications of this greater flexibility are not clear. For example, how does their departure from traditional gendered norms affect their peer relationships? Do they seek out other children who also adhere less rigidly to gendered roles? How are they affected by peers and teachers who actively enforce gendered role behavior (e.g., in the form of separate play spaces for boys and girls, and rules about boys' toys and girls' toys)? Second, many children with lesbian and gay parents must navigate their parents' coming out, which can be stressful. Little is known about how children's adjustment to their parents' coming out changes over time, and what factors facilitate an easier adjustment for children. Longitudinal research is needed to better understand these issues and to shed light on how family dynamics in general change after parents come out. Finally, the children of lesbian and gay parents lack many of the fundamental protections that are granted to children of heterosexual parents. In the event that parents dissolve their relationship, children's relationships with both parents are not necessarily protected, and the emotional, financial, practical, and symbolic consequences can be devastating for children. Research is needed that explores how parental relationship dissolution affects children and, likewise, addresses how legal protections might positively influence the postdissolution trajectories of children of lesbian and gay parents.

The research also has suggested that children of lesbian and gay parents may continue to be shaped by their family structure as adults and that they continue to have experiences that are unique to their family structure (e.g., they encounter situations in which they must decide whether to come out about their families). Furthermore, there is some evidence that at least some adults with lesbian and gay parents possess notably flexible ideas about gender, sexuality, and family. The potential impact of their family structure, then, may be felt across generations and decades. The offspring of adults with lesbian and gay parents, for example, may be exposed to more expansive notions about gender, sexual orientation, and family, from both their parents and their gay and lesbian grandparents. Research that explores the intergenerational dynamics of lesbian- and gay-parent families, then, would undoubtedly reveal fascinating insights about lesbian and gay family life.

KEY CONTENT GAPS IN EXISTING RESEARCH

Much of the research on lesbian and gay parents and their children has focused on lesbian mothers and their children, who were either conceived in the context of heterosexual relationships or by insemination. Significantly less research has been done on other types of families. For example, lesbian and gay adoptive families have received little attention thus far in the literature, with some exceptions (e.g., Bennett, 2003a, 2003b; Erich, Leung, & Kindle, 2005; Gianino, 2008; Leung, Erich, & Kanenberg, 2005; Shelley-Sireci & Ciano-Boyce, 2002). These families, who challenge basic assumptions of what a family is (e.g., that family members must be biologically related and heterosexual) face an array of unique issues, including navigating multiple aspects of difference within the family and coping with complex stigmas surrounding these multiple differences. Issues specific to adoption may also arise: For example, parents must decide how to talk about the facts of adoption with their children, their families, and individuals in the broader social context, such as their children's schools or their own workplaces. Furthermore, children with closed adoptions may have questions about their birth parents or express a desire to search for their birth parents as they grow older. Such issues must be navigated sensitively and with attention to the developmental stage of the child. Lesbian or gay adoptive parents who adopt children of color also face the task of socializing their children to develop healthy racial identities, in addition to helping them to understand and feel confident about their minority family structure and adoptive status. Research is needed that addresses the challenges and needs faced by lesbian and gay adoptive families, as well as their experiences during different phases of the life cycle.

More broadly, research on lesbian and gay multiracial couples and families has been relatively limited. Lesbian and gay multiracial couples and families necessarily possess multiple group identities that simultaneously position them within both dominant and nondominant groups in society (Eldridge & Barrett, 2003). For example, a White woman who is partnered with a Black woman and who has adopted a Black child with her partner occupies both privileged and nonprivileged statuses. By virtue of her status as a White woman, she possesses power. By virtue of her relationships with her partner and child, however, she is exposed to some of the same stigmas faced by Black people in the United States. A question to explore is how such a parent experiences these multiple identities and how the family, as a unit, navigates such a complex nexus of identities. Indeed, families in which multiple races are represented face particular challenges with regard to their visibility in society. They may experience frequent inquiries about the nature of their relationships to one another; alternatively, because of their visible differences from one another, they may not even be seen as members of the same family.

A related question to consider is how racial splits in the family, for example, when only one parent shares race with the child(ren), impact family dynamics. Specifically, how does the racial split impact ongoing parent–child relationships, as well as the partner relationship? Does it cause conflict, jealousy, or feelings of exclusion on the part of the racially dissimilar parent? How does the racial split within the family affect family members' relationships with strangers, extended family, and social institutions? Is the racially similar parent seen and treated by others as the primary or "real" parent to the child? If so, how do parents and children navigate these kinds of presumptions and misunderstandings? Much more research is needed that explores the complex identities and relationships of multiracial family members.

Gay-father families have also been vastly understudied, with some exceptions (e.g., Berkowitz, 2007; Mallon, 2004; Schacher, Auerbach, & Silverstein, 2005). Research on gay fathers has the potential to contribute valuable insights and move the field forward, in that gay fathers necessarily challenge conventional definitions of masculinity and paternity, as well as the dominant sexual norms of gay culture (Adam, 2006; Stacey, 2006). Because gay fathers are the targets of multiple stereotypes and stigmas (e.g., commonly portrayed as incapable of nurturance, sexually promiscuous, and irresponsible), how they navigate these stigmas during various stages of the life cycle is a subject of interest. Also of interest is how gay men, as couples and parents, navigate hegemonic norms about masculinity (Connell, 1992). As two men socialized to define themselves in terms of their earning capacities, how do they make decisions about who, if anyone, should stay home during their child's early months or years? Furthermore, what are the consequences of these decisions for men's sense of themselves as workers and fathers? Likewise, what are gay men's experiences of performing so-called mothering activities? That is, to what extent do they embrace these activities as fundamental to their roles and identities as parents, and to what extent do they experience discomfort, embarrassment, insecurity, or ambivalence regarding their roles as nurturers and providers? Additionally, because the children of gay fathers have rarely been studied (Erich et al., 2005; Leung et al., 2005), much more research on their adjustment and experiences is needed. Studies could explore the extent to which the existing research on children of lesbian mothers accurately encompasses, or reflects, the experiences of children of gay fathers; indeed, there may be certain challenges, strengths, and experiences that are unique to children of gay fathers.

Studies on transgender parents and their children have also been limited (R. Green, 1998; S. Hines, 2006a), and the research that exists has largely focused on the effects of parents' transgenderism on their children's gender identity (e.g., R. Green, 1978, 1998). Studies of transgender parents may yield important insights into the boundaries of existing gender classificatory systems, as well as highlighting new possibilities for the ways in which we think about, conceptualize, and define gender. Specifically, studies are needed that explore how transgender persons define and articulate their own gender identities: Research by S. Hines (2006a, 2006b) suggests that few transgender persons describe themselves as solely female or male but, rather, resist such labels and seek to define themselves in more complex ways. Another question is how transgender parents' own ideas about gender shape their parenting. For example, what messages about gender do they impart to their children, and, in turn, what messages about gender do their children internalize?

Indeed, very little is known about the family dynamics of transgender parents and their children. Of particular interest is how parents and children reconfigure their relationships in the wake of a parent's transition, and how this transition is subjectively experienced by all family members. For example, how do children come to comprehend and accept their parent's gender transition? What factors appear to promote children's understanding and acceptance, as well as their overall adjustment? Also of interest are the experiences of the nontransitioning parent. What specific challenges and struggles do such individuals face? What factors predict whether they will stay with a transitioning parent? What factors predict whether they will support or interfere with their children's relationship with a transitioning parent? What are the consequences of their support or nonsupport for the transitioning parent and their children?

Studies of transgender persons (both male-to-female and female-to-male) who become parents after they transition are especially needed. This area is virtually unexplored, although there is evidence that some women who are in the process of transitioning to be men may delay this transition in order to become pregnant (Lev, 2004), which may cause intrapsychic conflict as individuals struggle with the bodily changes that accompany pregnancy—changes that are fundamentally inconsistent with their gender identity (Lothstein, 1988). Many interesting questions can be asked about the experiences of transgender people who pursue parenthood. How do these men and women decide how, when, and with whom to become parents? What unique challenges do they encounter in realizing their parental identities?

How does their complex gendering impact their parenting? What are their experiences within the lesbian, gay, bisexual, and transgender (LGBT) community, the LGBT parent community, and their broader communities? These and other questions have yet to be explored.

Finally, lesbian- and gay-parent stepfamilies are also understudied (Baptiste, 1987; Lynch & Murray, 2000). Men and women who have or adopt a child in the context of one (heterosexual or same-sex) relationship, dissolve this relationship, and later enter into another (same-sex) relationship experience multiple changes and transitions that can be stressful for both parents and children. Research that follows families over time, as opposed to examining these transitions retrospectively (Lynch & Murray, 2000), is needed; such studies can track couple and parent–child processes as individuals reconfigure their families and relationships and can provide insights into the nature and consequences of these changes. Longitudinal research will permit greater understanding of the factors that contribute to successful stepfamily formation and integration. Further, studies should seek to include as many family members as possible (parent, stepparent, children, the noncustodial parent). Such studies can provide insights into the differing perspectives and experiences of individual family members.

METHODOLOGICAL ISSUES: FUTURE PROSPECTS

As described in chapter 1 and throughout the current volume, a number of methodological challenges characterize the research in this area. The lack of representative samples is one notable challenge. However, inroads are beginning to be made in this area. For example, some existing nationally representative datasets (e.g., the Adolescent Health Database, http:// www.cpc.unc.edu/projects/addhealth) do include questions concerning sexual orientation and family structure, and these datasets are increasingly being used to answer questions about the well-being and experiences of same-sex couples and households headed by same-sex couple (e.g., Wainright, Russell, & Patterson, 2004; Wainright & Patterson, 2008). Notably, the findings of these studies have validated and substantiated previously documented findings and patterns, as well as uncovering new areas of potential inquiry. Researchers are encouraged to draw on these existing databases to answer questions related to sexual orientation and family structure. Further, it is possible that federally funded national surveys may include more questions pertaining to sexual orientation. In the future, many of these surveys will utilize very large samples, which could yield enough sexual minority respondents to permit meaningful analyses.

A related sampling challenge is that studies in this area have tended to use samples that are predominantly White, middle-class, and urban. One potential solution to this problem may lie in greater use of the Internet as a recruitment device. The Internet is ideal for reaching a worldwide audience relatively effortlessly and quickly (e.g., by asking sexual minorities to fill out online surveys). While there are certainly drawbacks in using online surveys to gather information about the behaviors, experiences, and lives of sexual minorities (e.g., such methods may draw unwanted responses from persons who are not the intended sample; Internet usage patterns vary according to finances and accessibility; Harding & Peel, 2007), there is evidence that the Internet may be particularly useful in accessing understudied or hidden members of the LGBT population, such as rural lesbians and gay men, closeted lesbians and gay men, and transgender persons. For example, Rosser, Oakes, Bockting, and Miner (2007) recruited a geographically and economically diverse sample of more than 1,000 persons who self-identified as transgender, using Internet methods. Participants were recruited by banners placed on transgender community Web sites and in chat rooms, as well as messages posted to online mailing lists and forums. These banners displayed a revolving set of messages regarding their study on transgender health. By clicking on a banner or link, participants went directly to the transgender study Web site, where they could then complete the researchers' online survey. The authors noted that

> the anonymity, reach, and decreased burden on respondents that are inherent in Internet-based studies—where participants can complete a survey at times and places, as well as in the speed and manner, of their own choosing—all predict greater participation for online versus offline studies. The Internet may be the only way to reach certain sexual minorities . . . Indeed, the more hidden the population, the more likely Internet-based methods may be the appropriate or only way to reach a sexual minority (broadly defined). (p. 58)

Thus, the Internet may be ideal not only for accessing and studying transgender persons in particular but also for surveying sexual minorities in remote geographical areas, immigrant sexual minorities, disabled or home-bound sexual minorities, and other hard-to-reach sexual minorities.

Racial and ethnic minority sexual minorities are also underrepresented in samples of lesbians and gay men. It follows that novel or creative recruitment approaches may be necessary to ensure their adequate representation in sexual minority samples. As Moore (2006) noted, traditional methods for sampling lesbians (e.g., through advertisements in LGBT-oriented publications and postings at LGBT community centers) have not been successful in recruiting large numbers of non-White participants. Moore noted that given the tendency for researchers who study lesbians and gay men to be White themselves and to recruit participants from their own social networks, this strategy is simply not ideal for locating Black lesbians. Thus, Moore, a Black lesbian, used different methods in gathering participants for her study of predominantly Black lesbians. Specifically, she began her research by spending time at a variety of predominantly Black social events. These events, both private and public, included church meetings, book clubs, parties, poetry readings, and workshops on parenting. She also attended gay pride and Black gay pride events in several cities. Moore ultimately obtained a sample of approximately 100 participants, approximately 64% of whom were Black American, 20% of whom identified as West Indian or Caribbean, and 10% who identified as Latina. A. I. Green (2007) used similar methods, recruiting his sample of 30 gay Black men from a diverse range of local organizations in downtown Manhattan, including athletic teams, gyms, bars, churches, and civic associations. These data suggest that participating in community events and activities within the target community, as well as networking with members of the target community, may yield more success in the recruitment of racial/ethnic sexual minorities than traditional methods.

A very different type of challenge in research on sexual minorities and their families is the lack of public recognition of and support for this work. As described in chapter 1 of this volume, research on lesbians, gay men, and their families is inadequately funded and poorly represented in academic journals. Professional associations, academic journals, and private foundations can all play a valuable role in enhancing the visibility of sexual minority research, as well as increasing its methodological rigor and standards. Professional associations can include calls for proposals on topics related to LGBT families for their annual conferences. Establishing awards and grant programs aimed at stimulating LGBT-related research will also help to foster career development in this area. Academic journals can solicit manuscript submissions that explore LGBT-related themes and issues (e.g., by publishing special issues on topics such as sexual orientation, gender identity, and the family; sexual orientation and the law; and sexual orientation and the workplace). Finally, private foundations and granting agencies can play a crucial role in stimulating scholarship in this area. By offering funding opportunities to graduate students, junior scholars, and midcareer scholars, granting agencies can finance high-quality research that has the potential to move the field forward.

CONCLUDING THOUGHTS

Much has been learned from the existing research on lesbian- and gay-parent families. With regard to gender, the available data provide insights into some of the ways in which relationships and family processes are transformed when partners are of the same sex rather than of different sexes. At the same time, they provide striking evidence of the myriad ways in which gender is not only personally and relationally constructed but is also a fundamental part of the broader social structure. In this way, lesbian and gay couples and their families are constantly in a process of negotiation, balancing their own unique gender processes and configurations with the expectations and norms that are enforced by the broader systems in which they live (e.g., the workplace; the legal system; ideologies surrounding heterosexuality, marriage, family, the division of labor, and parenting). For example, a lesbian who was raised by egalitarian, dual-earner heterosexual parents and who has a strong desire to share parenthood equally with her female partner may nevertheless find herself considering her and her partner's current or future parental roles against the inescapable reference points of "mother" and "father." Yet by virtue of "doing gender" in the context of a same-sex relationship rather than a heterosexual relationship, sexual minorities are necessarily doing gender differently than members of heterosexual relationships, even if their labor arrangements and caretaking responsibilities, for example, seem to mirror that of the typical or traditional heterosexual couple. Because the social context in which a process occurs inevitably transforms that process (Bronfenbrenner, 1977, 1986), lesbians' and gay men's own gendering cannot wholly replicate or simulate the gendering processes of heterosexual couples. Thus, even when seemingly imitative of heterosexual relational dynamics, same-sex couples' gender processes are not equivalent to heterosexual dynamics—in structure, in meaning, or in purpose.

The research in this area also challenges fundamental and taken-for-granted notions about "the family," and therefore invites us to revisit and reexamine our current ideas about and definitions of family. Family is not a static institution but one that is constantly being reworked, reshaped, reimagined, and reenacted in complex and dynamic ways. Lesbian- and gay-parent families (re)vision the family by materially and theoretically destabilizing some of the basic assumptions about families: that they are heterosexual, biologically related, legally linked, and socially accepted. Indeed, parenting is often delimited as the natural consequence of biology (Donovan, 2000), and yet lesbian and gay parents clearly challenge and undermine this notion, thereby contributing to more expansive notions of parenting and family. Also, members of lesbian- and gay-parent families construct and perceive their family relationships in ways that defy traditional notions of family: For example, sexual minority adults may enjoy close familial relationships with friends, and children conceived by alternative insemination may view their lesbian or gay parent's partner as more of a parent than their donor, who is technically their biological father. Thus, such children's conceptions of family, which emphasize "the subjective meaning of intimate connections, rather than formal, objective ties based purely on biological or marriage ties," perfectly illustrate, and strongly support, the socially constructed nature of families (Hargreaves, 2006, p. 277). However, although lesbian- and gay-parent families construct and enact family in unique ways, they are not, by virtue of their family structure, essentially different from heterosexual-parent families. Rather, the research in this area provides considerable evidence that family processes—that is, the relationships and dynamics that exist among family members—are often more important than family structure in influencing the mental health and adjustment of family members (Murray & Golombok, 2005; C. J. Patterson, 2000).

A considerable number of studies have compared the adjustment outcomes of lesbian and gay parents and their children with those of heterosexual parents and their children. Scholars are increasingly calling for a more nondefensive stance with regard to research in this area (Goldberg, in press; Riggs, 2006; Stacey & Biblarz, 2001). These scholars acknowledge the utility of comparing lesbian and gay parents with heterosexual parents on various psychosocial and family process indicators, but they warn that this research may inadvertently treat heterosexual parenting as the gold standard against which any other form of parenting is measured (Riggs, 2006). By continuing to judge gay parents in terms of their similarity to heterosexual parents, we as researchers reify the discourse that the nuclear, two-parent heterosexual married family is both the ideal and the normative baseline with which same-sex couples should be compared. Such positioning also serves to uphold a theory of sexuality that views lesbians and gay men as essentially different from heterosexuals (S. Hicks, 2005c). Furthermore, while comparative studies can be beneficial in highlighting the similarities and differences between lesbian and heterosexual parents, such research can inevitably result in overgeneralizing or masking the experiences of and differences within lesbian parent–headed families (Goldberg, in press; Hequembourg & Farrell, 1999). Thus, what is increasingly needed is research that brings lesbian- and gay-parent families from the margins to the center of theorizing (Clarke, 2002). This sort of shift opens up new and exciting questions to be explored—such as, what is a family?—and facilitates the exploration and understanding of diversity within lesbian- and gay-parent families. Indeed, research that focuses on lesbian and gay parents and their families in their own right has the potential to significantly expand our understanding of parents, families, roles, gender, and sexuality.

Comparative studies, though, should not be abandoned entirely. Rather, what is needed is a change in focus. Specifically, I recommend that we shift our theorizing and analysis from focusing simply on family structure to considering the significance of family processes. Family structure (lesbian vs. heterosexual parent household) is worthy of examination, but, as demonstrated in this volume, structural variables may ultimately be less significant in shaping children's developmental outcomes than family processes such as family interaction patterns, parental well-being, relationships among family members, and so on (C. J. Patterson, 2000).

Finally, in reflecting on what we know from the research on lesbian and gay parents and their children, we must remain cognizant of all that we have yet to learn. For example, we must remember that what we know about lesbian- and gay-parent families is limited to research that largely references the experiences of White, middle-class families. Much more research is needed to fully capture the diversity that is inherent in this group, with regard to racial and ethnic makeup, social class, geographical location, family formation, and many other social settings. Further, it is essential that researchers think beyond what research has been done and what questions have been asked to carve out new and innovative areas of inquiry, in order to push the field forward. By asking difficult questions, pursuing unexplored areas, and probing the experiences of the "unseen" members of the LGBT community, we will gain a richer, deeper, and more accurate picture of the landscape of LGBT-parent families.

REFERENCES

Abidin, R. R., Jenkins, C. L., & McGaughey, M. C. (1992). The relationship of early family variables to children's subsequent behavioral adjustment. *Journal of Clinical Child Psychology, 21*, 60–69.

Adam, B. (2006). Relationship innovation in male couples. *Sexualities, 9*, 5–26.

Adams, H., & Phillips, L. (2006). Experiences of two-spirit lesbian and gay Native Americans: An argument for standpoint theory in identity research. *Identity, 6*, 273–291.

Advanced Fertility Center of Chicago. (2007). *In vitro fertilization*. Retrieved on August 1, 2007, from http://www.advancedfertility.com/ivfprice.htm

Agigian, A. (2004). *Baby steps: How lesbian alternative insemination is changing the world*. Middletown, CT: Wesleyan University Press.

Alderson, K. G. (2004). A phenomenological investigation of same-sex marriage. *The Canadian Journal of Human Sexuality, 13*, 107–122.

Alexander, C. J. (2001). Developmental attachment and gay and lesbian adoptions. *Journal of Gay and Lesbian Social Services, 13*, 93–97.

Allen, K. R. (2007). Ambiguous loss after lesbian couples with children break up: A case for same-gender divorce. *Family Relations, 56*, 175–183.

Allen, K. R., & Demo, D. H. (1995). The families of lesbians and gay men: A new frontier in family research. *Journal of Marriage and the Family, 57*, 111–127.

Almack, K. (2005). What's in a name? An exploration of the significance of the choice of surnames given to the children, born within female same sex families. *Sexualities, 8*, 239–254.

Almack, K. (2006). Seeking sperm: Accounts of lesbian couples' reproductive decision-making and understandings of the needs of the child. *International Journal of Law, Policy and the Family, 20*, 1–22.

Alpert-Gillis, L. J., & Connell, J. P. (1989). Gender and sex-role influence on children's self-esteem. *Journal of Personality, 57*, 97–114.

American Psychiatric Association. (1980). *Diagnostic and statistical manual of mental disorders* (3rd ed.). Washington, DC: Author.

American Psychiatric Association. (1994). *Diagnostic and statistical manual of mental disorders* (4th ed.). Washington, DC: Author.

Anderson, S. C., & Holliday, M. (2004). Normative passing in the lesbian community: An exploratory study. *Journal of Gay & Lesbian Social Services, 17*, 25–38.

Arendell, T. (2000). Conceiving and investigating motherhood: The decade's scholarship. *Journal of Marriage and Family, 62*, 1192–1207.

Ariel, J., & McPherson, D. (2000). Therapy with lesbian and gay families and their children. *Journal of Marital and Family Therapy, 26*, 421–432.

BabyCenter. (2007). *Fertility drugs: Clomiphene*. Retrieved on June 18, 2007, from http://www.babycenter.com/refcap/preconception/fertilityproblems/6186.html

Badgett, M. V. L. (1998). *Income inflation: The myth of affluence among gay, lesbian and bisexual Americans*. Washington, DC: The Institute for Gay and Lesbian Strategic Studies.

Badgett, M. V. L., & Rogers, M. A. (2003). *Left out of the count: Missing same-sex couples in Census 2000*. Washington, DC: The Institute for Gay and Lesbian Strategic Studies.

Baetens, P., Camus, M., & Devroey, P. (2002). Counseling lesbian couples: Requests for donor insemination on social grounds. *Reproductive BioMedicine Online, 6,* 75–83.

Bailey, J. M., Bobrow, D., Wolfe, M., & Mikach, S. (1995). Sexual orientation of adult sons of gay fathers. *Developmental Psychology, 31,* 124–129.

Bailey, J. M., Kim, P. Y., Hills, A., & Linsenmeier, J. A. W. (1997). Butch, femme, or straight acting? Partner preferences of gay men and lesbians. *Journal of Personality and Social Psychology, 73,* 960–973.

Baker, P. (2005). *Public discourses of gay men*. London: Routledge.

Ballard, C. G., Davis, R., Cullen, P. C., Mohan, R. N., & Dean, C. (1994). Postnatal depression in mothers and fathers. *British Journal of Psychiatry, 164,* 782–788.

Balsam, K. F., Beauchaine, T. P., Rothblum, E. D., & Solomon, S. E. (2008). Three-year follow-up of same-sex couples who had civil unions in Vermont, same-sex couples not in civil unions, and heterosexual married couples. *Developmental Psychology, 44,* 102–116.

Bandura, A. (1977). *Social learning theory*. Englewood Cliffs, NJ: Prentice-Hall.

Bandura, A., & Walters, R. (1963). *Social learning and personality development*. New York: Holt, Rinehart & Winston.

Baptiste, D. A. (1987). The gay and lesbian stepparent family. In F. W. Bozett (Ed.), *Gay and lesbian parents* (pp. 112–137). New York: Praeger.

Barrett, H., & Tasker, F. (2001). Growing up with a gay parent: Views of 101 gay fathers on their sons' and daughters' experiences. *Educational and Child Psychology, 18,* 62–77.

Barrett, S. E. (1997). Children of lesbian parents: The what, when, and how of talking about donor identity. *Women & Therapy, 20,* 43–55.

Baumeister, R. F., Catanase, K. R., & Vohs, K. D. (2001). Is there a gender difference in strength of sex drive? *Personality and Social Psychology Review, 5,* 242–273.

Belcastro, P. A., Gramlich, T., Nicholson, T., Price, J., & Wilson, R. (1993). A review of data-based studies addressing the effects of homosexual parenting on children's sexual and social functioning. *Journal of Divorce and Remarriage, 20,* 105–122.

Belsky, J. (1984). The determinants of parenting: A process model. *Child Development, 55,* 83–96.

Belsky, J., & Rovine, M. (1990). Patterns of marital change across the transition to parenthood: Pregnancy to three years postpartum. *Journal of Marriage and the Family, 52,* 5–19.

Ben-Ari, A., & Livni, T. (2006). Motherhood is not a given thing: Experiences and constructed meanings of biological and nonbiological lesbian mothers. *Sex Roles, 54,* 521–531.

Bengtson, V., & Allen, K. (1993). The life course perspective applied to families over time. In P. Boss, W. Doherty, R. LaRossa, W. Schumm, & S. Steinmetz (Eds.), *Sourcebook of family theories and methods: A contextual approach* (pp. 469–499). New York: Plenum Press.

Bennett, S. (2003a). International adoptive lesbian families: Parental perceptions of the influence of diversity on family relationships in early childhood. *Smith College Studies in Social Work, 7,* 73–91.

Bennett, S. (2003b). Is there a primary mom? Parental perceptions of attachment bond hierarchies within lesbian adoptive families. *Child & Adolescent Social Work Journal, 20,* 59–173.

Bepko, C., & Johnson, T. (2000). Gay and lesbian couples in therapy: Perspectives for the contemporary family therapist. *Journal of Marital & Family Therapy, 26,* 409–419.

Bergen, K. M., Suter, E. A., & Daas, K. L. (2006). "About as solid as a fish net": Symbolic construction of a legitimate parental identity for nonbiological lesbian mothers. *The Journal of Family Communication, 6,* 201–220.

Berkman, C., & Zinberg, G. (1997). Homophobia and heterosexism in social workers. *Social Work, 42,* 319–332.

Berkowitz, D. (2007). A sociohistorical analysis of gay men's procreative consciousness. *Journal of GLBT Family Studies, 3,* 157–190.

Berkowitz, D., & Marsiglio, W. (2007). Gay men: Negotiating procreative, father, and family identities. *Journal of Marriage and Family, 69,* 366–381.

Berscheid, E. (2006). *The changing reasons for marriage and divorce.* Mahwah, NJ: Erlbaum.

Bialeschki, M. D., & Pearce, K. D. (1997). "I don't want a lifestyle—I want a life": The effect of role negotiations on the leisure of lesbian mothers. *Journal of Leisure Research, 29,* 113–131.

Bigner, J. J., & Bozett, F. W. (1989). Parenting by gay fathers. *Marriage & Family Review, 14,* 155–175.

Bigner, J. J., & Bozett, F. W. (1990). Parenting by gay fathers. In F. W. Bozett & M. B. Sussman (Eds.), *Homosexuality and family relations* (pp. 155–176). New York: Harrington Park Press.

Bigner, J. J., & Jacobsen, R. B. (1989a). Parenting behaviors of homosexual and heterosexual fathers. *Journal of Homosexuality, 18,* 173–186.

Bigner, J. J., & Jacobsen, R. B. (1989b). Parenting behaviors of homosexual and heterosexual fathers. In F. W. Bozett (Ed.), *Homosexuality and the family* (pp. 173–186). New York: Harrington Park Press.

Biswas, U. N. (2007). Promoting health and well-being in lives of people living with HIV and AIDS. *Psychology and Developing Societies, 19,* 215–247.

Blankenhorn, D. (1995). *Fatherless America: Confronting our most urgent social problem*. New York: Basic Books.

Blasband, D., & Peplau, L. A. (1985). Sexual exclusivity versus openness in gay male couples. *Archives of Sexual Behavior, 14*, 395–412.

Blumenfeld, W. (1992). *Homophobia: How we all pay the price*. Boston: Beacon Press.

Blumstein, P., & Schwartz, P. (1983). *American couples: Money, work, sex*. New York: William Morrow.

Boggis, T. (2001). Affording our families: Class issues in family formation. In M. Bernstein & R. Reimann (Eds.), *Queer families, queer politics* (pp. 175–181). New York: Columbia University Press.

Boldizar, J. P. (1991). Assessing sex typing and androgyny in children: The children's sex role inventory. *Developmental Psychology, 27*, 505–515.

Boon, S., & Miller, R. J. (1999). Exploring the links between interpersonal trust and the reasons underlying gay and bisexual males' disclosure of their sexual orientation to their mothers. *Journal of Homosexuality, 30*, 89–112.

Bor, R., du Plessis, P., & Russell, M. (2004). The impact of disclosure of HIV on the index patient's self-defined family. *Journal of Family Therapy, 26*, 167–192.

Bos, H. M. W., & Hakvoort, E. M. (2007). Child adjustment and parenting in planned lesbian families with known and as-yet unknown donors. *Journal of Psychosomatic Obstetrics & Gynecology, 28*, 121–129.

Bos, H. M. W., & van Balen, F. (2008). Children in planned lesbian families: Stigmatization, psychological adjustment, and protective factors. *Culture, Health, & Sexuality, 10*, 221–236.

Bos, H. M. W., van Balen, F., & van den Boom, D. C. (2004). Experience of parenthood, couple relationship, social support, and child rearing goals in planned lesbian families. *Journal of Child Psychology and Psychiatry, 45*, 755–764.

Bos, H. M. W., van Balen, F., & van den Boom, D. C. (2007). Child adjustment and parenting in planned lesbian-parent families. *American Journal of Orthopsychiatry, 77*, 38–48.

Bowlby, J. (1951). *Maternal care and mental health*. Geneva: World Health Organization.

Bozett, F. W. (1980). How and why gay fathers disclose their homosexuality to their children. *Family Relations, 29*, 173–179.

Bozett, F. W. (1987). Children of gay fathers. In F. W. Bozett (Ed.), *Gay and lesbian parents* (pp. 39–57). New York: Praeger.

Bramlett, M. D., & Mosher, W. D. (2001). *First marriage, dissolution, divorce, and remarriage: United States: Advance data from vital and health statistics, No. 323*. Hyattsville, MD: National Center for Health Statistics.

Brewaeys, A., Ponjaert-Kristoffersen, I., Van Steirteghem, A. C., & Devroey, P. (1993). Children from anonymous donors: An inquiry into homosexual and heterosexual parents' attitudes. *Journal of Psychosomatic Obstetrics & Gynecology, 14*, 23–35.

Brodzinsky, D. M. (2003). *Adoption by lesbians and gay men: A national survey of adoption agency policies, practices, and attitudes*. Retrieved on September 1, 2007, from http://www.adoptioninstitute.org/whowe/Gay%20and%20Lesbian%20 Adoption1.html

Bronfenbrenner, U. (1977). Toward an experimental ecology of human development. *American Psychologist, 32,* 513–531.

Bronfenbrenner, U. (1986). Ecology of the family as a context for human development: Research perspectives. *Developmental Psychology, 22,* 723–742.

Brooks, D., & Goldberg, S. (2003). Gay and lesbian adoptive and foster care placements: Can they meet the needs of waiting children? *Social Work, 46,* 147–157.

Brooks, D., Simmel, C., Wind, L. & Barth, R. (2005). Contemporary adoption in the United States: Implications for the next wave of adoption theory, research, and practice. In D. Brodzinsky & J. Palacios (Eds.), *Psychological issues in adoption: Theory, research, and application* (pp. 1–26). Westport, CT: Greenwood Publishing Group.

Brown, R., & Perlesz, A. (2007). Not the "other" mother: How language constructs lesbian co-parenting relationships. *Journal of GLBT Family Studies, 3,* 267–308.

Brubaker, L. L. (2002). Comment on Cameron and Cameron (2002): "Children of homosexual parents report childhood difficulties." *Psychological Reports, 91,* 331–332.

Bryant, A. S., & Demian (1994). Relationship characteristics of American gay and lesbian couples: Findings from a national survey. *Journal of Gay and Lesbian Social Services, 1,* 101–117.

Burch, B. (1985). Another perspective on merger in lesbian relationships. In L. B. Rosewater & L. E. A. Walker (Eds.), *Handbook of feminist therapy: Women's issues in psychotherapy* (pp. 100–109). New York: Springer.

Butler, J. (1991). Imitation and gender insubordination. In D. Fuss (Ed.), *Inside/out: Lesbian theories, gay theories.* New York: Routledge.

Byne, W. (1997). Why we cannot conclude that sexual orientation is primarily a biological phenomenon. *Journal of Homosexuality, 34,* 73–80.

Cahill, S., Battle, J., & Meyer, D. (2003). Partnering, parenting, and policy: Family issues affecting Black lesbian, gay, bisexual, and transgender (LGBT) people. *Race & Society, 6,* 85–98.

Cain, R. (1991a). Stigma management and gay identity development. *Social Work, 36,* 67–73.

Cain, R. (1991b). Relational contexts and information management among gay men. *Families in Society, 72,* 344–352.

Caldwell, M. A., & Peplau, L. A. (1984). The balance of power in lesbian relationships. *Sex Roles, 10,* 587–600.

Calhoun, C. (1997). Family outlaws: Rethinking connections between feminism, lesbianism, and the family. In H. L. Nelson (Ed.), *Feminism and families* (pp. 131–150). New York: Routledge.

Cameron, J., & Hargreaves, K. (2005). Managing family secrets: Same-sex relationships. *New Zealand Journal of Sociology, 20,* 102–121.

Cameron, P. (1999). Homosexual parents: Testing "common sense"—A literature review emphasizing the Golombok and Tasker longitudinal study of lesbians' children. *Psychological Reports, 85,* 282–322.

Cameron, P. (2006). Children of homosexuals and transsexuals are more apt to be homosexual. *Journal of Biosocial Science, 38,* 413–418.

Cameron, P., & Cameron, K. (1996). Homosexual parents. *Adolescence, 31,* 757–776.

Cameron, P., & Cameron, K. (1998). Homosexual parents: A comparative forensic study of character and harms to children. *Psychological Reports, 82,* 1155–1191.

Cameron, P., & Cameron, K. (2002). Children of homosexual parents report childhood difficulties. *Psychological Reports, 90,* 71–82.

Card, C. (2007). Gay divorce: Thoughts on the legal regulation of marriage. *Hypatia, 22,* 24–38.

Cardell, M., Finn, S., & Marecek, J. (1981). Sex-role identity, sex-role behavior, and satisfaction in heterosexual, lesbian, and gay male couples. *Psychology of Women, 5,* 488–494.

Caron, S. L., & Ulin, M. (1997). Closeting and the quality of lesbian relationships. *Families in Society, 78,* 413–419.

Carrington, C. (2002). *No place like home: Relationships and family life among lesbians and gay men.* Chicago: University of Chicago Press.

Carter, B., & McGoldrick, M. (Eds.) (2005). *The expanded family life cycle* (3rd ed.). Boston: Allyn & Bacon.

Casper, V., & Schultz, S. (1999). *Gay parents/straight schools: Building communication and trust.* New York: Teachers College Press.

Casper, V., Schultz, S., & Wickens, E. (1992). Lesbian and gay parents and the schools. *Teachers College Record, 94,* 109–137.

Cass, V. (1979). Homosexual identity formation: A theoretical model. *Journal of Homosexuality, 4,* 219–235.

Chabot, J. M., & Ames, B. D. (2004). "It wasn't 'let's get pregnant and go do it'": Decision-making in lesbian couples planning motherhood via donor insemination. *Family Relations, 53,* 348–356.

Chan, R., Brooks, R., Raboy, B., & Patterson, C. (1998). Division of labor among lesbian and heterosexual parents: Associations with children's adjustment. *Journal of Family Psychology, 12,* 402–419.

Chan, R., Raboy, B., & Patterson, C. (1998). Psychosocial adjustment among children conceived via donor insemination by lesbian and heterosexual mothers. *Child Development, 69,* 443–457.

Cheal, D. (1993). Unity and difference in postmodern families. *Journal of Family Issues, 14,* 5–19.

Child Welfare Information Gateway. (2004). *Costs of adopting: Factsheet for families.* Retrieved on June 18, 2007, from http://www.childwelfare.gov/pubs/s_cost/s_costb.cfm

Chrisp, J. (2001). That four letter word—sons: Lesbian mothers and adolescent sons. *Journal of Lesbian Studies, 5*, 195–209.

Christopher, F. S., & Sprecher, S. (2000). Sexuality in marriage, dating, and other relationships: A decade review. *Journal of Marriage and Family, 62*, 999–1027.

Ciano-Boyce, C., & Shelley-Sireci, L. (2002). Who is Mommy tonight? Lesbian parenting issues. *Journal of Homosexuality, 43*, 1–13.

Clarke, V. (2001). What about the children? Arguments against lesbian and gay parenting. *Women's Studies International Forum, 24*, 555–570.

Clarke, V. (2002). Sameness and difference in research on lesbian parenting. *Journal of Community and Applied Social Psychology, 12*, 210–222.

Clarke, V., & Kitzinger, C. (2005). "We're not living on planet lesbian": Constructions of male role models in debates about lesbian families. *Sexualities, 8*, 137–152.

Clarke, V., Kitzinger, C., & Potter, J. (2004). 'Kids are just cruel anyway': Lesbian and gay parents' talk about homophobic bullying. *British Journal of Social Psychology, 43*, 531–550.

Clarke, V., & Turner, K. (2007). Clothes maketh the queer? Dress, appearance, and the construction of lesbian, gay, bisexual identities. *Feminism & Psychology, 17*, 267–276.

Clarkson, J. (2006). "Everyday Joe" versus "pissy, bitchy queens": Gay masculinity on StraightActing.com. *Journal of Men's Studies, 14*, 191–207.

Clarkson-Freeman, P. A. (2004). The Defense of Marriage Act (DOMA): Its impact on those seeking same-sex marriage. *Journal of Homosexuality, 48*, 1–19.

Coleman, E. (1981). Developmental stages of the coming out process. *Journal of Homosexuality, 7*, 31–43.

Coleman, M., Ganong, L., & Leon, K. (2006). Divorce and postdivorce relationships. In A. L. Vangelisti & D. Perlman (Eds.), *The Cambridge handbook of personal relationships* (pp. 157–173). New York: Cambridge University Press.

Collins, P. H. (1992). Black women and motherhood. In B. Thorne & M. Yalom (Eds.), *Rethinking the family: Some feminist questions* (pp. 215–245). New York: Longman.

Coltrane, S. (2000). Research on household labor. *Journal of Marriage and Family, 62*, 1209–1233.

Connell, R. W. (1992). A very straight gay: Masculinity, homosexual experience, and the dynamics of gender. *American Sociological Review, 57*, 735–751.

Connell, R. W. (1995). *Masculinities*. Berkeley: University of California Press.

Connolly, C. M. (2002a). Lesbian and gay parenting: A brief history of legal and theoretical issues. *Studies in Law, Politics, & Society, 26*, 189–208.

Connolly, C. M. (2002b). The voice of the petitioner: The experiences of gay and lesbian parents in successful second-parent adoption proceedings. *Law & Society Review, 36*, 325–346.

Connolly, C. M. (2005). A qualitative exploration of resilience in long-term lesbian couples. *The Family Journal, 13,* 266–280.

Cordova, J. V., Gee, C. B., & Warren, L. Z. (2005). Emotional skillfulness in marriage: Intimacy as a mediator of the relationship between emotional skillfulness and marital satisfaction. *Journal of Social & Clinical Psychology, 24,* 218–235.

Corrigan, P. W. (2005). Dealing with stigma through personal disclosure. In P. W. Corrigan (Ed.), *On the stigma of mental illness: Practical strategies for research and social change* (pp. 257–280). Washington, DC: American Psychological Association.

Costello, C. Y. (1997). Conceiving identity: Bisexual, lesbian, and gay parents consider their children's sexual orientations. *Journal of Sociology and Social Welfare, 24,* 63–89.

Costigan, C. L., Cox, M. J., & Cauce, A. M. (2003). Work–parenting linkages among dual-earner couples at the transition to parenthood. *Journal of Family Psychology, 17,* 397–408.

Cowan, C. P., & Cowan, P. A. (1988). Who does what when partners become parents: Implications for men, women, and marriage. In C. P. Cowan & P. A. Cowan (Eds.), *Transitions to parenthood* (pp. 105–131). New York: Haworth Press.

Cowan, P. A., & Cowan, C. P. (2003). Normative family transitions, normal family processes, and healthy child development. In F. Walsh (Ed.), *Normal family processes: Growing diversity and complexity* (3rd ed., pp. 424–459). New York: Guilford Press.

Crawley, S. L. (2001). Are butch and fem working-class and antifeminist? *Gender & Society, 15,* 175–196.

Croteau, J. M. (1996). Research on the work experiences of lesbian, gay, and bisexual people: An integrative review of methodology and findings. *Journal of Vocational Behavior, 48,* 195–209.

Croteau, J. M., Talbot, D. M., Lance, T. S., & Evans, N. J. (2002). A qualitative study of the interplay between privilege and oppression. *Journal of Multicultural Counseling and Development, 24,* 239–258.

Cusick, L., & Rhodes, T. (2000). Sustaining sexual safety in relationships: HIV positive people and their sexual partners. *Culture, Health, & Sexuality, 2,* 473–487.

Dalton, S. E., & Bielby, D. D. (2000). That's our kind of constellation: Lesbian mothers negotiate institutionalized understandings of gender within the family. *Gender & Society, 14,* 36–61.

Daniels, K. R. (1994). Adoption and donor insemination: Factors influencing couples' choices. *Child Welfare, 73,* 5–14.

D'Augelli, A. R., Rendina, H. J., Grossman, A. H., & Sinclair, K. O. (2006/2007). Lesbian and gay youths' aspirations for marriage and raising children. *Journal of LGBT Issues in Counseling 1,* 77–98.

Davis, M., Hart, G., Bolding, G., Sherr, L., & Elford, J. (2006). Sex and the Internet: Gay men, risk reduction, and serostatus. *Culture, Health & Sexuality, 8,* 161–174.

DeMino, K. A., Appleby, G., & Fisk, D. (2007). Lesbian mothers with planned families: A comparative study of internalized homophobia and social support. *American Journal of Orthopsychiatry, 77,* 165–173.

Devor, H. (1997). *FTM: Female-to-male transsexuals in society.* Bloomington: Indiana University Press.

Devor, H. (2002). Who are "we"? Where sexual orientation meets gender identity. *Journal of Gay and Lesbian Psychotherapy, 6,* 5–21.

Diamond, L. M. (2000). Passionate friendships among adolescent sexual-minority women. *Journal of Research on Adolescence, 10,* 191–209.

Diamond, L. M., & Dube, E. M. (2002). Friendship and attachment among heterosexual and sexual minority youths. *Journal of Youth and Adolescence, 31,* 155–166.

DiLapi, E. M. (1989). Lesbian mothers and the motherhood hierarchy. *Journal of Homosexuality, 18,* 101–121.

Dindia, K. (1998). "Going into and coming out of the closet": The dialectics of stigma disclosure. In B. M. Montgomery & L. A. Baxter (Eds.), *Dialectical approaches to studying personal relationships* (pp. 83–108). Mahwah, NJ: Erlbaum.

Dobson, J. (2004). *Marriage under fire: Why we must win this battle.* Portland, OR: Multnomah.

Donovan, C. (2000). Who needs a father? Negotiating biological fatherhood in British lesbian families using self-insemination. *Sexualities, 3,* 149–164.

Downing, J. B., & Goldberg, A. E. (2008, August). *Lesbian mothers' perceptions of paid work and family obligations.* Poster presented at the American Psychological Association annual conference, Boston.

Downing, J. B., Richardson, H., & Goldberg, A. E. (2008, August). *Gay men's decision-making in choosing an adoption path.* Poster presented at the American Psychological Association annual conference, Boston.

Dreschler, C. (2003). "We are all others": An argument for queer. *Journal of Bisexuality, 3,* 265–275.

Dundas, S., & Kaufman, M. (2000). The Toronto lesbian family study. *Journal of Homosexuality, 40,* 65–79.

Dunne, G. A. (2000). Opting into motherhood: Lesbians blurring the boundaries and transforming the meaning of parenthood and kinship. *Gender & Society, 14,* 11–35.

Editors of the *Harvard Law Review.* (1990). *Sexual orientation and the law.* Cambridge, MA: Harvard University Press.

Edser, S. J., & Shea, J. D. (2002). An exploratory study of bisexual men in monogamous, heterosexual marriages. *Journal of Bisexuality, 2,* 5–29.

Ehrensaft, D. (1990). *Parenting together: Men and women sharing the care of their children.* Champaign: The University of Illinois Press.

Ehrensaft, D. (2005). *Daddies, donors, surrogates: Answering tough questions and building strong families.* New York: Guilford Press.

Eisenberg, N., Martin, C. L., & Fabes, R. A. (1996). Gender development and gender effects. In D. C. Berliner & R. C. Calfee (Eds.), *Handbook of educational psychology* (pp. 358–396). New York: Prentice-Hall.

Elder, G. H. (1996). Human lives in changing societies: Life course and developmental insights. In R. B. Cairns, G. H. Elder, & J. Costello (Eds.), *Developmental science* (pp. 31–62). New York: Cambridge University Press.

Elder, G. H. (1998a). The life course and human development. In W. Damon & R. M. Lerner (Eds.), *Handbook of child psychology: Vol. 1. Theoretical models of human development* (5th ed., pp. 939–991). Hoboken, NJ: Wiley.

Elder, G. H. (1998b). The life course as developmental theory. *Child Development, 69*, 1–12.

Eldridge, N. S., & Barrett, S. (2003). Biracial lesbian-led adoptive families. In L. B. Silverstein, & T. J. Goodrich (Eds.), *Feminist family therapy* (pp. 307–318). Washington, DC: American Psychological Association.

Eldridge, N. S., & Gilbert, L. A. (1990). Correlates of relationship satisfaction in lesbian couples. *Psychology of Women Quarterly, 14*, 43–62.

Elizur, Y., & Mintzer, A. (2003). Gay males' intimate relationship quality: The roles of attachment security, gay identity, social support, and income. *Personal Relationships, 10*, 411–435.

Epstein, R. (2002). Butches with babies: Reconfiguring gender and motherhood. *Journal of Lesbian Studies, 6*, 41–57.

Erel, O., & Burman, B. (1995). Interrelatedness of marital relations and parent–child relations: A meta-analytic review. *Psychological Bulletin, 118*, 108–132.

Erich, S., Leung, P., & Kindle, P. (2005). A comparative analysis of adoptive family functioning with gay, lesbian, and heterosexual parents and their children. *Journal of GLBT Family Studies, 14*, 43–60.

Erwin, T. M. (2007). Two moms and a baby: Counseling lesbian couples choosing motherhood. *Women & Therapy, 30*, 99–149.

Faderman, L. (1991). *Odd girls and twilight lovers: A history of lesbian life in twentieth-century America.* New York: Penguin.

Fassinger, R. (1995). From invisibility to integration: Lesbian identity in the workplace. *The Career Development Quarterly, 44*, 148–167.

Fassinger, R. (2008). Workplace diversity and public policy: Challenges and opportunities for psychology. *American Psychologist, 63*, 252–268.

Fassinger, R., & Arseneau, J. R. (2007). "I'd rather get wet than be under that umbrella": Differentiating the experiences and identities of lesbian, gay, bisexual, and transgendered people. In K. J. Bieschke, R. M. Perez, & K. A. DeBord (Eds.), *Handbook of counseling and psychotherapy with lesbian, gay, bisexual, and transgendered clients* (2nd ed., pp. 19–49). Washington, DC: American Psychological Association.

Feldman, R., Sussman, A. L., & Zigler, E. (2004). Parental leave and work adaptation at the transition to parenthood: Individual, marital, and social correlates. *Applied Developmental Psychology, 25*, 459–479.

Ferree, M. M. (1990). Beyond separate spheres: Feminism and family research. *Journal of Marriage and the Family, 52,* 866–884.

Firestein, B. A. (2007). Cultural and relational contexts of bisexual women: Implications for therapy. In K. J. Bieschke, R. M. Perez, & K. A. DeBord (Eds.), *Handbook of counseling and psychotherapy with lesbian, gay, bisexual, and transgendered clients* (2nd ed., pp. 91–117). Washington, DC: American Psychological Association.

Flaks, D. K., Ficher, I., Masterpasqua, F., & Joseph, G. (1995). Lesbians choosing motherhood: A comparative study of lesbian and heterosexual parents and their children. *Developmental Psychology, 31,* 105–114.

Freedman, D., Tasker, F., & di Ceglie, D. (2002). Children and adolescents with transsexual parents referred to a specialist gender identity development service: A brief report of key developmental features. *Clinical Child Psychology and Psychiatry, 7,* 423–432.

Fulcher, M., Sutfin, E. L., & Patterson, C. J. (2008). Individual differences in gender development: Associations with parental sexual orientation, attitudes, and division of labor. *Sex Roles, 58,* 330–341.

Furstenberg, F. F., & Cherlin, A. (1991). *Divided families: What happens to children when parents part.* Cambridge, MA: Harvard University Press.

Gabb, J. (1999). Imag(in)ing the queer lesbian family. *Journal of the Association for Research on Mothering, 1,* 9–20.

Gabb, J. (2004a). Critical differentials: Querying the incongruities within research on lesbian parent families. *Sexualities, 7,* 167–182.

Gabb, J. (2004b). Sexuality education: How children of lesbian mothers "learn" about sex/uality. *Sex Education, 4,* 19–34.

Gabb, J. (2005). Lesbian M/Otherhood: Strategies of familial–linguistic management in lesbian parent families. *Sociology, 39,* 585–603.

Gagnon, A. C., Riley, A., Toole, M., & Goldberg, A. E. (2007, August). *Motivations to parent in lesbian adoptive couples.* Poster presented at the American Psychological Association annual conference, San Francisco.

Gamson, J., & Moon, D. (2004). The sociology of sexualities: Queer and beyond. *Annual Review of Sociology, 30,* 47–64.

Garcia, O. (2008, February 11). Agency, birth mother try to take baby back from adoptive parents. *JournalStar.com.* Retrieved May 20, 2008 from: www.journalstar.com/articles/2008/02/11/news/nebraska/doc47b069ddd7cb2681253863.xt

Garner, A. (2004). *Families like mine: Children of gay parents tell it like it is.* New York: Harper.

Garnets, L., & Kimmel, D. (2003). *Psychological perspectives on lesbian and gay male experience.* New York: Columbia University Press.

Gartrell, N., Banks, A., Hamilton, J., Reed, N., Bishop, H., & Rodas, C. (1999). The National Lesbian Family Study: 2. Interviews with mothers of toddlers. *American Journal of Orthopsychiatry, 69,* 362–369.

Gartrell, N., Banks, A., Reed, N., Hamilton, J., Rodas, C., & Deck, A. (2000). The National Lesbian Family Study: 3. Interviews with mothers of five-year-olds. *American Journal of Orthopsychiatry, 70,* 542–548.

Gartrell, N., Deck, A., Rodas, C., Peyser, H., & Banks, A. (2005). The National Lesbian Family Study: 4. Interviews with the 10-year-old children. *American Journal of Orthopsychiatry, 75,* 518–524.

Gartrell, N., Deck, A., Rodas, C., Peyser, H., & Banks, A. (2006). The USA National Lesbian Family Study: Interviews with mothers of 10-year-olds. *Feminism & Psychology, 16,* 175–192.

Gartrell, N., Hamilton, J., Banks, A., Mosbacher, D., Reed, N., Sparks, C. H., et al. (1996). The National Lesbian Family Study: 1. Interviews with prospective mothers. *American Journal of Orthopsychiatry, 66,* 272–281.

Gates, G. (2007, November). *Geographic trends among same-sex couples in the U.S. Census and the American Community Survey.* Los Angeles: The Williams Institute.

Gates, G., Badgett, M. V. L., Macomber, J. E., & Chambers, K. (2007). *Adoption and foster care by gay and lesbian parents in the United States.* Washington, DC: The Urban Institute.

Gates, G., & Ost, J. (2004). *The gay and lesbian atlas.* Washington, DC: The Urban Institute.

Gershon, T. D., Tschann, J. M., & Jemerin, J. M. (1999). Stigmatization, self-esteem, and coping among the adolescent children of lesbian mothers. *Journal of Adolescent Health, 24,* 437–445.

Giammattei, S. V. (2008). Family relations and emotional intelligence of children raised by lesbian or heterosexual parents. *Dissertation Abstracts International: Section B: The Sciences and Engineering, 68*(7-B), 4823.

Gianino, M. (2008). Adaptation and transformation: The transition to adoptive parenthood for gay male couples. *Journal of GLBT Family Studies, 4,* 205–243.

Gil de Lamadrid, M. (Ed.). (1991). *Lesbians choosing motherhood: Legal implications of donor insemination and co-parenting.* San Francisco: National Center for Lesbian Rights.

Gilligan, C. (1982). *In a different voice: Psychological theory and women's development.* Cambridge, MA: Harvard University Press.

Gjerdingen, D. K., & Chaloner, K. (1994). Mothers' experiences with household roles and social support during the first postpartum year. *Women and Health, 21,* 57–74.

Goffman, E. (1963). *Stigma: Notes on the management of spoiled identity.* Englewood Cliffs, NJ: Prentice-Hall.

Goldberg, A. E. (2006). The transition to parenthood for lesbian couples. *Journal of GLBT Family Studies, 2,* 13–42.

Goldberg, A. E. (2007a). (How) does it make a difference? Perspectives of adults with lesbian, gay, and bisexual parents. *American Journal of Orthopsychiatry, 77,* 550–562.

Goldberg, A. E. (2007b). Talking about family: Disclosure practices of adults raised by lesbian, gay, and bisexual parents. *Journal of Family Issues, 28,* 100–131.

Goldberg, A. E. (2009). Lesbian and heterosexual preadoptive couples' openness to transracial adoption. *American Journal of Orthopsychiatry, 79,* 103–117.

Goldberg, A. E. (in press). Lesbian parents and their families: Complexity and intersectionality from a feminist perspective. In S. Lloyd, A. Few, & K. R. Allen (Eds.), *Feminist theory, methods and praxis in family studies.* Thousand Oaks, CA: Sage.

Goldberg, A. E., & Allen, K. R. (2007). Lesbian mothers' ideas and intentions about male involvement across the transition to parenthood. *Journal of Marriage and Family, 69,* 352–365.

Goldberg, A. E., Downing, J. B., & Richardson, H. (in press). From infertility to adoption: Experiences of lesbian and heterosexual preadoptive couples. *Journal of Social and Personal Relationships.*

Goldberg, A. E., Downing, J. B., & Sauck, C. C. (2007). Choices, challenges, and tensions: Perspectives of lesbian prospective adoptive parents. *Adoption Quarterly, 10,* 33–64.

Goldberg, A. E., Downing, J. B., & Sauck, C. C. (2008). Perceptions of children's parental preferences in lesbian two-mother households. *Journal of Marriage and Family, 70,* 419–434.

Goldberg, A. E., & Perry-Jenkins, M. (2004). The division of labor and working-class women's well-being across the transition to parenthood. *Journal of Family Psychology, 18,* 225–236.

Goldberg, A. E., & Perry-Jenkins, M. (2007). The division of labor and perceptions of parental roles: Lesbian couples across the transition to parenthood. *Journal of Social and Personal Relationships, 24,* 297–318.

Goldberg, A. E., & Sayer, A. G. (2006). Lesbian couples' relationship quality across the transition to parenthood. *Journal of Marriage and Family, 68,* 87–100.

Goldberg, A. E., & Smith. J. Z. (2008a). Social and psychological resources in prospective adoptive parents. *Family Relations, 57,* 281–294.

Goldberg, A. E., & Smith, J. Z. (2008b). The social context of lesbian mothers' anxiety during early parenthood. *Parenting: Science & Practice, 8,* 213–239.

Goldhaber, O. (2007). "I want my mommies": The cry for mini-DOMAs to recognize the best interest of the children of same-sex couples. *Family Court Review, 45,* 287–301.

Golombok, S., Perry, B., Burston, A., Murray, C., Mooney-Somers, J., Stevens, M., & Golding, J. (2003). Children with lesbian parents: A community study. *Developmental Psychology, 39,* 20–33.

Golombok, S., Spencer, A., & Rutter, M. (1983). Children in lesbian and single-parent households: Psychosexual and psychiatric appraisal. *Journal of Child Psychology and Psychiatry, 24,* 551–572.

Golombok, S., & Tasker, F. (1994). Children in lesbian and gay families: Theories and evidence. *Annual Review of Sex Research, 5,* 73–100.

Golombok, S., & Tasker, F. (1996). Do parents influence the sexual orientation of their children? Findings from a longitudinal study of lesbian families. *Developmental Psychology, 32*, 3–11.

Goodman, C. (1999). Intimacy and autonomy in long term marriage. *Journal of Gerontological Social Work, 32*, 83–97.

Gordon, L. E. (2006). Bringing the U-Haul: Embracing and resisting sexual stereotypes in a lesbian community. *Sexualities, 9*, 171–192.

Gottman, J. (1990). Children of gay and lesbian parents. In F. W. Bozett & M. B. Sussman (Eds.), *Homosexuality and family relations* (pp. 177–196). New York: Harrington Park Press.

Gottman, J. M., Levenson, R. W., Swanson, C., Swanson, K., Tyson, R., & Yoshimoto, D. (2003). Observing gay, lesbian, and heterosexual couples' relationships: Mathematical modeling of conflict interaction. *Journal of Homosexuality, 45*, 65–91.

Green, A. I. (2007). On the horns of a dilemma: Institutional dimensions of the sexual career in a sample of middle-class, urban, Black, gay men. *Journal of Black Studies, 37*, 753–774.

Green, R. (1974). *Sexual identity conflict in children and adults*. New York: Basic Books.

Green, R. (1978). Sexual identity of 37 children raised by homosexual or transsexual parents. *American Journal of Psychiatry, 135*, 692–697.

Green, R. (1998). Transsexuals' children. *The International Journal of Transgenderism, 2*(4). Retrieved on February 20, 2008, from http://www.symposion.com/ijt/ijtc0601.htm

Green, R. (2000). "Lesbians, gay men, and their parents": A critique of LaSala and the prevailing clinical "wisdom." *Family Process, 39*, 257–266.

Green, R., Mandel, J. B., Hotvedt, M. E., Gray, J., & Smith, L. (1986). Lesbian mothers and their children: A comparison with solo parent heterosexual mothers and their children. *Archives of Sexual Behavior, 15*, 167–184.

Greene, B. (2000a). African American lesbian and bisexual women. *Journal of Social Issues, 56*, 239–249.

Greene, B. (2000b). African-American lesbian and bisexual women in feminist psychodynamic psychotherapies: Surviving and thriving between a rock and a hard place. In L. Jackson & B. Greene (Eds.), *Psychotherapy with African-American women: Innovative psychodynamic perspectives and practice* (pp. 82–125). New York: Guilford Press.

Greene, B., & Boyd-Franklin, N. (1996). African American lesbians: Issues in couples therapy. In J. Laird & R. Green (Eds.), *Lesbians and gays in couples and families: A handbook for therapists* (pp. 251–271). San Francisco: Jossey-Bass.

Gross, H., & Pattison, H. (2007). *Sanctioning pregnancy: A psychological perspective on the paradoxes and culture of research*. London: Routledge.

Guastello, D. D., & Guastello, S. J. (2003). Androgyny, gender role behavior, and emotional intelligence among college students and their parents. *Sex Roles, 49*, 663–673.

Haas, S. (2002). Social support as relationship maintenance in gay male couples coping with HIV or AIDS. *Journal of Social and Personal Relationships, 19,* 87–112.

Haddock, S. A. (2003). A conversation with Christopher Carrington, PhD: Family life among lesbians and gay men. *Journal of Feminist Family Therapy, 14,* 65–76.

Haimes, E., & Weiner, K. (2000). 'Everybody's got a dad . . . ': Issues for lesbian families in the management of donor insemination. *Sociology of Health and Illness, 22,* 477–499.

Halkitis, P. N. (2001). An exploration of perceptions of masculinity among gay men living with HIV. *The Journal of Men's Studies, 9,* 413–429.

Hall, R. L., & Greene, B. (2002). The complex legacy of social class on African American lesbian relationships. *Journal of Lesbian Studies, 6,* 65–74.

Han, C. (2007). They don't want to cruise your type: Gay men of color and the racial politics of exclusion. *Social Identities, 13,* 51–67.

Harding, R., & Peel, E. (2007). Surveying sexualities: Internet research with non-heterosexuals. *Feminism & Psychology, 17,* 277–285.

Hardt, J., & Rutter, M. (2004). Validity of adult retrospective reports of adverse childhood experiences: Review of the evidence. *Journal of Child Psychology & Psychiatry, 45,* 260–273.

Hare, J. (1994). Concerns and issues faced by families headed by a lesbian couple. *The Journal of Contemporary Human Services, 75,* 27–35.

Hargreaves, K. (2006). Constructing families and kinship through donor insemination. *Sociology of Health and Illness, 28,* 261–283.

Harper, G. W., Jernewall, N., & Zea, M. C. (2004). Giving voice to emerging science and theory for lesbian, gay, and bisexual people of color. *Cultural Diversity and Ethnic Minority Psychology, 10,* 187–199.

Harris, M. B., & Turner, P. H. (1986). Gay and lesbian parents. *Journal of Homosexuality, 12,* 101–113.

Hart, T. A., Wolitski, R. J., Purcell, D. W., Gomez, C., & Halkitis, P. (2003). Sexual behavior among HIV-positive men who have sex with men: What's in a label? *The Journal of Sex Research, 40,* 179–188.

Harvey, S. M., Carr, C., & Bernheine, S. (1989). Lesbian mothers: Health care experiences. *Journal of Nurse Midwifery, 34,* 115–119.

Haugen, E. N., Schmutzer, P. A., & Wenzel, A. (2004). Sexuality and the partner relationship during pregnancy and the postpartum period. In J. H. Harvey, A. Wenzel, & S. Sprecher (Eds.), *The handbook of sexuality in close relationships* (pp. 411–435). Mahwah, NJ: Erlbaum.

Hays, R., Catania, J., McKusick, L., & Coates, T. (1990). Help-seeking for AIDS-related concerns: A comparison of gay men with various HIV diagnoses. *American Journal of Community Psychology, 18,* 743–745.

Heineman, T. V. (2004). A boy and two mothers: New variations on an old theme or a new story. *Psychoanalytic Psychology, 21,* 99–115.

Henrickson, M. (2005). Lavender parents. *Social Policy Journal of New England, 26,* 68–83.

Henrickson, M. (2007). Reaching out, hooking up: Lavender netlife in a New Zealand study. *Sexuality Research & Social Policy, 4,* 38–49.

Hequembourg, A., & Farrell, M. (1999). Lesbian motherhood: Negotiating marginal–mainstream identities. *Gender & Society, 13,* 540–555.

Herdt, G. (1992). *Gay culture in America: Essays from the field.* Boston: Beacon.

Herek, G. M. (1986). On heterosexual masculinity: Some psychical consequences of the social construction of gender and sexuality. *American Behavioral Scientist, 29,* 563–577.

Herek, G. M. (1996). Why tell if you're not asked? Self-disclosure, intergroup contact, and heterosexual's attitudes toward lesbians and gay men. In L. Garnets & D. C. Kimmel (Eds.), *Psychological perspectives on lesbian, gay, and bisexual issues* (pp. 270–298). New York: Columbia University Press.

Herek, G. M. (2006). Legal recognition of same-sex relationships in the United States: A social science perspective. *American Psychologist, 61,* 607–621.

Herek, G. M. (2007). Confronting sexual stigma and prejudice: Theory and practice. *Journal of Social Issues, 63,* 905–925.

Herrmann-Green, L. K., & Gehring, T. M. (2007). The German lesbian family study: Planning for parenthood via donor insemination. *Journal of GLBT Family Studies, 3,* 351–395.

Hertz, R. (2002). The father as an idea: A challenge to kinship boundaries by single mothers. *Symbolic Interaction, 25,* 1–31.

Hicks, S. (2005a). Queer genealogies: Tales of conformity and rebellion amongst lesbian and gay foster carers and adopters. *Qualitative Social Work: Research & Practice, 4,* 293–308.

Hicks, S. (2005b). Maternal men—perverts and deviants? Making sense of gay men as foster carers and adopters. *Journal of GLBT Family Studies, 2,* 93–114.

Hicks, S. (2005c). Is gay parenting bad for kids? Responding to the 'very idea of difference' in research on lesbian and gay parents. *Sexualities, 8,* 153–168.

Hicks, G. R., & Lee, T. (2006). Public attitudes toward gays and lesbians: Trends and predictors. *Journal of Homosexuality, 51,* 57–77.

Hickson, F. C., Davies, P. M., Hunt, A. J., Weatherburn, P., McManus, T. J., & Coxon, A. P. (1992). Maintenance of open gay relationships: Some strategies for protection against HIV. *AIDS Care, 4,* 409–419.

Hill, C. (1999). Fusion and conflict in lesbian relationships? *Feminism & Psychology, 9,* 179–189.

Hines, M. (2004). Androgen, estrogen, and gender: Contributions of the early hormone environment to gender-related behavior. In A. H. Eagly, A. E. Beall, & R. J. Sternberg (Eds.), *The psychology of gender* (2nd ed., pp. 9–37). New York: Guilford.

Hines, S. (2006a). Intimate transitions: Transgender practices of partnering and parenting. *Sociology, 40,* 353–371.

Hines, S. (2006b). What's the difference? Bringing particularity to queer studies of transgender. *Journal of Gender Studies, 15*, 49–66.

Hoeffer, B. (1981). Children's acquisition of sex-role behavior in lesbian-mother families. *American Journal of Orthopsychiatry, 51*, 536–544.

Hollandsworth, M. J. (1995). Gay men creating families through surro-gay arrangements: A paradigm for reproductive freedom. *Journal of Gender & Law, 3*, 183–246.

Holt, M., & Stephenson, N. (2006). Living with HIV and negotiating psychological disclosure. *Health: An Interdisciplinary Journal for the Social Study of Health, Illness and Medicine, 10*, 211–231.

Huggins, S. L. (1989). A comparative study of self-esteem of adolescent children of divorced lesbian mothers and divorced heterosexual mothers. In F. W. Bozett (Ed.), *Homosexuality and the family* (pp. 123–135). New York: Harrington Park Press.

Human Rights Campaign Foundation. (2002). *The state of the family*. Washington, DC: Author.

Hunter, J., & Mallon, G. P. (1998). Social work practice with gay men and lesbians within communities. In G. P. Mallon (Ed.), *Foundations of social work practice with lesbian and gay persons* (pp. 229–248). Binghamton, NY: Haworth Press.

Israel, G. (2004). Supporting transgender and sex reassignment issues: Couple and family dynamics. *Journal of Couples and Relationship Therapy, 3*, 53–63.

Jager, A. M. (1989). Love and knowledge: Emotion in feminist epistemology. *Inquiry, 32*, 151–176.

James, S. E. (2002). Clinical themes in gay and lesbian parented adoptive families. *Clinical Child Psychology & Psychiatry, 7*, 475–486.

James, S. E., & Murphy, B. C. (1998). Gay and lesbian relationships in a changing social context. In C. J. Patterson & A. R. D'Augelli (Eds.), *Lesbian, gay, and bisexual identities in families: Psychological perspectives* (pp. 75–98). New York: Oxford University Press.

Javaid, G. A. (1993). The children of homosexual and heterosexual single mothers. *Child Psychiatry & Human Development, 23*, 235–248.

Jay, K., & Young, A. (1979). *Out of the closets: Voices of gay liberation*. New York: BJ Publishing Group.

Johnson, S. M., & O'Connor, E. (2002). *The gay baby boom: The psychology of gay parenthood*. New York: New York University Press.

Jones, C. (2005). Looking like a family: Negotiating bio-genetic continuity in British lesbian families using licensed donor insemination. *Sexualities, 8*, 221–237.

Jones, R. W., & de Cecco, J. P. (1982). The femininity and masculinity of partners in heterosexual and homosexual relationships. *Journal of Homosexuality, 8*, 37–44.

Joos, K. E., & Broad, K. L. (2007). Coming out of the family closet: Stories of adult women with LGBTQ parent(s). *Qualitative Sociology, 30*, 275–295.

Julien, D., Chartrand, E., & Begin, J. (1996). Male couples' dyadic adjustment and the use of safer sex within and outside of primary relationships. *Journal of Family Psychology, 10*, 89–96.

Julien, D., Chartrand, E., Simard, M. C., Bouthillier, D., & Begin, J. (2003). Conflict, social support, and relationship quality: An observational study of heterosexual, gay male, and lesbian couples' communication. *Journal of Family Psychology*, *17*, 419–428.

Kadushin, G. (1996). Gay men with AIDS and their families of origin: An analysis of social support. *Health & Social Work*, *21*, 141–149.

Kane, E. (2006). "No way my boys are going to be like that!": Parents' responses to children's gender nonconformity. *Gender & Society*, *20*, 149–176.

Kendell, K. (1999). Sexual orientation and child custody. *Trial*, *35*, 42.

Kendler, K. S., Thornton, L. M., Gilman, S. E., & Kessler, R. C. (2000). Sexual orientation in a U.S. national sample of twin and nontwin sibling pairs. *American Journal of Psychiatry*, *157*, 1843–1846.

Kenney, J. W., & Tash, D. T. (1992). Lesbian childbearing couples' dilemmas and decisions. *Health Care for Women International*, *13*, 209–219.

Kindle, P. A., & Erich, S. (2005). Perceptions of social support among heterosexual and homosexual adopters. *Families in Society*, *86*, 541–546.

King, M., & Bartlett, A. (2005). What same sex civil partnerships may mean for health. *Journal of Epidemiology and Community Health*, *60*, 188–191.

Kippax, S. C., Aggleton, P., Moatti, J. P., & Delfraissy, J. F. (2007). Living with HIV: Recent research from France and the French Caribbean (VESPA study), Australia, Canada, and the United Kingdom. *AIDS*, *21*, S1–S3.

Kirkpatrick, M., Smith, C., & Roy, R. (1981). Lesbian mothers and their children: A comparative study. *American Journal of Orthopsychiatry*, *51*, 545–551.

Kitterod, R. H., & Pettersen, S. V. (2006). Making up for mothers' employed working hours? Housework and childcare among Norwegian fathers. *Work, Employment & Society*, *20*, 473–492.

Klinkenberg, D., & Rose, S. (1994). Dating scripts of lesbians and gay men. *Journal of Homosexuality*, *26*, 23–35.

Kluwer, E. S., Heesink, J. A. M., & van de Vliert, E. (2002). The division of labor across the transition to parenthood: A justice perspective. *Journal of Marriage and Family*, *64*, 930–943.

Koepke, L., Hare, J., & Moran, P. (1992). Relationship quality in a sample of lesbian couples with children and child-free lesbian couples. *Family Relations*, *41*, 224–229.

Kosciw, J. G., & Diaz, E. M. (2008). *Involved, invisible, ignored: The experiences of lesbian, gay, bisexual, and transgender parents and their children in our nation's K–12 schools*. New York: Gay, Lesbian and Straight Education Network. Retrieved June 3, 2008, from http://www.glsen.org/cgi-bin/iowa/all/news/record/2271.html

Kranz, K. C., & Daniluk, J. C. (2006). Living outside of the box: Lesbian couples conceived through the use of anonymous donor insemination. *Journal of Feminist Family Therapy*, *18*, 1–33.

Krieg, D. B. (2007). Does motherhood get easier the second time around? Examining parenting stress and marital quality among mothers having their first or second child. *Parenting: Science & Practice, 7,* 149–175.

Kurdek, L. A. (1988). Relationship quality of gay and lesbian cohabiting couples. *Journal of Homosexuality, 15,* 93–118.

Kurdek, L. A. (1993). The allocation of household labor in gay, lesbian, and heterosexual married couples. *Journal of Social Issues, 49,* 127–139.

Kurdek, L. A. (1994). Areas of conflict for gay, lesbian, and heterosexual couples: What couples argue about influences relationship satisfaction. *Journal of Marriage and the Family, 56,* 923–934.

Kurdek, L. A. (1995). Developmental changes in relationship quality in gay and lesbian cohabiting couples. *Developmental Psychology, 31,* 86–94.

Kurdek, L. A. (1996). The deterioration of relationship quality for gay and lesbian cohabiting couples: A five-year prospective longitudinal study. *Personal Relationships, 3,* 417–442.

Kurdek, L. A. (1998). Relationship outcomes and their predictors: Longitudinal evidence from heterosexual married, gay cohabiting, and lesbian cohabiting couples. *Journal of Marriage and the Family, 60,* 553–568.

Kurdek, L. A. (2000). Attractions and constraints as determinants of relationship commitment: Longitudinal evidence from gay, lesbian, and heterosexual couples. *Personal Relationships, 7,* 245–262.

Kurdek, L. A. (2001). Differences between heterosexual non-parent couples and gay, lesbian, and heterosexual parent couples. *Journal of Family Issues, 22,* 727–754.

Kurdek, L. A. (2003). Differences between gay and lesbian cohabiting couples. *Journal of Social Personal Relationships, 20,* 411–436.

Kurdek, L. A. (2005). What do we know about gay and lesbian couples? *Current Directions in Psychological Science, 14,* 251–254.

Kurdek, L. A. (2006). Differences between partners from heterosexual, gay, and lesbian cohabiting couples. *Journal of Marriage and Family, 68,* 509–528.

Kurdek, L. A. (2007). The allocation of household labor by partners in gay and lesbian couples. *Journal of Family Issues, 28,* 132–148.

Kurdek, L. A., & Schmitt, J. P. (1987). Perceived emotional support from family and friends in members of homosexual, married, and heterosexual cohabiting couples. *Journal of Homosexuality, 14,* 57–68.

Kuvalanka, K. A. (2007). Coping with heterosexism and homophobia: Young adults with lesbian parents reflect on their adolescence. *Dissertation Abstracts International Section A: Humanities and Social Sciences, 68*(4-A), 1677.

Kuvalanka, K. A., & Goldberg, A. E. (2008). [Queer youth with queer parents]. Unpublished data.

Kuvalanka, K. A., & Goldberg, A. E. (in press). "Second generation": Queer youth with queer parents. *Journal of Youth & Adolescence.*

Kuvalanka, K. A., Teper, B., & Morrison, O. (2006). COLAGE: Providing community, education, leadership, and advocacy by and for children of GLBT parents. *Journal of GLBT Family Studies, 2,* 71–92.

Kweskin, S. L., & Cook, A. S. (1982). Heterosexual and homosexual mothers' self-described sex-role behavior and ideal sex-role behavior in children. *Sex Roles*, 8, 967–975.

Lane, J. D., & Wegner, D. M. (1995). The cognitive consequences of secrecy. *Journal of Personality and Social Psychology*, 69, 237–253.

LaSala, M. C. (2002). Walls and bridges: How coupled gay men and lesbians manage their intergenerational relationships. *Journal of Marital and Family Therapy*, 28, 327–339.

Lassiter, P. S., Dew, B. J., Newton, K., Hays, D. G., & Yarbrough, B. (2006). Self-defined empowerment for gay and lesbian parents: A qualitative explanation. *The Family Journal*, 14, 245–252.

Lauer, R. H., & Lauer, J. C. (1987). Factors in long-term marriages. *Journal of Family Issues*, 7, 382–390.

Lemieux, R., & Hale, J. L. (2000). Intimacy, passion, and commitment among married individuals: Further testing of the triangular theory of love. *Psychological Reports*, 87, 941–948.

Lerner, R., & Nagai, A. (2001). No basis: What the studies don't tell us about same-sex parenting. *Marriage Law Project*. Washington, DC: Ethics and Public Policy Center.

Leung, P., Erich, S., & Kanenberg, H. (2005). A comparison of family functioning in gay/lesbian, heterosexual and special needs adoptions. *Children & Youth Services Review*, 27, 1031–1044.

Lev, A. I. (2004). *The complete lesbian and gay parenting guide*. New York: Penguin.

Lev, A. I. (2006). Gay dads: Choosing surrogacy. *Lesbian & Gay Psychology Review*, 7, 73–77.

Lev, A. I., Dean, G., DeFilippis, L., Everham, K., McLaughlin, L., & Phillips, C. (2005). Dykes and tykes: A virtual lesbian parenting community in lesbian communities: Festivals, RVs, and the Internet. *Journal of Lesbian Studies*, 9, 81–94.

Levitt, H. M., & Hiestand, K. (2005). Enacting a gendered sexuality: Butch and femme perspectives. *Journal of Constructivist Psychology*, 18, 39–51.

Levitt, H. M., & Horne, S. G. (2002). Explorations of lesbian-queer genders: Butch, femme, androgynous, or "other." *Journal of Lesbian Studies*, 6, 25–39.

Levine, M. (1979). *Gay men: The sociology of male homosexuality*. New York: Harper & Row.

Lewin, E. (1993). *Lesbian mothers: Accounts of gender in American culture*. Ithaca, NY: Cornell University Press.

Lewis, K. G. (1980). Children of lesbians: Their point of view. *Social Work*, 23, 198–203.

Lewis, L. (1984). The coming-out process for lesbians: Integrating a stable identity. *Social Work*, 29, 464–469.

Liau, A., Millett, G., & Marks, G. (2006). Meta-analytic examination of online sex seeking and sexual risk behavior among men who have sex with men. *Sexually Transmitted Diseases*, 33, 576–584.

Lindsay, J., Perlesz, A., Brown, R., McNair, R., de Vaus, D., & Pitts, M. (2006). Stigma or respect: Lesbian-parented families negotiating school settings. *Sociology, 40*, 1059–1077.

Litovich, M. L., & Langhout, R. D. (2004). Framing heterosexism in lesbian families: A preliminary examination of resilient coping. *Journal of Community and Applied Social Psychology, 14*, 411–435.

Liu, C., Ostrow, D., Detels, R., Hu, Z., Johnson, L., Kingsley, L., & Jacobson, L. P. (2006). Impacts of HIV infection and HAART use on quality of life. *Quality of Life Research: An International Journal of Quality of Life Aspects of Treatment, Care & Rehabilitation, 15*, 941–949.

Llewelyn, S. (2007). A neutral feminist observer? Observation-based research and the politics of feminist knowledge making. *Gender & Development, 15*, 299–310.

Loiacano, D. K. (1989). Gay identity issues among Black Americans: Racism, homophobia, and the need for validation. *Journal of Counseling and Development, 68*, 21–25.

Lothstein, L. M. (1988). Female-to-male transsexuals who have delivered and reared their children. *Annals of Sex Research, 1*, 151–166.

Lynch, J., & Murray, K. (2000). For the love of children: The coming out process of lesbian and gay parents and stepparents. *Journal of Homosexuality, 39*, 1–24.

Lynch, J. M. (2004a). Becoming a stepparent in gay/lesbian stepfamilies: Integrating identities. *Journal of Homosexuality, 48*, 45–60.

Lynch, J. M. (2004b). The identity transformation of biological parents in lesbian/gay stepfamilies. *Journal of Homosexuality, 47*, 91–107.

Lytton, H., & Romney, D. M. (1991). Parents' differential socialization of boys and girls: A meta-analysis. *Psychological Bulletin, 109*, 267–296.

MacCallum, F., & Golombok, S. (2004). Children raised in fatherless families from infancy: A follow-up of children of lesbian and single heterosexual mothers at early adolescence. *Journal of Child Psychology & Psychiatry, 45*, 1407–1419.

Maccoby, E. (1988). Gender as a social category. *Developmental Psychology, 45*, 513–530.

Mackey, R. A., Diemer, M. A., & O'Brien, B. A. (2000). Psychological intimacy in the lasting relationships of heterosexual and same-gender couples. *Sex Roles, 43*, 201–227.

Mackey, R. A., Diemer, M. A., & O'Brien, B. A. (2004). Relational factors in understanding satisfaction in the lasting relationships of same-sex and heterosexual couples. *Journal of Homosexuality, 47*, 111–136.

Mackey, R. A., O'Brien, B. A., & Mackey, E. F. (1997). *Gay male and lesbian couples: Voices from lasting relationships*. Westport, CT: Praeger.

Mallon, G. P. (2004). *Gay men choosing parenthood*. New York: Columbia University Press.

Mallon, G. P. (2007). Assessing lesbian and gay prospective foster and adoptive families: A focus on the home study process. *Child Welfare, 86*, 67–86.

Man who was formerly a woman claims to be five months pregnant. (2008, March 29). *New York Daily News*. Retrieved June 5, 2008, from http://www.nydailynews.com/news/us_world/2008/03/28/2008-03-28_man_who_was_formerly_a_woman_claims_to_b.html

Martin, A. (1998). Clinical issues in psychotherapy with lesbian-, gay-, and bisexual-parented families. In C. J. Patterson & A. R. D'Augelli (Eds.), *Lesbian, gay, and bisexual identities in families: Psychological perspectives* (pp. 270–291). New York: Oxford University Press.

Martin, C. L., & Ruble, D. (2004). Children's search for gender cues: Cognitive perspectives on gender development. *Current Directions in Psychological Science, 13*, 67–70.

Mason, J. (2006). Mixing methods in a qualitatively driven way. *Qualitative Research, 6*, 9–25.

Matteson, D. R. (1985). Bisexual men in marriage: Is a positive homosexual identity and stable marriage possible? *Journal of Homosexuality, 11*, 149–171.

Matthews, A. K., Tartaro, J., & Hughes, T. L. (2003). A comparative study of lesbian and heterosexual women in committed relationships. *Journal of Lesbian Studies, 7*, 101–114.

Matthews, C. R., & Lease, S. H. (2000). Focus on lesbian, gay, and bisexual families. In R. M. Perez, K. A. DeBord, & K. J. Bieschke (Eds.), *Handbook of counseling and psychotherapy with lesbian, gay, and bisexual clients* (pp. 249–273). Washington, DC: American Psychological Association.

Matthews, J. D., & Cramer, E. P. (2006). Envisaging the adoption process to strengthen gay and lesbian-headed families: Recommendations for adoption professionals. *Child Welfare, 85*, 317–340.

Matthey, S., Barnett, B., Ungerer, J., & Waters, B. (2000). Paternal and maternal depressed mood during the transition to parenthood. *Journal of Affective Disorders, 60*, 75–85.

Mayes, L. C., & Leckman, J. F. (2007). Parental representations and subclinical changes in postpartum mood. *Infant Mental Health Journal, 28*, 281–297.

Mayne, T. J., Acree, M., Chesney, M. A., & Folkman, S. (1998). HIV sexual risk behavior following bereavement in gay men. *Health Psychology, 17*, 403–411.

Mays, V., Chatters, L. M., Cochran, S. D., & Mackness, J. (1998). African American families in diversity: Gay men and lesbians as participants in family networks. *Journal of Comparative Family Studies, 29*, 73–87.

Mays, V., Cochran, S., & Rhue, S. (1993). The impact of perceived discrimination on the intimate relationships of Black lesbians. *Journal of Homosexuality, 25*, 1–14.

McCandlish, B. (1987). Against all odds: Lesbian mother family dynamics. In F. Bozett (Ed.), *Gay and lesbian parents* (pp. 23–38). New York: Praeger.

McDermott, E. (2006). Surviving in dangerous places: Lesbian identity performances in the workplace, social class, and psychological health. *Feminism & Psychology, 16*, 193–211.

McGovern, M. A. (1990). Sensitivity and reciprocity in the play of adolescent mothers and young fathers with their infants. *Family Relations, 39,* 427–431.

McIntyre, D. H. (2004). Gay parents and child custody: A struggle under the legal system. *Mediation Quarterly, 12,* 135–149.

McMahon, C., Barnett, B., Kowalenko, N., Tennant, C., & Don, N. (2001). Postnatal depression, anxiety and unsettled infant behaviour. *Australian and New Zealand Journal of Psychiatry, 35,* 581–588.

McManus, A. J., Hunter, L. P., & Renn, H. (2006). Lesbian experiences and needs during childbirth: Guidance for health care providers. *Journal of Obstetric, Gynecologic, & Neonatal Nursing, 35,* 13–23.

McNeill, K., Rienzi, B., & Kposowa, A. (1998). Families and parenting: A comparison of lesbian and heterosexual mothers. *Psychological Reports, 82,* 59–62.

McPheeters, A., Carmi, M., & Goldberg, A. E. (2008, August). *Gay men's experiences of sexism and heterosexism in the adoption process.* Poster presented at the American Psychological Association annual conference, Boston.

Meezan, W., & Martin, J. I. (2003). Exploring current themes in research on gay, lesbian, bisexual, and transgender populations. *Journal of Gay & Lesbian Social Services, 15,* 1–14.

Meezan, W., & Rauch, J. (2005). Gay marriage, same-sex parenting, and America's children. *The Future of Children, 15,* 97–115.

Mercier, L. R., & Harold, R. D. (2003). At the interface: Lesbian-parent families and their children's schools. *Children & Schools, 25,* 35–47.

Merighi, J. R., & Grimes, M. D. (2000). Coming out to families in a multicultural context. *Families in Society, 81,* 32–41.

Meyer, I. H. (2003). Prejudice, social stress, and mental health in lesbian, gay, and bisexual populations: Conceptual issues and research evidence. *Psychological Bulletin, 129,* 674–697.

Meyer, J. (1989). Guess who's coming to dinner this time? A study of gay intimate relationships and the support for those relationships. *Marriage & Family Review, 14,* 59–82.

Michelle, C. (2006). Transgressive technologies? Strategies of discursive containment in the representation and regulation of assisted reproductive technologies in Aotearoa/New Zealand. *Women's Studies International Forum, 29,* 109–124.

Miller, J. A., Jacobsen, R. B., & Bigner, J. J. (1981). The child's home environment for lesbian vs. heterosexual mothers: A neglected area of research. *Journal of Homosexuality, 7,* 49–56.

Money, J., & Ehrhardt, A. (1972). *Man and woman; boy and girl.* Baltimore: Johns Hopkins University Press.

Mooney-Somers, J., & Golombok, S. (2000). Children of lesbian mothers: From the 1970s to the new millennium. *Sexual and Relationship Therapy, 15,* 121–126.

Moore, M. (2006). Lipstick or Timberlands? Meanings of gender presentation in Black lesbian communities. *Signs, 32,* 113–129.

Moore, M. R. (2008). Household decision making in lesbian stepfamilies. *American Sociological Review, 73,* 335–356.

Morgan, K. S., & Brown, L. S. (1991). Lesbian career development, work behavior, and vocational counseling. *The Counseling Psychologist, 19,* 273–291.

Morningstar, B. (1999). Lesbian parents: Understanding developmental pathways. In J. Laird (Ed.), *Lesbians and lesbian families* (pp. 197–212). New York: Columbia University Press.

Morris, J. F., Waldo, C. R., & Rothblum, E. D. (2001). A model of predictors and outcomes of outness among lesbians and bisexual women. *American Journal of Orthopsychiatry, 71,* 61–71.

Morse, C. A., Buist, A., & Durkin, S. (2000). First-time parenthood: Influences on pre- and post-natal adjustment in fathers and mothers. *Journal of Psychosomatic Obstetrics & Gynecology, 21,* 109–120.

Morton, S. B. (1998). Lesbian divorce. *American Journal of Orthopsychiatry, 68,* 410–419.

Moskowitz, D. A., Rieger, G., & Roloff, M. E. (2008). Tops, bottoms, and versatiles. *Sexual and Relationship Therapy, 23,* 191–202.

Moyle, G., Gatell, J., Perno, C. F., Ratanasuwan, W., Schechter, M., & Tsoukas, C. (2008). Potential for new antiretrovirals to address unmet needs in the management of HIV-1 infection. *AIDS Patient Care, 22,* 459–471.

Murray, C., & Golombok, S. (2005). Going it alone: Solo mothers and their infants conceived by donor insemination. *American Journal of Orthopsychiatry, 75,* 242–253.

Muzio, C. (1995). Lesbians choosing children: Creating families, creating narrative. *Journal of Feminist Family Therapy, 7,* 33–45.

Nestle, J. (Ed.). (1992). *The persistent desire: A femme–butch reader.* Boston: Alyson Books.

Nugent, K., & Goldberg, A. E. (2008). *Choosing a type of adoption: Experiences of gay, lesbian, and heterosexual couples.* Unpublished manuscript.

Nungesser, L. G. (1980). Theoretical bases for research on the acquisition of social sex-roles by children of lesbian mothers. *Journal of Homosexuality, 5,* 177–187.

O'Connell, A. (1993). Voices from the heart: The developmental impact of a mother's lesbianism on her adolescent children. *Smith College Studies in Social Work, 63,* 281–299.

Oerton, S. (1998). Reclaiming the 'housewife'? Lesbians and household work. *Journal of Lesbian Studies, 2,* 69–83.

Orel, N. A., & Fruhauf, C. A. (2006). Lesbian and bisexual grandmothers' perceptions of the grandparent–grandchild relationship. *Journal of GLBT Family Studies, 2,* 43–70.

Oswald, R. (2002). Resilience within the family networks of lesbians and gay men: Intentionality and redefinition. *Journal of Marriage and Family, 64,* 374–383.

Oswald, R., Blume, L., & Marks, S. (2005). Decentering heteronormativity: A model for family studies. In V. Bengtson, A. Acock, K. Allen, D. Klein, & P. Dilworth-

Anderson (Eds.), *Sourcebook of family theory and research* (pp. 143–165). Thousand Oaks, CA: Sage.

Oswald, R., & Culton, L. (2003). Under the rainbow: Rural gay life and its relevance for family providers. *Family Relations, 52,* 72–79.

Oswald, R. F., Goldberg, A. E., Kuvalanka, K., & Clausell, E. (2008). Structural and moral commitment among same-sex couples: Relationship duration, religiosity, and parental status. *Journal of Family Psychology, 22,* 411–419.

Paechter, C. (2000). Growing up with a lesbian mother: A theoretically-based analysis of personal experiences. *Sexualities, 3,* 395–408.

Pagenhart, P. (2006). Confessions of a lesbian dad. In H. Aizley (Ed.), *Confessions of the other mother: Nonbiological lesbian mothers tell all* (pp. 35–58). Boston: Beacon.

Palmer, R., & Bor, R. (2001). The challenges to intimacy and sexual relationships for gay men in HIV serodiscordant relationships: A pilot study. *Journal of Marital and Family Therapy, 27,* 419–431.

Patterson, C. J. (1993). Children of lesbian and gay parents. In L. D. Garnets & D. C. Kimmel (Eds.), *Perspectives on lesbian, gay and bisexual experiences* (2nd ed., pp. 497–548). New York: Columbia University Press.

Patterson, C. J. (1995). Families of the lesbian baby boom: Parents' division of labor and children's adjustment. *Developmental Psychology, 31,* 115–123.

Patterson, C. J. (1997). Children of lesbian and gay parents. In T. Ollendick & R. Prinz (Eds.), *Advances in clinical child psychology: Vol. 19* (pp. 235–282). New York: Plenum Press.

Patterson, C. J. (1998). The family lives of children born to lesbian mothers. In C. J. Patterson & A. R. D'Augelli (Eds.), *Lesbian, gay, and bisexual identities in families* (pp. 154–176). New York: Oxford University Press.

Patterson, C. J. (2000). Family relationships of lesbians and gay men. *Journal of Marriage and Family, 62,* 1052–1069.

Patterson, C. J. (2006). Children of lesbian and gay parents. *Current Directions in Psychological Science, 15,* 241–244.

Patterson, C. J., Hurt, S., & Mason, C. D. (1998). Families of the lesbian baby boom: Children's contact with grandparents and other adults. *American Journal of Orthopsychiatry, 68,* 390–399.

Patterson, C. J., Sutfin, E. L., & Fulcher, M. (2004). Division of labor among lesbian and heterosexual parenting couples: Correlates of specialized versus shared patterns. *Journal of Adult Development, 11,* 179–189.

Patterson, D. G., Ciabattari, T., & Schwartz, P. (1999). The constraints of innovation: Commitment and stability among same-sex couples. In J. Adams & W. Jones (Eds.), *Handbook of interpersonal commitment and relationships stability* (pp. 339–359). New York: Plenum.

Pawelski, J. G., Perrin, E. C., Foy, J. M., Allen, C. F., Crawford, M. D. M., Kaufman, M., et al. (2006). The effects of marriage, civil union, and domestic partnership laws on the health and well-being of children. *Pediatrics, 118,* 349–364.

Pearlman, S. F. (1996). Loving across race and class divides: Relational challenges and the interracial lesbian couple. *Women & Therapy, 19,* 25–35.

Pedrick, J., & Goldberg, A. E. (2008, August). *Gay men's experiences during the transition to parenthood.* Poster presented at the American Psychological Association annual conference, Boston.

Peel, E., & Harding, R. (2004a). Civil partnerships: A new couple's conversation. *Feminism & Psychology, 14,* 41–46.

Peel, E., & Harding, R. (2004b). Divorcing romance, rights, and radicalism: Beyond pro and anti in the lesbian and gay marriage debate. *Feminism & Psychology, 14,* 588–599.

Pellegrini, A. D., & Long, J. D. (2002). A longitudinal study of bullying, dominance, and victimization during the transition from primary school through secondary school. *British Journal of Developmental Psychology, 20,* 259–280.

Pennington, S. B. (1987). Children of lesbian mothers. In F. Bozett (Ed.), *Gay and lesbian parents* (pp. 58–73). New York: Praeger.

Peplau, L. A. (2003). Human sexuality: How do men and women differ? *Current Directions in Psychological Science, 12,* 37–40.

Peplau, L. A., & Cochran, S. (1981). Value orientations in the intimate relationships of gay men. *Journal of Homosexuality, 6,* 1–19.

Peplau, L. A., Cochran, S. D., & Mays, V. M. (1997). A national survey of the intimate relationships of African American lesbians and gay men: A look at commitment satisfaction, sexual behavior, and HIV disease. In B. Greene (Ed.), *Ethnic and cultural diversity among lesbians and gay men* (pp. 11–38). Thousand Oaks, CA: Sage.

Peplau, L. A., Cochran, S., Rook, K., & Padesky, C. (1978). Loving women: Attachment and autonomy in lesbian relationships. *Journal of Social Issues, 34,* 7–27.

Peplau, L. A., & Fingerhut, A. (2004). The paradox of the lesbian worker. *Journal of Social Issues, 60,* 719–735.

Peplau, L. A., & Fingerhut, A. (2007). The close relationships of lesbians and gay men. *Annual Review of Psychology, 58,* 405–424.

Peplau, L. A., Fingerhut, A., & Beals, K. P. (2004). Sexuality in the relationships of lesbians and gay men. In J. Harvey, A. Wenzel, & S. Sprecher (Eds.), *Handbook of sexuality in close relationships* (pp. 233–248). Mahwah, NJ: Erlbaum.

Perlesz, A., Brown, R., Lindsay, J., McNair, R., de Vaus, D., & Pitts, M. (2006). Families in transition: Parents, children, and grandparents in lesbian families give meaning to 'doing family.' *Journal of Family Therapy, 28,* 175–199.

Perren, S., von Wyl, A., Burgin, D., Simoni, H., & von Klitzing, K. (2005). Depressive symptoms and psychosocial stress across the transition to parenthood: Associations with parental psychopathology and child difficulty. *Journal of Psychosomatic Obstetrics & Gynecology, 26,* 173–183.

Perrin, E. C. (1998). Children whose parents are lesbian or gay. *Contemporary Pediatrics, 115,* 113–130.

The Pew Research Center. (2006). *Survey report: Pragmatic Americans liberal and conservative on social issues*. Retrieved October 15, 2008, from http://people-press.org/report/283/pragmatic-americans-liberal-and-conservative-on-social-issues

Pharr, S. (1988). *Homophobia: A weapon of sexism*. Little Rock, AR: Chardon Press.

Pies, C. (1988). *Considering parenthood*. San Francisco: Spinsters/Aunt Lute.

Pies, C. (1990). Lesbians and the choice to parent. *Marriage and Family Review, 14,* 137–154.

Polikoff, N. (1990). This child does have two mothers: Redefining parenthood to meet the needs of children in lesbian-mother and other nontraditional families. *Georgetown Law Journal, 78,* 459–515.

Popenoe, D. (1993). American family decline, 1960–1990: A review and appraisal. *Journal of Marriage and the Family, 55,* 527–541.

Prager, K. J., & Buhrmester, D. (1998). Intimacy and need fulfillment in couple relationships. *Journal of Social and Personal Relationships, 15,* 435–469.

Prestage, G., Jin, F., Zablotska, I., Grulich, A., Imrie, J., Kaldor, J., et al. (2008). Trends in agreements between regular partners among men in Sydney, Melbourne and Brisbane, Australia. *AIDS and Behavior, 12,* 513–520.

Rand, C., Graham, D. L. R., & Rawlings, E. I. (1982). Psychological health and factors the court seeks to control in lesbian mother custody trials. *Journal of Homosexuality, 8,* 27–39.

Ray, V., & Gregory, R. (2001). School experiences of the children of lesbian and gay parents. *Family Matters, 59,* 28–34.

Reimann, R. (1997). Does biology matter? Lesbian couples' transition to parenthood and their division of labor. *Qualitative Sociology, 20,* 153–185.

Reinhardt, R. U. (2002). Bisexual women in heterosexual relationships. *Journal of Bisexuality, 2,* 163–171.

Rich, A. (1981). *Compulsory heterosexuality and lesbian existence*. London: Onlywoman Press.

Ricketts, W., & Achtenberg, R. (1987). The adoptive and foster gay and lesbian parent. In F. Bozett (Ed.), *Gay and lesbian parents* (pp. 89–111). New York: Praeger.

Ridge, S. R., & Feeney, J. A. (1998). Relationship history and relationship attitudes in gay males and lesbians: Attachment style and gender differences. *Australian and New Zealand Journal of Psychiatry, 32,* 848–859.

Ridgeway, C. L., & Correll, S. R. (2004). Unpacking the gender system: A theoretical perspective on gender beliefs and social relations. *Gender & Society, 18,* 510–531.

Riggle, E. D. B., & Rostosky, S. S. (2005). For better or for worse: Psycholegal soft spots and advance planning for same-sex couples. *Professional Psychology: Research and Practice, 36,* 90–96.

Riggle, E. D. B., Whitman, J. S., Olson, A., Rostosky, S. S., & Strong, S. (2008). The positive aspects of being a lesbian or gay man. *Professional Psychology: Research and Practice, 39,* 210–217.

Riggs, D. (2006). Developmentalism and the rhetoric of best interest of the child: Challenging heteronormative constructions of families and parenting in foster care. *Journal of GLBT Family Studies, 2*, 57–73.

Risman, B. J. (1987). Intimate relationships from a microstructural perspective: Men who mother. *Gender & Society, 1*, 6–32.

Risman, B. J. (2004). Gender as social structure: Theory wrestling with social transformation. *Gender & Society, 18*, 429–450.

Rivers, I., Poteat, V. P., & Noret, N. (2008). Victimization, social support, and psychosocial functioning in same-sex and opposite-sex couples in the United States. *Developmental Psychology, 44*, 127–134.

Roisman, G. I., Clausell, E., Holland, A., Fortuna, K., & Elieff, K. (2008). Adult romantic relationships as contexts of human development: A multimethod comparison of same-sex couples with opposite-sex dating, engaged, and married couples. *Developmental Psychology, 44*, 91–101.

Romesburg, D. (2001, January 30). November 26, 1996: Bottoms's worst-case scenario for gay families. *The Advocate*. Retrieved June 9, 2009, from http://www.thefreelibrary.com/November+26%2c+1996%3a+Bottoms's+worst-case+scenario+for+gay+families.-a069661500

Rose, S., & Zand, D. (2000). Lesbian dating and courtship from young adulthood to midlife. *Journal of Gay and Lesbian Social Services, 11*, 77–104.

Ross, L. E., & Steele, L. S. (2006). Lesbian and bisexual women's recommendations for improving the provision of assisted reproductive technology services. *Fertility & Sterility, 86*, 735–738.

Ross, L. E., Steele, L. S., & Epstein, R. (2006). Service use and gaps in services for lesbian and bisexual women during donor insemination, pregnancy, and the postpartum period. *Journal of Obstetrics and Gynecology Canada, 28*, 505–511.

Rosser, B. R., Oakes, J. M., Bockting, W. O., & Miner, M. (2007). Capturing the social demographics of hidden sexual minorities: An Internet study of the transgender population in the United States. *Sexuality Research & Social Policy, 4*, 50–64.

Rostosky, S. S., Korfhage, B. A., Duhigg, J. M. Stern, A. J., Bennett, L., & Riggle, E. D. B. (2004). Same-sex couple perceptions of family support: A consensual qualitative study. *Family Process, 43*, 43–57.

Rothblum, E. D., Balsam, K. F., & Solomon, S. E. (2008). Comparison of same-sex couples who were married in Massachusetts, had domestic partnerships in California, or had civil unions in Vermont. *Journal of Family Issues, 29*, 48–78.

Rubin, G. (1992). Of catamites and kings: Reflections on butch, gender, and boundaries. In J. Nestle (Ed.), *The persistent desire: A femme–butch reader* (pp. 466–482). Boston: Alyson Books.

Russell, G. (1978). The father role and its relation to masculinity, femininity, and androgyny. *Child Development, 49*, 1174–1181.

Rust, P. C. (1993). Neutralizing the political threat of the marginal woman: Lesbians' beliefs about bisexual women. *Journal of Sex Research, 30*, 214–228.

Rust, P. C. (1995). *The challenge of bisexuality to lesbian politics: Sex, loyalty, and revolution*. New York: New York University Press.

Rutledge, S. E. (2007). Enacting personal HIV disclosure policies for sexual situations: HIV-positive gay men's experiences. *Qualitative Health Research, 17*, 1040–1059.

Rutter, V., & Schwartz, P. (1996). Same-sex couples: Courtship, commitment, context. In A. E. Auhagen & M. von Salisch (Eds.), *The diversity of human relationships* (pp. 197–226). New York: Cambridge University Press.

Ryan, S., & Cash, S. (2004). Adoptive families headed by gay or lesbian parents: A threat . . . or hidden resource? *University of Florida Journal of Law and Public Policy, 15*, 443–465.

Ryan, S. D. (2000). Examining social workers' placement recommendations of children with gay and lesbian adoptive parents. *Families in Society, 81*, 517–528.

Ryan-Flood, R. (2005). Contested heteronormativities: Discourses of fatherhood among lesbian parents in Sweden and Ireland. *Sexualities, 8*, 189–204.

Saad, L. (2008). *Americans evenly divided on morality of homosexuality*. Retrieved on October 8, 2008, from http://www.gallup.com/poll/108115/Americans-Evenly-Divided-Morality-Homosexuality.aspx

Safer, J., & Riess, B. F. (1975). Two approaches to the study of female homosexuality: A critical and comparative review. *International Mental Health Research Newsletter, 17*(1), 11–13.

Saffron, L. (1998). Raising children in an age of diversity: Advantages of having a lesbian mother. *Journal of Lesbian Studies, 2*, 35–47.

Sanderson, S. L. (2000). Factors influencing paternal involvement in childrearing. *Dissertation Abstracts International: Section B: The Sciences and Engineering, 60*(11-B), 5790.

Savin-Williams, R. C. (1995). Dating and romantic relationships among gay, lesbian, and bisexual youths. In R. C. Savin-Williams & K. M. Cohen (Eds.), *The lives of lesbians, gays, and bisexuals: Children to adults* (pp. 166–180). New York: Harcourt Brace.

Savin-Williams, R. C. (1998). *" . . . And then I became gay": Young men's stories*. New York: Routledge.

Savin-Williams, R. C. (2008). Then and now: Recruitment, definition, diversity, and positive attributes of same-sex populations. *Developmental Psychology, 44*, 135–138.

Schacher, S. J., Auerbach, C. F., & Silverstein, L. B. (2005). Gay fathers expanding the possibilities for us all. *Journal of GLBT Family Studies, 1*, 31–52.

Scheib, J. E., Riordan, M., & Rubin, S. (2005). Adolescents with open-identity sperm donors: Reports from 12–17 year olds. *Human Reproduction, 20*, 239–252

Schope, R. D. (2002). The decision to tell: Factors influencing the disclosure of sexual orientation by gay men. *Journal of Gay and Lesbian Social Services, 14*, 1–21.

Schreurs, K. M. G. (1994). Intimacy, autonomy, and relationship satisfaction in Dutch lesbian couples and heterosexual couples. *Journal of Psychology & Human Sexuality, 7*, 41–57.

Schuck, K. D., & Liddle, B. J. (2001). Religious conflicts experienced by lesbian, gay, and bisexual individuals. *Journal of Gay and Lesbian Psychotherapy, 5*, 63–82.

Schulz, M. S., Cowan, P. A., Cowan, C. P., & Brennan, R. T. (2004). Coming home upset: Gender, marital satisfaction, and the daily spillover of workday experience into couple interactions. *Journal of Family Psychology, 18*, 250–263.

Schumm, W. (2004). What was really learned from Tasker and Golombok's (1995) study of lesbian and single parent mothers? *Psychological Reports, 94*, 422–424.

Shelley-Sireci, L., & Ciano-Boyce, C. (2002). Becoming lesbian adoptive parents: An explanatory study of lesbian adoptive, lesbian birth, and heterosexual adoptive parents. *Adoption Quarterly, 6*, 33–43.

Shimonaka, Y., Nakazato, K., Kawaai, C., & Sato, S. (1997). Androgyny and successful adaptation across the life span among Japanese adults. *Journal of Genetic Psychology, 158*, 389–400.

Short, L. (2007). Lesbian mothers living well in the context of heterosexism and discrimination: Resources, strategies and legislative changes. *Feminism & Psychology, 17*, 57–74.

Signorella, M. L., Bigler, R. S., & Liben, L. S. (1993). Developmental differences in children's gender schemata about others: A meta-analytic review. *Developmental Psychology, 13*, 106–126.

Silverstein, L. B. (1996). Fathering is a feminist issue. *Psychology of Women Quarterly, 20*, 3–37.

Silverstein, L. B., & Auerbach, C. F. (1999). Deconstructing the essential father. *American Psychologist, 54*, 397–409.

Silverstein, L. B., Auerbach, C. F., & Levant, R. F. (2002). Contemporary fathers reconstructing masculinity: Clinical implications of gender role strain. *Professional Psychology: Research and Practice, 33*, 361–369.

Simmons, T., & O'Neil, G. (2001, September). *Households and families: 2000* (U.S. Census Bureau Publication No. C2KBR/01–8). Washington, DC: U.S. Census Bureau.

Singh, D., Vidaurri, M., Zambarano, R. J., & Dabbs, J. M. (1999). Lesbian erotic role identification: Behavioral, morphological, and hormonal correlates. *Journal of Personality and Social Psychology, 75*, 1035–1049.

Smith, C. A., & Stillman, S. (2002). Butch/femme in the personal advertisements of lesbians. *Journal of Lesbian Studies, 6*, 45–61.

Smith, R. B., & Brown, R. A. (1997). The impact of social support on gay male couples. *Journal of Homosexuality, 33*, 39–61.

Solomon, S. E., Rothblum, E. D., & Balsam, K. F. (2004). Pioneers in partnership: Lesbian and gay male couples in civil unions compared with those not in civil unions, and married heterosexual siblings. *Journal of Family Psychology, 18*, 275–286.

Solomon, S. E., Rothblum, E. D., & Balsam, K. F. (2005). Money, housework, sex, and conflict: Same-sex couples in civil unions, those not in civil unions, and heterosexual married siblings. *Sex Roles, 52,* 561–575.

Sourander, A., Helstela, L., Helenius, H., & Piha, J. (2000). Persistence of bullying from childhood to adolescence: A longitudinal 8-year follow-up study. *Child Abuse & Neglect, 24,* 873–881.

Sourander, A., Jensen, P., Ronning, J., Niemela, S., Helenius, H., Sillanmaki, L., et al. (2007). What is the early adulthood outcome of boys who bully or are bullied in childhood? The Finnish "From a Boy to a Man" study. *Pediatrics, 120,* 397–404.

Sprecher, S., & Hendrick, S. (2004). Self-disclosure in intimate relationships: Associations with individual and relationship characteristics over time. *Journal of Social and Clinical Psychology, 23,* 857–877.

Stacey, J. (2006). Gay parenthood and the decline of paternity as we knew it. *Sexualities, 9,* 27–55.

Stacey, J., & Biblarz, T. (2001). (How) does the sexual orientation of parents matter? *American Sociological Review, 66,* 159–183.

Stein, A. (1992). All dressed up, but no place to go? Style wars and the new lesbianism. In J. Nestle (Ed.), *The persistent desire: A femme–butch reader* (pp. 431–439). Boston: Alyson Books.

Stein, A. (2005). Make room for Daddy: Anxious masculinity and emergent homophobias in neopatriarchal politics. *Gender & Society, 19,* 601–620.

Steinberg, L., & Monahan, K. (2007). Age differences in resistance to peer influence. *Developmental Psychology, 53,* 1531–1543.

Steinbugler, A. C. (2005). Visibility as privilege and danger: Heterosexual and same-sex interracial intimacy in the 21st century. *Sexualities, 8,* 425–443.

Sullivan, M. (1996). Rozzie and Harriet? Gender and family patterns of lesbian coparents. *Gender & Society, 10,* 747–767.

Surra, C., Gray, C., Boettcher, T. M. J., Cottle, A., & West, C. (2006). From courtship to universal properties: Research on dating and mate selection, 1950–2003. In A. Vangelisti & D. Perlman (Eds.), *The Cambridge handbook of personal relationships* (pp. 113–130). New York: Cambridge University Press.

Sutfin, E. L., Fulcher, M., Bowles, R. P., & Patterson, C. J. (2008). How lesbian and heterosexual parents convey attitudes about gender to their children: The role of gendered environments. *Sex Roles, 58,* 501–513.

Szymanksi, D. M. (2005). Heterosexism and sexism as correlates of psychological distress in lesbians. *Journal of Counseling & Development, 83,* 355–360.

Tasker, F. L. (1999). Children in lesbian-led families: A review. *Clinical Child Psychology and Psychiatry, 4,* 153–166.

Tasker, F. L., & Golombok, S. (1997). *Growing up in a lesbian family: Effects on child development.* London: Guilford Press.

Tasker, F. L., & Golombok, S. (1998). The role of co-mothers in planned lesbian-led families. *Journal of Lesbian Studies, 2,* 61–79.

Taylor, Y. (2005). Real politik or real politics? Working-class lesbians' political 'awareness' and activism. *Women's Studies International Forum, 28*, 484–494.

Thorne, B. (1992). Feminism and the family: Two decades of thought. In B. Thorne & M. Yalom (Eds.), *Rethinking the family: Some feminist questions* (pp. 1–24). Boston: Northeastern University Press.

Thornton, A., & Young-DeMarco, L. (2001). Four decades of trends in attitudes toward family issues in the United States: The 1960s through the 1990s. *Journal of Marriage and Family, 63*, 1009–1037.

Tolman, D. L., & Diamond, L. M. (2001). Desegregating sexuality research: Cultural and biological perspectives on gender and desire. *Annual Review of Sex Research, 12*, 33–74.

Touroni, E., & Coyle, A. (2002). Decision-making in planned lesbian parenting: An interpretative phenomenological analysis. *Journal of Community & Applied Social Psychology, 12*, 194–209.

Tower, R. B., & Krasner, M. (2006). Marital closeness, autonomy, mastery, and depressive symptoms in a U.S. Internet sample. *Personal Relationships, 13*, 429–449.

Troiden, R. R. (1979). Becoming homosexual: A model of gay identity acquisition. *Psychiatry: Journal for the Study of Interpersonal Processes, 42*, 362–373.

Turner, P. H., Scadden, L., & Harris, M. B. (1990). Parenting in gay and lesbian families. *Journal of Gay & Lesbian Psychotherapy, 1*, 55–66.

Turteltaub, G. L. (2002). The effects of long-term primary relationship dissolution on the children of lesbian parents. *Dissertation Abstracts International: Section B: The Sciences and Engineering, 63*(5-B), 2610.

Tye, M. C. (2003). Lesbian, gay, bisexual, and transgendered parents: Special considerations for the custody and adoption evaluator. *Family Court Review, 41*, 92–103.

Van Dam, M. A. (2004). Mothers in two types of lesbian families: Stigma experiences, supports, and burdens. *Journal of Family Nursing, 10*, 450–484.

Vanfraussen, K., Ponjaert-Kristoffersen, I., & Brewaeys, A. (2002). What does it mean for youngsters to grow up in a lesbian family created by means of donor insemination? *Journal of Reproductive and Infant Psychology, 20*, 237–252.

Vanfraussen, K., Ponjaert-Kristoffersen, I., & Brewaeys, A. (2003a). Family functioning in lesbian families created by donor insemination. *American Journal of Orthopsychiatry, 73*, 78–90.

Vanfraussen, K., Ponjaert-Kristoffersen, I., & Brewaeys, A. (2003b). Why do children want to know more about the donor? The experiences of youngsters raised in lesbian families. *Journal of Psychosomatic & Obstetric Gynecology, 24*, 31–38.

Vyncke, J. D., & Julien, D. (2007). Social support, coming out, and adjustment of lesbian mothers in Canada and France: An exploratory study. *Journal of GLBT Family Studies, 3*, 397–424.

Wade, J. C., & Donis, E. (2007). Masculinity ideology, male identity, and romantic relationship ideology among heterosexual and gay men. *Sex Roles, 57*, 775–786.

Wainright, J. L., & Patterson, C. J. (2006). Delinquency, victimization, and substance use among adolescents with female same-sex parents. *Journal of Family Psychology, 20*, 526–530.

Wainright, J. L., & Patterson, C. J. (2008). Peer relations among adolescents with female same-sex parents. *Developmental Psychology, 44*, 117–126.

Wainright, J., Russell, S., & Patterson, C. (2004). Psychosocial adjustment, school outcomes, and romantic relationships of adolescents with same-sex parents. *Child Development, 75*, 1886–1898.

Wald, D. (2007). *Gay surrogacy: A legal perspective (March, 2007)*. Retrieved September 30, 2007, from http://gaylife.about.com/od/gayparentingadoption/a/gayparent.htm

Walters, S. D. (2000). Wedding bells and baby carriages: Heterosexuals imagine gay families, gay families imagine themselves. In M. Andrews, S. D. Sclater, & C. Squire (Eds.), *Lines of narrative: Psychosocial perspectives* (pp. 48–63). New York: Routledge.

Wardle, L. D. (1997). The potential impact of homosexual parenting on children. *University of Illinois Law Review, 1997*, 833–819.

Wayment, H. A., & Peplau, L. A. (1995). Social support and well-being among lesbian and heterosexual women: A structural modeling approach. *Personality and Social Psychology Bulletin, 21*, 1189–1199.

Weber, J. C. (1996). Social class as a correlate of gender identity among lesbian women. *Sex Roles, 35*, 271–280.

Wegesin, D. J., & Meyer-Bahlburgh, H. F. L. (2000). Top/bottom self-label, anal sex practices, HIV risk and gender role identity in gay men in New York City. *Journal of Psychology & Human Sexuality, 12*, 43–62.

Wendland, C. L., Byrn, F., & Hill, C. (1996). Donor insemination: A comparison of lesbian couples, heterosexual couples and single women. *Fertility & Sterility, 65*, 764–770.

West, C., & Zimmerman, D. H. (1987). Doing gender. *Gender & Society, 1*, 125–151.

West, R., & Turner, L. H. (1995). Communication in lesbian and gay families: Building a descriptive base. In T. J. Socha & G. H. Stamp (Eds.), *Parents, children, and communication* (pp. 148–167). Mahwah, NJ: Erlbaum.

Weston, K. (1991). *Families we choose: Lesbians, gays, kinship.* New York: Columbia University Press.

Weston, K. (1992). The politics of gay families. In B. Thorne & M. Yalom (Eds.), *Rethinking the family* (pp. 119–139). Boston: Northeastern University Press.

Whisman, M. A., Uebelacker, L. A., & Weinstock, L. M. (2004). Psychopathology and marital satisfaction: The importance of evaluating both partners. *Journal of Consulting and Clinical Psychology, 72*, 830–838.

Wilton, T., & Kaufman, T. (2000). Lesbian mothers' experiences of maternity care in the UK. *Midwifery, 17*, 203–211.

Witt, S. D. (1997). Parental influence on children's socialization to gender roles. *Adolescence, 32,* 253–259.

Wohlfeiler, D., & Potterat, J. (2005). Using gay men's sexual networks to reduce sexually transmitted disease (STD)/human immunodeficiency virus (HIV) transmission. *Sexually Transmitted Diseases, 32,* 48–52.

Wood, W., & Eagly, A. H. (2002). A cross-cultural analysis of the behavior of women and men: Implications for the origins of sex differences. *Psychological Bulletin, 128,* 699–727.

Yep, G. A., Lovaas, K. E., & Elia, J. P. (2003). A critical appraisal of assimilationist and radical ideologies underlying same-sex marriage in LGBT communities in the United States. *Journal of Homosexuality, 45,* 45–64.

Yip, A. K. T. (2004). Same-sex marriage: Contrasting perspectives among lesbian, gay, and bisexual Christians. *Feminism & Psychology, 14,* 173–180.

INDEX

Academic functioning, 141–142
Adolescent Health Database, 183
Adolescents of gay and lesbian parents
    disclosure to peers, 147
    in lesbian stepfamilies, relationship, 151
    parents' disclosure of orientation to, 141, 146
    psychological adjustment, 140–141
    sexual minority identification, 170–172
        research sampling issues, 171, 171n3
    social functioning, 135–138
        developmental aspects, 136–138
    in transracial adoptions, 172–173
Adoption. *See also specific types*
    barriers, 68–70
    child characteristics, 66–68
    child's need for privacy, 91, 91n
    choices and challenges, 65–70, 81–82
    costs, 55–56
    court decisions, research implications of, 122
    lesbian couples' division of labor, 100
    motivations for, 57
    practice-related implications, 85–86
    public attitude trends, 3n
    research gaps, 180
    type of, 65–66
    unique context, 81–82
    U.S. Census data, 50
Adoption agencies
    attitudes and practices, 68
    practice implications, 85–86, 86n14
    selection of, 69
Adult children of lesbian and gay parents, 157–175
    community constructions of, 165–166
    coping with heterosexism, 159–161
    culturally queer identification, 166
    disclosure practices, 161–164
    family construction of, 165–166
    major research findings, 179–180
    parents' coming out, recollections of, 148, 161
    peer hostility, recollections of, 136, 160
    practical resources, 175

"protecting our families" sentiment, 168–169
    research needs, 174
    research rationale, 158
    sexual minority identification, 170–172
    sexuality and gender attitudes, 167–169
    toleration of differences, 164–165
    transracial adoptions, recollections of, 172–173
Age factors, lesbian dating script, 22
AIDS. *See* HIV/AIDS
Alternative insemination. *See also* Known donors; Unknown donors
    barriers to, 62–64
    biological mother decision, 58–59, 59n6
    choices and challenges, 57–65, 81
    costs, 54
    couple asymmetries, 81
    donor characteristics, 62
    donor type, 59–62
    known versus unknown donors, 59–62
    legal barriers, 64–65
Androgynous behavior/interests
    Black lesbian study, 35, 35n
    gendered role behavior modeling effect, 130–131
    and parenting, 112
Anonymous donors. *See* Unknown donors
Assimilationism, in parenthood representations, 108–109
Attitudes. *See* Public attitudes
Autonomy, in gay and lesbian relationships, 27–29

Biogenetic relationship to child
    and alternative insemination, 62
    in parenthood decisions, 56, 56n5, 57
Biological mother. *See also* Birth mother; Nonbiological mother
    children's affection for, 104, 151
    children's language about, 150
    children's relationship with, 151
    division of labor, 99–102
    family support, 118
    heterosexual mothers comparison, parenting, 111

parental role negotiations, 103–105
parenting abilities, 111
Birth mother. *See also* Biological mother
    and gender identity, 56n1
    lesbian couple decision, 58–59, 58n6
    naming practices, 77–78
    transition to parenthood period, 75–77
Bisexual parents
    terminology issues, 4–5
    U.S. Census data, 50, 50n
Bisexuality, social rejection of, 43
Black lesbians
    role playing and gender performance, 35
    stepparenting, 83, 83n13
Bonding, and open adoption, 82
"Bottoms" role, and gender identity, 37
Bottoms, Sharon, 110
Boundary control, children of gay parents, 146–147
Boys. *See also* Sons of lesbian mothers
    adoption preference, 67–68
    father-absent families, 131–132
        heterosexism, 132
Bullying
    adolescents of gay and lesbian parents, 136, 141–142
    children of gay and lesbian parents, 135–138, 153
        developmental aspects, 136–138
Butch–femme identities
    lesbian couple role playing, 33–36
    "opposite" couple pairing, 35
    and social class, 36

Career commitment, lesbian mothers, 100–101
Child care
    division of labor, 99–102
    gender identity aspects, 101–102
Child welfare adoption
    costs, 55
    disadvantages, 55–56
    practice recommendations, 86n14
    special needs children, 82
Children of lesbian and gay parents, 125–156
    disclosure to others, 146–148
    donor relationships, 151–153
        developmental outcomes, 152–153
    gendered role behavior, 128–134
    limitations as informants, 157–158
    major research findings, 179
    parents' coming out effect, 144–148

practical resources, 155–156
    "protecting our families" sentiment, 169
    psychological adjustment, 138–142
    research sampling issues, 12
    secrecy consequences, 148
    sexual identity,127–128, 170
    sexual orientation, 132–134
    social functioning, 134–138
        developmental patterns, 136–138, 142–147
    stigma protection methods, 146–147
    unique benefits, 97–98
Children of Lesbians and Gays Everywhere (COLAGE), 156
Children of transgendered parents, gender identity, 128
Children's development. *See* Developmental patterns
Children's parental preference, 104–105
Civil unions
    dissolution of, 26–27
    public attitude trends, 3n
    and relationship quality, 39–40
    social–legal context, 38–41
Closed relationships, 23–25
Closeting, risks and benefits, 19–20
Cohort effects, and life course perspective, 8
Coming out
    adult children of gay and lesbian parents, 161–164
    contextual forces, 18
    lesbian and gay parents, 91–93, 144–148
        children's experiences and reactions, 144–148
        timing effects on children, 141, 144
    protecting family concerns, 169
    racial/ethnic factors, 18–19
    risks and benefits, 19–20
    stage model, 18
Commitment ceremonies, function, 108–109
Community support, lesbian and gay parents, 119–120
Comparative studies, heterosexual parents, 143–144, 187
Complex gendering attitudes, 168
Conflict in relationships, 29–31
    gay and lesbian couples, 29–31
    interracial couples, 30
    and "out" differences, 30–31
    in transition to parenthood period, 78–80
Coparent adoption, 68–69

Coparenting agreements, 115n8
Costs, in routes to parenthood, 54–56
Coupling, social–historical perspective, 16–17
Courting and coupling. *See also* Dating
    scripts, 21–22
    social–historical perspective, 16–17
Cultural factors, gendered role behavior, 128–129
Culturally queer identification, 166
Custody decisions
    legal safeguards, 115–116
    parenting research context, 110
    research implications, 122

Data collection, sampling issues, 11–13
Dating, 20–22
    gendered scripts, 20–22
    life stage and age factors, 22
    trends, 17
Daughters of lesbians
    career aspirations, 130–131, 167
    gendered role behavior, 167–168
Decision-making
    routes to parenthood, 54–72
    to parent or not to parent, 51–54
    who should carry the child, 58–59, 59n6
Delinquency, adolescents of lesbian parents, 140
Depression, adolescents of lesbian parents, 139–140
Developmental patterns
    gender role behavior, 129
    known versus unknown donors effect, 152–153
    peer teasing/bullying effect, 136–138
    research needs, 142–143
Diagnostic and Statistical Manual of Mental Disorders (3rd ed.), 15
Differential reinforcement, gendered role behavior, 129
Disclosure practices
    children of gay and lesbian parents, 161–164
    gay and lesbian parents, 161–164
Dissolution rates, 26–27
Diversity attitudes
    adult children of gay and lesbian parents, 164–165
    children in minority family studies, 97–98
Division of labor

lesbian and gay male parents, 99–102
    children's psychological adjustment, 140–141
    ethnographic/observational studies, 101–102
    and gender identity, 101–102
    lesbian parent families, 10–11
    transition to parenthood period, 75–76
Divorce
    lesbian and gay parents, 114–116
    and parenting ability, 111–112
"Doing gender," 186
Domestic duties
    lesbian and gay parents, 99–102
    lesbian and gay relationships, 31–33
Domestic partnerships, advocates of, 41
Donors. *See also* Known donors; Unknown donors
    alternative insemination, choices, 59–62
    children's relationships with, 151–153
Dual-earner relationships, 32n

Ecological perspective
    definition, 7
    research context, 7–8
Egalitarianism, children of lesbian parents, 140–141, 168
Elementary school students, bullying, 137–138
Emotional difficulties, children, 138–142
Empathy, children in minority family structure, 98
Employment rates, lesbian couples, 32n
Equality issues
    couples' division of labor, 31–32
    lesbian and gay intimate relationships, 31–37
    and naming practices, 77–78
    transition to parenthood period, 75–77
Ethnographic research, division of labor, 101–102
Exosystem, ecological perspective, 7
Extended family
    heterosexism, 160
    support role, 118

Family, construction of
    adult children of same-sex parents, 165–166
    children's ideas about, 149–153

research findings, 186–187

social constructionist perspective, 9–11, 186

Family life cycle, transitions, 8–9

Family support

adult children of same-sex parents memories of, 161

lesbian and gay intimate relationships, 41–43

lesbian and gay parents, 117–119

during the transition to parenthood, 74–75

Father absence

boys' gendered role behavior, 131

role model concerns, 94–97, 126, 131

Father role. *See* Gay fathers

Father word, lesbian mothers' use of, 96

Fatherhood, social constructivism, 10, 106

Femme women, gender performance, 33–36

Fertility services, barriers, 63

Finances. *See* Costs

Foster care adoption

disadvantages, 55–56

same-sex couples, percentages, 50

special needs children, 82

Friendship script, 21–22

Friends, children's disclosure to, 147

Friendship support

adult memories of, 161

lesbian and gay parents, 119–120

same-sex relationships, 41–43

during the transition to parenthood, 74–75

Funding, sexual minority research, 13

Fusion, lesbian relationships, 27–28

Gallup polls, 3n, 17

Gay bars, trends in use of, 17

Gay community, and gay parenthood, 119–120, 166–167

Gay fathers. *See* Gay men as parents

Gay, Lesbian and Straight Education Network survey, 92–94, 93n2, 136

Gay men as parents, 89–123

coming out to children, 145

friend support, 119–120

heterosexism concerns, 90–116

homophobia concerns, 90–94

major research findings, 178–179

mothering skills, 106–107

parental role construction, 105–107

parenting ability, 109–113

public representations, 107–109

research needs, 154, 181–182

role negotiation, 105–107

transition to parenthood, 72–85

and male versus female stereotypes, 84

relationship conflicts, 79–80

work orientation, 107

Gender identity

children of lesbian and gay parents, 127–128

definition, 127

and division of labor, parents, 101–102

lesbian biological mother, 58n6

Gender performance, gay and lesbian couples, 33–37

Gender role behavior

adult children of same-sex parents, memories, 167–169

children of gay and lesbian parents, 128–132

parent role model concerns, 94–97

cultural factors, 128–129

definition, 127

developmental theory, 129

father/mother absence model concerns, 94–97

gay and lesbian couples, 33–37

lesbian mothers, 130–131

parent division of labor, 101–102, 186

social constructionist perspective, 9–11

Gender socialization

father/mother absence concerns, 94–97

lesbian parents, 101–101

Gendered scripts, 20–22

Generational effects, male sexual exclusivity, 23

Genetics, and sexual orientation, 132–133. *See also* Biogenetic relationship to child

Geographical location, parenthood barrier, 52–53

Gestational surrogacy, 70n11

Girls

adoption preference, 67–68

gendered role modeling effect, 130

sexuality effect of lesbian mothers, 134

Grandparents, family support of, 117–118, 165

Growing Generations, 56, 56n4

Hegemonic masculinity, well-being implications, 37, 37n

Heterosexism
    adult children of same-sex parents
        memories of, 159–161
    definition, 18n
    parenting concern, 90–116
Heterosexual-parent families
    comparative research framework, 143–
        144, 187
    as research gold standard, 187
Heterosexual sex for pregnancy, risks, 55
High school students, bullying, 137–138
HIV/AIDS
    gay couples challenge, 43–45
    medication improvements effect, 44
Home study process, 64
Homophobia
    children's coping with, 159–160
    and coming out, 18–19
    definition, 18n
    parental concern, 90–94
Homophobic bullying, 92
Homosexuality, public attitude surveys, 3n
"Housewife" identity of lesbians, 102
Housework
    lesbian and gay couples, 32–33
    lesbian and gay parents, 99–102
    and gender identity, 101–102

In vitro fertilization, costs, 55
Infertility, stress of, 81
"Inserter" role, and gender identity, 37
Institutionalized heterosexism/homophobia,
    160
Insurance, alternative insemination cover-
    age, 63
"Intergeneration transmission," sexual orien-
    tation, 134
Intergenerational attitudes
    adult children of same-sex parents, 165,
        168
    gender and sexuality, 168
Internalized homophobia
    definition, 19n
    parenthood barrier, 51–52
International adoption
    choice of, 65–66
    costs, 55
Internet
    dating use, 22
    survey use, 183–184
Interracial couples
    challenges, 30

family and community lack of support,
    43
Intimate relationships
    lesbian and gay couples, 15–48
    lesbian and gay parents, 113–116

Joint adoption, 68–69
Journal publications, sexual minority exclu-
    sion, 13

Kinship, assimilationist aspects, 108–109
Known donors, 59–62
    children's developmental outcomes,
        152–153
    children's relationships, 152–153
    choice of, 59–62
    as gender role model, 96
    involvement with children, 61–62

Language about family, in children, 149–151
Learning theory, gendered role behavior, 129
Legal context
    alternative insemination, 63–64
    civil unions and marriage, 38–41
        practical resources, 47–48
    gay and lesbian couples, 38–41
    parenting decisions, 110
    surrogacy, 71
Legal partner, separating parents, 114–115
Lesbian, gay, bisexual parents, terminology,
    4–5
Lesbian mothers. *See also* Biological mother;
    Birth mother; Nonbiological mother
    adolescent children's adjustment, 141
    alternative insemination barriers, 62–
        64, 63n8
    division of labor, 99–102
    family support, 117–118
    gendered role behavior effects, 130–131
    male role model concerns, 94–96
    and male versus female stereotypes, 84
    parental role negotiation, 102–105
    route to parenthood motivation, 56–57
    sexual orientation of children, 133–134
    transition to parenthood, 72–85
Lesbian parents, 89–123. *See also* Lesbian
    mothers
    children's psychological adjustment,
        140–141
    children's relationship with, 150–151
    coming out to children, 144–148
    division of labor, 99–102

family functioning, 109–113
heterosexism concerns, 90–116
homophobia concerns, 90–94
intimate relationships, 113–116
major research findings, 178–179
meaning and content of parenthood, 102–105
motivations for parenthood, 56–57
negotiating roles, 102–105
parental role negotiation, 102–105
parenting abilities, 109–113
public representations, 107–109
social support, 116–120
transition to parenthood, 72–85
    adjustment, 78–80
U.S. Census data, 50, 50n1
Lesbian stepfamilies. *See* Stepmothers
Lesbians, terminology issues, 4
LGB parents, terminology issues, 4–5
LGBT parents, terminology issues, 5
Life course perspective, 8–9

Macrosystem, ecological perspective, 7
Male role models
    father absence concern, 94–97
    lesbian mothers' pursuit of, 95–96
Marriage. *See* Same-sex marriage
Masculine role models, 95
Masculinity in boys, and father absence, 131
Maternal role, negotiation, 102–105
Medical heterosexism, 63
Mental health
    children of gay and lesbian parents, 138–142
    meta-analysis, 111, 111n6
    and parenting ability, 110–111
    transition to parenthood period, 80
Mesosystem, in ecological perspective, 7
Methodological limitation, in research, 11–13
Microsystem, in ecological perspective, 7
Middle-class status
    and butch–femme identity, 36
    family support factor, 119
    victimization factor, 137
Monogamy
    lesbian and gay relationships, 23–25
    and male–female differences, 24–25
Mother absence, role model concerns, 94–97
Mother role. *See* Lesbian mothers
Motherhood, as social construct, 10

Mothering
    gay male parents, 106–107
    as social construct, 106
Motivation, in transition to parenthood, 52
Multiracial couples/families, research need, 180–181

Naming practices, parental roles link, 77–78, 108
Native Americans, 43
Nonbiological mother
    children's language about, 150
    and children's preferences, 104
    children's relationship with, 151
    division of labor, 99–101
    family support, 118
    heterosexual fathers comparison, parenting, 111
    lesbian couples naming practices, 77–78
    parental role negotiation, 103–105
    paternal role choice, 105
    transition to parenthood stage, 79–80
Nondisclosure, children of same-sex parents, 146–147

Observational research
    need for, 13
    parents' division of labor, 101–102
Online surveys, 184
Open adoption
    choice of, 65
    female role model, desire for, as motive, 97
    unique challenges, 82
Open relationships
    lesbians and gay males, 23–25
    male–female differences, 24–25

Paid work, parent division of labor, 99–102
Parental roles
    gay male couples, 105–107
    lesbian couples, 102
    and naming practices, 77–78
    negotiation of, 102–107
    public representations, 107–109
Parenthood
    public representations, 107–109
    social constructivism, 10–11
Parenthood transition. *See* Transition to parenthood
Parenting, 109–113

abilities, 109–113
   heterosexual parenting comparisons, 111–112
   legal decisions, 110
   practical resources, 122–123
   practice implications, 121
   research implications, 120–121
   in transition to parenthood stage, 75–77
   values, 112–113
Paternal role
   negotiation, 102–105
   nonbiological mother, 105
Peer relationships
   adult children of same-sex parents, memories, 160
   children of same-sex parents, 134–138, 141
Peers, adolescents' disclosure to, 147
Poll data, trends, 3n
Popularity, children of same-sex parents, 135
Postmodern perspective. *See* Social constructivist perspective
Power issues
   and division of labor, 31–33
   gay and lesbian intimate relationships, 31–37
   gender performance and role playing, 33–37
Private adoptions
   choice of, 66
   costs, 55
Private domestic, open adoption, 65
Psychological adjustment
   adolescents of gay and lesbian parents, 140–142
   children of gay and lesbian parents, 138–142
   research issues, 142–143
Public attitudes
   historical shifts, 8
   same-sex sexuality, 17
   survey data, 3n
Public representations, parenthood, 107–109

Qualitative research
   children of gay and lesbian parents, needs, 143
   children's ideas about family, 149–151
   need for, 13–14
   parents' division of labor, 101–102
Queer, terminology issues, 4

Racial/ethnic factors
   adoption decision, 67
   and coming out, 18–19
   family support role, 117–118
   gay and lesbian relationships, 30
   multi-racial couples/families, 180–181
   research underrepresentation, 184–185
   same-sex relationships support, 43
Racial splits, in families, 181
"Receiver" role, and gender identity, 37
Relationship conflicts. *See* Conflict in relationships
Relationship dissolution
   children as constraint, 116
   lesbian and gay parents, 114–116
     rates of, 115, 115n9
   lesbian and gay relationships, 26–27
Relationship satisfaction, lesbian parents, 113–114
Religion, and coming out, 18–19
Research, 3–14, 177–188
   ecological perspective, 7–8
   funding problems, 13, 185
   gaps in, 180–183
   life course perspective, 8–9
   major findings, 177–180
   methodological issues, 11–13, 183–185
   publication outlets problem, 13
   sampling challenges, 183–185
   social constructivist perspective, 9–13
Resilience, in adult memories of childhood, 160–161
Role model concerns, father/mother absence, 94–97
Role playing. *See* Gender role behavior
Romance script, gendered aspects, 21–22

Safe school policies, 93–94, 154
Same-sex marriage
   negative views of, 40–41
   practical resources, 47
   and relationship quality, 40
   social–legal context, 38–41
Sampling issues
   children of lesbian and gay parents, 12
   research limitations, 11–13, 183–185
School environment
   children's coping with heterosexism, 159–160
   parental challenge, 92–94
   practical resources, 123
   stigmatization reduction, 154–155

Scripts, first date, 20–21
Second-parent adoptions
    family support factor, 118
    function of, 64, 64n9, 108, 118
    home-study step in, 64
Secrecy consequences, children and families, 148
Selective disclosure, children, 146–147
Self-esteem, children of lesbian parents, 141
Self-insemination, 55
Separation rates, gay couples, 26–27. *See also* Relationship dissolution
Sexual exclusivity, 23–25
Sexual identity
    adult children of gay and lesbian parents, 167
    children of gay and lesbian parents, 127–128
    research issues, 142–143
Sexual intimacy
    lesbian parents, 113, 113n7
    transition to parenthood period, 79
Sexual orientation
    children of gay and lesbian parents, 132–134
    research issues, 142–143
    definition, 127
Sexuality, social constructivist perspective, 9–11
Sexually-explicit scripts, 21–22
Single-mother home, 94, 94n3
Single parents, versus coupled, 84–85
Social class. *See* Socioeconomic status effects
Social constructivist perspective, 9–11
    family, gender, and sexuality, 9–11
    mothering and fathering roles, 106
    parenthood conception, 9–10
Social functioning/relationships. *See also specific aspects*
    adolescents of gay and lesbian parents, 135–136
    children of gay and lesbian parents, 134–138
    research needs, 142–143
Social learning theory, gendered role behavior, 129
Social support
    adult memories of, 161
    lesbian and gay parents, 116–120
    same-sex intimate relationships, 41–43
    transition to parenthood, 74–75
Sociocultural attitudes. *See* Public attitudes

Socioeconomic status effects, 137
    and butch–femme identity, 36
    family support factor, 119
    and marriage rights, 41, 41n
    victimization factor, 137
Sons of lesbian mothers
    gender role behavior, 131–132, 167n
    heterosexism, 132
    sexuality effect, 134
    teasing of, 136
Special needs children, adoption, 66–67, 82
"Specialized" housework labor, 32
Sperm donors. *See* Donors
Stepfamilies
    parenting challenges, 83
    research need, 183
Stepmothers
    adolescent children of, 151
    division of labor, 100
    parental role negotiation, 103
Stigmatization, children of lesbian parents, 141, 154–155, 160–161
Substance abuse, adolescents of lesbian parents, 140
Surrogacy, 70–72
    choice of, 70–72
    costs, 56
    genetic asymmetry in, 71–72
    options, 70n11
Survey data
    committed relationships, 23
    same-sex sexuality, 17
    trends, 3n

Teachers, heterosexism, 159–160
Teasing
    adolescents of gay and lesbian parents, 136
    children of gay and lesbian parents, 134–138, 153
    developmental aspects, 136–138
Terminology issues, 5–6
Tolerance for diversity
    adult children of gay and lesbian parents, 164–165
    children in minority family structure, 97–98
"Tops" role, and gender identity, 37
Transgender parents
    children's disclosure to friends, 147
    children's sexual identity, 128
    coming out to children, 145

naming practices, 78
research needs, 182–183
terminology issues, 5
transition to parenting, 83–84
Transition to parenthood, 49–88
    barriers, 51–54
    decision-making, 51–72
    definition, 51
    division of labor, 75–76
    equality issue, 75–78
    male versus female stereotypes, 84
    mental health, 80
    naming practices, 77–78
    parenting roles, 75–77
    practical resources, 87–88
    practice-related implications, 85–87
    relationship adjustment, 78–80
    social supports, 74–75
    turning points, 53–54
    U.S. Census data, 50, 50n1
Transracial adoptions
    decision, 67
    and family support, 118
    young adults' perception, 172–173
Turning points, parenthood decision, 53–54

Unknown donors
    children's developmental outcome,
        152–153

children's relationship, 152–153
choice of, 59–60
U.S. Census data
    lesbian couple employment rates, 32n
    same-sex committed relationships, 23
    same-sex parenthood, 50, 50n1

Victimization
    children/adolescents of gay and lesbian
        parents, 134–138
        psychological adjustment, 138–142
    transracially adopted young adults, 172

Well-being. *See* Psychological adjustment
Working class context
    and butch–femme identity, 36
    family support factor, 119
    and marriage rights, 41, 41n
    and victimization, 137
Workplace, same-sex parents supports, 121–
    122

Y chromosome, insemination choice factor,
    67n10
"Yes" donors, 152

ABOUT THE AUTHOR

Abbie E. Goldberg is an assistant professor in the Department of Psychology at Clark University in Worcester, Massachusetts. She received her PhD in clinical psychology from the University of Massachusetts at Amherst and completed a clinical psychology internship at Yale Medical School. Her research has examined the transition to parenthood in diverse families, including lesbian-parent families and adoptive-parent families. In particular, her work has focused on how families' relationships and identities change across the transition to parenthood and how gender and sexual orientation figure into individuals' adjustment and experience of parenthood. In addition, she has studied the experiences of adults raised by lesbian, gay, and bisexual parents. She has received funding for her research from the National Institutes of Health, the American Psychological Association, the Alfred P. Sloan Foundation, the Williams Institute, the Gay and Lesbian Medical Association, and the Society for the Psychological Study of Social Issues.